To my wife Shirley and son Oliver

MURDOCH BOOKS

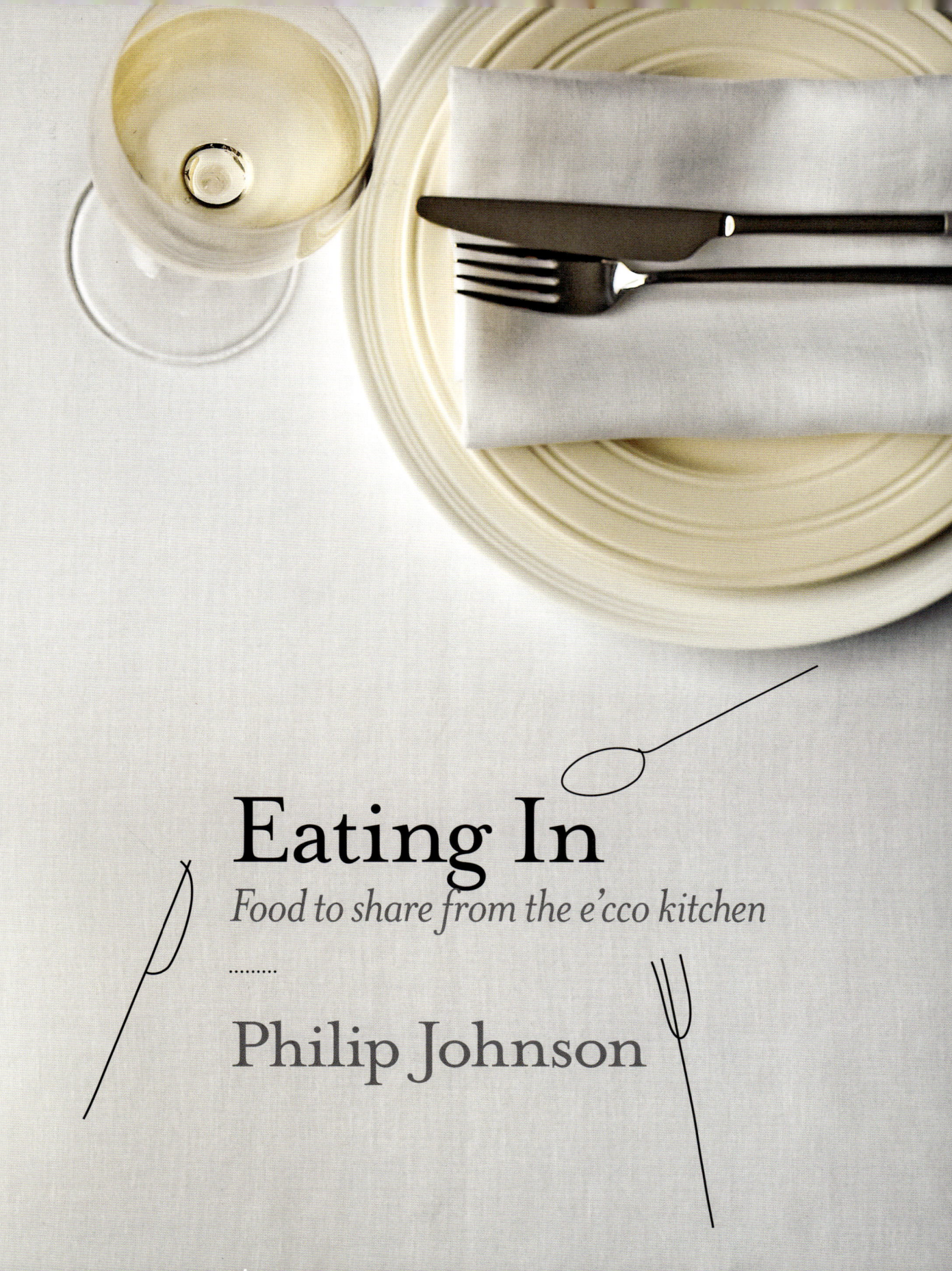

Eating In
Food to share from the e'cco kitchen

Philip Johnson

Introduction 6

Contents

Planning 8

Starters 18

Menus 10
Party Advice 14

Salads & Vegetarian 20
Seafood 36
Poultry & Meat 58

Mains 76

Seafood 78
Poultry & Meat 98

Sides 136

Desserts 172

Basics 226

Glossary 246

Index 250

From my kitchen to yours

For those of us who are passionate about food, there is no better feeling than cooking great meals for people. This is what I do every day of my life. In the e'cco kitchen my crew and I create more than a hundred meals for people each day and there is immense satisfaction gained from watching people enjoy the food we serve. It springs from the thrill of the pace of restaurant service combined with an innate nurturing quality inside every chef. We love to feed people, it's in our blood!

It's exactly the same at home. When we invite friends and family to dine with us, although we go to a lot of effort to prepare delicious food, the rewards of seeing people come together at the table, to talk, laugh and indulge, make it worthwhile. The inspiration for this book has come from some of our regular customers who frequently get together to cook for their family and friends, using the recipes from my previous books. They share my passion, not just for food, but for entertaining. Many of the dishes in this book are ones served at the restaurant, and they will work just as well in your home kitchen as they do at e'cco.

The recipes here are divided into starters, mains, sides and desserts. Pick and mix to create your own e'cco at home experience, or use one of the tempting menus I've provided as a guide — I have designed these for an elegant yet casual style of dining, perfectly suited to feeding the family or hosting a gathering of friends. Whether it's a big dinner party, a lazy summer Sunday lunch, a wintry night in front of the fire or an Asian-inspired soirée, you can prepare any of these dishes ahead of time or bring everyone together to cook with you.

Whatever the occasion, use these recipes to suit your own style of cooking and entertaining in your own home, complementing your skill as a cook and embracing the joy of being a host. Enjoy!

Philip Johnson

Planning

Menus
Party Advice

Menus

Creating a menu is the chef's equivalent of an artist's canvas — the dishes you select might reflect your technique or flair, and almost always reflect the mood you are in, all of which helps to create a certain atmosphere at the dining table. Think about what flavours you want your guests to taste in each dish, but also what you want them to feel when they eat it.

These menus are meant to be used as a guideline to show you that you can mix and match recipes to create a menu to suit any occasion. Don't be afraid to jump out of your comfort zone. You can add as many side dishes as you like; each addition will add a new dimension to the experience and help keep the conversation flowing — for that is the true art of entertaining.

The shared table

Throw your favourite tablecloth over your largest table, decorate it with flowers from the garden or even seasonal vegetables and lay out this spread to feed a casual gathering.

Carpaccio of beef, horseradish cream & chorizo oil (page 74)
Wet polenta, sand crab, chilli, garlic & basil (page 42)
Warm chicken salad with avocado, apple, celery
  & pecans (page 64)
Beetroot risotto, goat's cheese, pickled golden beetroot
  & candied walnuts (page 20)
Steamed greens with salted lemon, white anchovies
  & toasted almonds (page 162)

Feeding a crowd

As Australians, we love throwing a party — it's part of our national psyche. Enjoy the carefree aspect of handing around plates of shared food that you can prepare ahead of time, so you can entertain your guests instead of getting stuck in the kitchen.

Seared prawns with a salad of melon, ginger, lime
  & mint (page 47)
Duck liver crostini with fried duck egg (page 72)
Saganaki & lemon (page 148)
Prawn & chickpea fritters, tomato & coriander
  salsa (page 54)
Roast quail with a salad of witlof, dates, hazelnuts
  & saffron dressing (page 69)
Chocolate meringues with cassis cream & fresh
  raspberries (page 225)

Spring late lunch

As the days start to grow longer, the nights become warmer and the markets fill with spring greens and tender lamb. Get inspired to mark the end of winter with a late lunch and make the most of the sun's warmth, eating outdoors with friends as the afternoon turns to evening.

Pan-fried asparagus, Ligurian olives, garlic
  & chilli (page 154)
Lamb cutlets, scorched tomatoes, sumac croutons,
  Persian feta, sugarsnap peas & olives (page 119)
Orange & coconut syrup cake (page 221)

Vegetarian delights

You don't need to be a vegetarian to enjoy a meal without meat. Beautifully constructed, these dishes are stunning in their own right and really do not need to be served with much, other than a great glass of wine, to accompany them. Enjoy the offerings of the season and make the most of good home-grown produce whenever you can.

Open ravioli with artichokes, pan-roasted tomatoes, basil,
  goat's curd & olives (page 26)
Blue cheese soufflé with a pear, hazelnut & truffle honey
  salad (page 32)
Grilled polenta with red pepper jam (pages 157 & 235)
Roast pumpkin, wild rocket, pine nuts, honey & cumin
  dressing (page 164)

Asia after dark

With its myriad flavours and aromas, Asian food can evoke a variety of moods and emotions, whether it's the lightness of herbs, the sweetness of sauces or the fiery touch of chillies. This is a dinner menu for those with an adult palate.

Thai red curry of prawns with Asian salad
  & peanuts (page 44)
Sichuan pork belly, black bean broth
  & Asian greens (page 103)
Coconut tapioca, caramelised bananas, pineapple
  sorbet & sesame cookies (page 196)

Cocktail hour

For a party with a difference, think outside the square. Serve a selection of starters that have been cleverly minimised to bite-sized morsels, a mid-course that is small enough to eat one-handed but big enough to satisfy hungry guests and finish with a decadent mouthful of something sweet.

Seared prawns, sautéed potatoes, fennel, watercress,
  avocado, saffron and vanilla beurre blanc (page 50)
Steamed scallops, leeks, rice wine vinegar & soy (page 45)
Soy-braised beef cheek, Asian herb salad & fried
  shallots (page 61)
Risotto of slow-cooked rabbit, peas & mascarpone (page 135)
Ginger kisses with espresso cream (page 203)
Lemon & white chocolate mousse with lemon curd (page 216)

Long summer days

Lay a rug under the trees on the back lawn, plunge a bottle of rosé into a bucket of ice and celebrate the long days of summer. Lay strips of prosciutto over slices of melon or slivers of piquant blue cheese and chunks of juicy nectarine to get you started, then follow with these dishes — relax and enjoy.

Tomato salad with salted ricotta & basil (page 144)
Grilled swordfish with warm kipfler potato salad
   & salsa verde (page 87)
Coconut cake with mango mousse & milk gelato (page 187)

Middle Eastern feast

The air of any Middle Eastern souk (market) is always fragrant with the aroma of spices garnered from across the globe. Bring the luxurious slow-cooked fare and sweet delights from the exotic Middle East into your kitchen at home — a perfect feast for sharing.

Moroccan spiced quail, carrot purée, feta
   & olives (page 62)
Lamb tagine with couscous & harissa (page 115)
Saffron & almond cake with milk gelato & saffron
   syrup (page 193)

Barbecue in style

When it's hot, too hot to cook inside, but you still have an appetite for good food, take the heat out of the kitchen and fire up the barbecue. Revolutionise your outdoor space and share the cooking with friends and family.

Barbecue bug tails with a salad of green mango,
   chilli, coriander & lime (page 41)
Marinated eggplant with labneh & balsamic (page 145)
Palliard of chicken with a mixed leaf salad (page 130)
Warm potato salad with lemon & grain mustard (page 152)
Grilled bananas, banana bread & burnt butter
   ice cream (page 175)

Memories of the Mediterranean

The cuisines of the people who live along the shores of the Mediterranean are dictated by the foods that can be harvested from the beautiful but sometimes harsh landscape. Nuts, herbs, cheese from goats and sheep, fish from the azure waters and sweet ripe fruit — simple but delicious food.

Baked fig & goat's curd with a salad of rocket, hazelnuts
   & vincotto (page 23)
Rare-seared tuna, zucchini, pecorino, salted lemon,
   olives & salsa verde (page 78)
Baked date tart, caramelised oranges & crème fraîche
   ice cream (page 195)

Rich autumn spread

With the sting of the summer sun gone and an extra rug needed on the bed at night, autumn is a season in which to enjoy food that is a touch richer. This is a great collection of dishes to match with your favourite wines.

Sugar-cured ocean trout, celeriac rémoulade, salted lemon & basil oil (page 51)
Roast pork belly, caramelised pear purée, potato fondant, silverbeet & pomegranate jus (page 106)
Green apple, raisin & polenta crumble pie (page 188)

Nourishing winter warmers

We don't really have a winter to speak of in Brisbane, but I've experienced enough freezing nights in London to know that these dishes will warm the soul, warm the heart and inspire lively conversation around the dinner table.

Potato gnocchi, pine mushrooms, cavolo nero, porcini butter, peas & pecorino (page 31)
Braised lamb shanks, red wine risotto & roast garlic (page 131)
Steamed golden syrup & ginger puddings (page 176)

The big night in

The deceptively effortless dinner party is an art form in itself. With the glassware polished, the table laid and the food prepared, the focus moves to the charm, wit and humour of your dining companions. This menu gives you maximum flavour and eye appeal for the effort you put in.

Pancetta-wrapped scallops, parsnip purée & curry vinaigrette (page 56)
Eye fillet of beef, truffled kipfler potatoes, buttered spinach, sauce soubise & crisp sweetbreads (page 124)
Pistachio & caramel ice cream, poached pears & butterscotch sauce (page 199)

A laidback Christmas

Who wants to cook on Christmas Day? This is a rich, festive dinner with most of the preparation occurring the days before the big event — perfect for impressing your loved ones, creating memories and allowing you to enjoy the day at your leisure.

Parmesan wafer stack with lobster, watercress & lime mayonnaise (page 36)
Ibérico ham with burrata, rocket, vincotto, tomato fondue & toasted ciabatta (page 66)
Whole rainbow trout baked in sea salt with salsa verde (page 83)
Cherry & Drambuie semifreddo (page 214)

Advice from an old pro

The art of entertaining at home will come naturally to many of you so please feel free to skip this chapter if you want to. Having said that, I find (with much sadness) that entertaining at home has become a lost art.

When I take a night off and take the opportunity to dine in my own restaurant, I am constantly reminded of how important it is to create a hospitable environment.

I watch my staff as they go about their numerous tasks — polishing glassware, smoothing down linen, pouring water or wiping plates clean as they leave the kitchen. The result of all this effort is a beautiful dining experience where guests are free to let the evening play out over the table.

Here are a few lessons I have learned over the years that may make life easier for you in the kitchen and can help make for a seamless evening for you and your guests.

Lesson one: planning the menu

Aim to plan and prepare as much as you can in advance. Set a menu keeping in mind a few important factors — the climate, the setting, the number of people you are catering for, the preparation (including the shopping), and finally, consider the cooking and serving time.

Be realistic

There's an old oriental expression that says, 'You can create the hell you want'. This definitely applies in the kitchen. Want a stressful dinner party? Then set out to serve a meal with lots of different sauces that involve a lot of last-minute cooking when you don't have the time to prepare properly or the skills to create the kind of dinner you are dreaming about.

Consider your skills
To make cooking easier, judge how much effort you're willing to put in and how much time you have. Gauge the level of your kitchen skills and match it to the recipes you choose. The recipes in this book range from easy to slightly challenging, and also include those that will appeal to good home cooks who aren't afraid to spend a reasonable amount of time in the kitchen to create a memorable dining experience.

Remember your guests
It is courteous for guests to let you know if they have any dietary requirements, preferably prior to the evening. Nothing rattles the cook more than serving someone a plate of prawns only to learn they have a shellfish allergy. In a commercial kitchen it's easy to rectify, at home it's not so easy.
To keep things simple, some hosts ask people if they have any special considerations they need to make when they invite them — that way you can avoid disappointment on the night.

Select the best produce
Consider the weather and choose food that's appropriate to the season. If you're experiencing a heatwave then gnocchi and roast beef might not be your first choice. There's also the consideration of eating food that is in season — lamb is great in spring and rhubarb is at its best in late summer. Look to your local markets to find the best of regional produce and make the most of it while it's at its seasonal best.

Create a balanced meal
I always like to consider that a meal should be balanced in itself, starting with lighter food, moving onto something heavier and finishing with a dessert that is both satisfying, yet in a way, palate cleansing.

Key ingredients

Be careful not to double up on key ingredients and be mindful of things such as too much spice or too many carbohydrates. I once created a menu that focused solely on just a few of my favourite dishes — it turned out every one of them had nuts in them! I love nuts but it really was overkill.

No set rules

There are no real rules — the recipes in this book all fall into the category of modern Australian cuisine. A lot of people however, particularly men, don't feel like they've had a good feed unless they've had some protein and carbohydrates. So as a rule of thumb, aim to incorporate about 200 g (7 oz) of meat or fish in the meal for each person.

Create your own style

Try not to start with a pastry dish as there's nowhere to go after this and your guests will be half full by the time you get to the main course. Having said that, feel free to select recipes from within these pages that use a range of dishes to reflect your own style. Sometimes I make three starters and a main, put them on the table and let people help themselves, then finish with a great dessert.

The finer details

May I also add at this point that I am a believer in cloth napkins — it just feels right when you wipe your mouth. I also can't stress enough the quality of coffee you serve. Some people have short memories and can only remember the last course. Don't worry if you don't have an espresso machine, freshly ground good-quality coffee made in a plunger can also be a thing of beauty at the end of a meal.

Lesson two: on the night

Make sure you allow yourself plenty of time for the other important aspects of a dinner party or gathering. Having the table set, wine chilled, music on and candles lit before your guests arrive will make all the difference to how the rest of your meal pans out. And remember that your presence as the host is just as important as the food, so allow yourself plenty of time to freshen up.

Timing is everything

In my experience one of the biggest problems with entertaining a group is waiting and hoping that people will arrive on time. There are some people who are habitually late, I am one of them. My wife worked this out long ago and will always tell me a function starts an hour before it actually does. Clever. Once your guests have arrived and have a glass in their hand, give them time to settle into the surroundings. When you are ready to start serving food, give them a hint perhaps, by asking them to take a bowl or plate as they make their way to the table to sit down.

Prepare in advance

The more you plan ahead the more relaxed you'll be on the night and the more time you can spend with your guests. Make life easier for yourself by placing all the prepared ingredients in front of you before you start cooking. Arrange the ingredients or components of each course on different shelves of the refrigerator. If you need to, make a list with all the chores in order of necessity and tick them off as you go. Prepare whatever you can the previous day. Prepare a 'dirty area' — a place to put the plates and cutlery after use and deal with them afterwards.

Sit back and enjoy

The way the evening (or lunch) unfolds is up to you and your guests. The flavour of beautiful food, great wine and the satisfaction of eating together is a really wonderful human experience. Bringing people together to share a meal in your home should be celebrated and celebrated often, simply for what it is. If you are lucky, you will get to enjoy the experience of being a guest in other people's homes, sharing their great food, as often as you play host.

Starters

Salads & Vegetarian
Seafood
Poultry & Meat

Beetroot risotto, goat's cheese, pickled golden beetroot & candied walnuts

SERVES 6

2 tablespoons olive oil
1 tablespoon unsalted butter
4 French shallots (eschalots), diced
2 garlic cloves, crushed
500 g (1 lb 2 oz/2¼ cups) risotto (arborio) rice
500 ml (17 fl oz/2 cups) vegetable stock (Basics, page 228)
500 ml (17 fl oz/2 cups) freshly juiced beetroot juice
200 ml (7 fl oz) red wine
50 g (1¾ oz/½ cup) freshly grated Italian parmesan cheese
60 g (2¼ oz) unsalted butter
1 large beetroot (beet), cooked in salted boiling water, cooled, peeled and cut into 1 cm (½ inch) dice
sea salt and freshly ground black pepper
red wine vinegar, to taste
100 g (3½ oz/1 cup) candied walnuts (Basics, page 239), to serve
100 g (3½ oz) goat's curd, to serve
15 g (½ oz/½ cup) small watercress sprigs, to serve
extra virgin olive oil, for drizzling

PICKLED GOLDEN BEETROOT

50 ml (1¾ fl oz) white wine
80 ml (2½ fl oz/⅓ cup) white wine vinegar
80 g (2¾ oz/⅓ cup) caster (superfine) sugar
a pinch of saffron threads
3 baby golden beetroot (beets), peeled

To make the pickled golden beetroot, put the white wine in a small saucepan and bring to the boil. Reduce the heat and simmer until the wine reduces slightly. Add the vinegar, sugar, saffron and 125 ml (4 fl oz/½ cup) water, stirring until the sugar has dissolved. Remove from the heat. Use a mandolin or very sharp knife to thinly slice the golden beetroot into rounds. Put the slices in a non-reactive bowl and pour over the pickling liquid. Set aside to cool to room temperature. The beetroot is best pickled the day before use. Refrigerate until required.

To make the beetroot risotto, heat the olive oil and butter in a large heavy-based saucepan over low–medium heat. Add the eschalot and garlic and sauté for 8–10 minutes, or until soft and translucent. Add the rice and stir until the rice is well coated with oil. Reduce the heat to low.

Meanwhile, in a separate saucepan, bring the vegetable stock and beetroot juice to the boil.

Add the red wine to the rice and stir briefly. Allow the risotto to cook until the wine is almost completely absorbed by the rice before adding 250 ml (9 fl oz/1 cup) of the combined vegetable stock and beetroot juice. Allow the risotto to cook until the stock is almost completely absorbed by the rice before adding another cup of stock. Continue to gradually add the stock, stirring frequently, until the rice is almost cooked.

Fold in the parmesan cheese, butter and diced beetroot. Season to taste with sea salt, black pepper and a little red wine vinegar.

To serve, divide the risotto among serving bowls. Garnish with the pickled golden beetroot, candied walnuts, teaspoons of goat's curd and the watercress sprigs. Drizzle with a little extra virgin olive oil and finish with a grind of black pepper.

Baked fig & goat's curd with a salad of rocket, hazelnuts & vincotto

The perfect eating fig is sweet and luscious — almost bursting at its well-rounded bottom. As the figs on this plate are going to take a little heat during cooking, look for figs that are just ripe but still a little firm.

SERVES 6
12 thin slices prosciutto
12 firm but ripe figs
120 g (4¼ oz) goat's curd or soft goat's cheese
olive oil, for drizzling
100 g (3½ oz) wild rocket (arugula) leaves
70 g (2½ oz/½ cup) hazelnuts, roasted, skinned and roughly chopped
vincotto (see Note), for drizzling

LEMON DRESSING
50 ml (1¾ fl oz) freshly squeezed lemon juice
1 teaspoon wholegrain mustard
½ tablespoon thyme leaves
150 ml (5 fl oz) extra virgin olive oil
sea salt and freshly ground black pepper

To make the lemon dressing, whisk together the lemon juice, mustard and thyme in a bowl until combined. Whisk in the extra virgin olive oil and season to taste with sea salt and black pepper. Set aside until needed.

Preheat the oven to 200°C (400°F/Gas 6).

Lay the prosciutto slices on a clean work surface. Take a thin slice off the base of each fig so they sit flat. Remove the top of each fig and cut a cross incision, 1–1.5 cm (½–⅝ inch) from the top down. Gently open each fig and place a generous teaspoon of goat's curd inside, then wrap a slice of prosciutto around the outside.

Sit the figs on a baking tray lined with baking paper, drizzle with a little olive oil and bake for 10–12 minutes, or until the prosciutto is cooked and the goat's curd begins to colour — you may need to give them a few minutes under a hot grill (broiler).

To serve, dress the rocket with the lemon dressing, then arrange to one side of each serving plate and scatter over the hazelnuts. Sit two figs alongside and drizzle with a little vincotto.

Note: Vincotto is a grape syrup made by cooking musts (pulped grapes), then reducing the volume by one-fifth. The syrup is then left to age in oak barrels for up to four years, producing quite a unique, sweet and sour flavour. It is available from most good delicatessens.

Pumpkin, feta, sage & walnut dumplings

SERVES 6

500 g (1 lb 2 oz) butternut pumpkin (winter squash), skin on, seeded and cut into large wedges
extra virgin olive oil, for drizzling
1 teaspoon cumin seeds, toasted and ground
sea salt and freshly ground black pepper
70 g (2½ oz) feta cheese
a few sage leaves, roughly chopped
100 g (3½ oz/1 cup) walnuts, roasted and chopped
30 round gow gee (egg) dumpling wrappers
1 egg, beaten
semolina, for dusting
100 g (3½ oz) rocket (arugula) leaves, to serve
juice of 1 lemon, to serve
shaved Italian parmesan cheese, to serve

Preheat the oven to 200°C (400°F/Gas 6). Put the pumpkin wedges on a baking tray lined with baking paper. Drizzle with a little extra virgin olive oil and season with cumin, sea salt and black pepper. Roast for about 20 minutes or until tender. Allow to cool completely, then scrape the flesh into a bowl, discarding the skins. Crumble over the feta and add the sage and half the walnuts. Lightly mix together and adjust the seasoning, to taste.

Lay the dumpling wrappers out on a clean work surface. Place a heaped teaspoon of the pumpkin mixture into the centre of each wrapper. Brush the edges with the beaten egg, then fold over to form a half-moon shape. You can leave them this shape, or pull each end around, brush the ends with beaten egg and pinch together to form a tortellini shape. Store the dumplings on a tray dusted with semolina, until required.

When ready to serve, steam the dumplings, in batches, in a steamer basket over a saucepan of boiling water or simply boil in salted water for 3–5 minutes, until the pastry is cooked and the filling has heated through — the dumplings should float to the top when cooked. Drain.

To serve, arrange the rocket leaves over the base of each serving plate, scatter over the remaining walnuts and dress with a squeeze of fresh lemon, a drizzle of extra virgin olive oil, sea salt and black pepper. Arrange four or five dumplings over the rocket and top with some shaved parmesan.

Leek tart, roasted pears, blue cheese & hazelnuts

SERVES 6
375 g (13 oz) block store-bought butter puff pastry
plain (all-purpose) flour, for dusting
1 egg yolk
sea salt and freshly ground black pepper
200 ml (7 fl oz) extra virgin olive oil
2 leeks, white part only, sliced into 1 cm (½ inch) rounds
2 tablespoons soft brown sugar, plus 3 tablespoons extra
75 g (2¾ oz) unsalted butter
60 ml (2 fl oz/¼ cup) white chicken stock (Basics, page 228)
3 nashi pears, seeded, cored and each cut into 8 wedges
50 ml (1¾ fl oz) balsamic vinegar
500 ml (17 fl oz/2 cups) verjuice (Glossary)
1 teaspoon Dijon mustard
3 teaspoons caster (superfine) sugar
100 g (3½ oz) Gorgonzola Dolcelatte or your favourite blue cheese
1 large handful of baby tatsoi leaves, or similar baby Asian greens
70 g (2½ oz/½ cup) hazelnuts, roasted, skinned and roughly chopped

Preheat the oven to 200°C (400°F/Gas 6). Grease and line two baking trays with baking paper.

Roll the pastry out on a lightly floured surface to make a 26 x 38 cm (10½ x 15 inch) rectangle. Use a pastry cutter to cut out six circles, each with a 12 cm (4½ inch) diameter. Lay the pastry discs on the trays, ensuring they don't touch. Whisk the egg yolk with 1 tablespoon of water to make an egg wash and use a pastry brush to brush over the top of each pastry round. Lightly season with sea salt and black pepper. Bake for 10 minutes, then reduce the oven temperature to 160°C (315°F/Gas 2–3) and bake for a further 15 minutes to cook through. Remove from the oven and set aside until ready to use.

Heat 1½ tablespoons of the extra virgin olive oil in a nonstick frying pan over medium heat. Add the leek and sauté for 2 minutes, then add the brown sugar and one-third of the butter, swirling the pan a little. Season with sea salt and black pepper. Add the chicken stock and reduce the heat to a gentle simmer. Cover and simmer for 5 minutes until the leek is just tender. Remove from the heat and keep warm until ready to use.

Heat 1 tablespoon of the extra virgin olive oil in a separate large nonstick frying pan over medium-high heat. Add the pear and sauté, tossing frequently, until well coloured. Reduce the heat to medium and add the extra brown sugar and remaining butter and season with sea salt and black pepper. Swirl the pan often to bring the butter and brown sugar together, then deglaze the pan with the balsamic vinegar. You may need to finish the pear in a moderate oven for 5 minutes until tender.

Meanwhile, in a small saucepan, bring the verjuice to a simmer over low heat and reduce to 50 ml (1¾ fl oz). Remove from the heat and whisk in the remaining extra virgin olive oil, and Dijon mustard and caster sugar. Set aside.

To serve, place a pastry base in the centre of each serving plate. Divide the warm leeks among the pastries, then arrange four pear wedges over the leeks. Crumble over a little Gorgonzola. Moisten the tatsoi leaves with a little of the verjuice dressing and place on top of the tart. Drizzle the remaining dressing around the plate and scatter with the roasted hazelnuts.

Open ravioli with artichokes, pan-roasted tomatoes, basil, goat's curd & olives

SERVES 6
375 g (13 oz) dried lasagne sheets (6 in total)
olive oil
9 good-quality bottled Italian artichokes, preferably with stems attached, drained
200 g (7 oz) cherry tomatoes
80 g (2¾ oz/½ cup) pitted kalamata olives
1 large handful of basil leaves
150 g (5½ oz) goat's curd
50 g (1¾ oz/½ cup) shaved Italian parmesan cheese

TOMATO VINAIGRETTE
2 kg (4 lb 8 oz) tomatoes
50 ml (1¾ fl oz) red wine vinegar
2 red chillies, seeded and finely diced
a pinch of cumin seeds, toasted and ground
150 ml (5 fl oz) extra virgin olive oil
sea salt and freshly ground black pepper
a splash of balsamic vinegar
caster (superfine) sugar, to taste

To make the tomato vinaigrette, put the tomatoes in a food processor and process until puréed, then pass through a fine sieve into a shallow frying pan. Simmer over medium heat until reduced by half. Remove from the heat, transfer to a bowl and cool to room temperature. Whisk in the red wine vinegar, chilli, ground cumin and fennel. Gradually whisk in the extra virgin olive oil until well combined. Season to taste with sea salt, black pepper and balsamic vinegar. You may need to adjust the acidity with a little caster sugar. Set aside until needed.

Cook the lasagne sheets in a large saucepan of salted boiling water until tender. Refresh in iced water, drain, then toss with the olive oil. Set aside to cool slightly. Cut each sheet into two 8–10 cm (3¼–4 inch) squares.

Heat a little olive oil in a large nonstick frying pan over medium heat. Sauté the artichokes briefly, achieving a little colour. Add the cherry tomatoes and cook until they begin to split. Add enough tomato vinaigrette to moisten, stirring to heat through, then remove from the heat and add the olives.

Meanwhile, reheat the lasagne sheets in boiling water. Drain well.

To serve, place a square of lasagne on each serving plate. Toss the basil leaves through the artichokes and tomatoes then spoon over the lasagne. Use a teaspoon to place small spoonfuls of goat's curd over the vegetables. Top with another square of lasagne and scatter the parmesan over the top. Drizzle the remaining tomato vinaigrette over and around the ravioli.

Salad of sautéed potatoes, mixed leaves, pancetta & poached egg

This is what I'd have for my last breakfast. Potatoes sautéed in butter with a poached egg, crisp pancetta and a sharp little salad. Just add coffee, fresh juice and get ready for anything.

SERVES 6

1 tablespoon white wine vinegar
6 eggs
a knob of unsalted butter
6 yellow-fleshed potatoes, such as southern gold (pink-eye), steamed in their skins and cut into thick slices
1 small baguette, cut into thin slices
extra virgin olive oil, for drizzling
150 g (5½ oz) mixed leaves, such as radicchio, witlof (chicory/Belgian endive) and frisée (curly endive)
2 spring onions (scallions), thinly sliced diagonally
12 thin slices flat pancetta, grilled

DRESSING

1 teaspoon wholegrain mustard
juice of ½ lemon
100 ml (3½ fl oz) extra virgin olive oil
sea salt and freshly ground black pepper

To soft poach the eggs, bring 2 litres (70 fl oz) water to the boil in a large shallow saucepan, then reduce the heat to a simmer and add the vinegar.

Break the eggs, one at a time, onto a saucer, then slide them into the gently simmering water. Cook no more than three or four eggs at a time. The eggs are cooked when the whites are set but the yolks are still soft — this usually takes 3–4 minutes. Remove from the water with a slotted spoon and place in a bowl of iced water. Set aside.

Heat the butter in a heavy-based frying pan over medium heat. Add the potato slices and sauté on both sides until golden.

Drizzle the baguette slices with extra virgin olive oil and toast on both sides under a hot grill (broiler) until golden.

To make the dressing, whisk together the mustard, lemon juice and extra virgin olive oil, and season with sea salt and black pepper.

In a large mixing bowl, combine the mixed leaves, spring onion and toasted baguette and drizzle over just enough of the dressing to moisten the leaves.

To serve, arrange about three slices of potato on each plate, and top with the salad. Place two slices of pancetta over the top. Briefly reheat the poached eggs in boiling water, then place on top of the salad. Drizzle the remaining dressing over the top and finish with a grind of black pepper.

Note: Always use the freshest eggs possible for poaching. If they're old, the egg white will separate from the yolk as soon as it is placed in the water.

Eggplant & feta agnolotti, cherry tomatoes, spinach & olives

SERVES 6

500 g (1 lb 2 oz) eggplant (aubergine)
sea salt and freshly ground black pepper
600 g (1 lb 5 oz) cherry tomatoes
950 g (2 lb 2 oz/3 cups) rock salt
1 egg
7 egg yolks
2 tablespoons olive oil
300 g (10½ oz/2 cups) strong baker's or '00' flour, sifted, plus extra for dusting
125 g (4½ oz) feta cheese, crumbled
1 small handful of flat-leaf (Italian) parsley leaves
15 g (½ oz/¼ cup) snipped chives
1 egg, extra, beaten
olive oil
400 g (14 oz) baby English spinach leaves
185 g (6½ oz/1 cup) chopped pitted kalamata olives

BURNT BUTTER VINAIGRETTE

100 g (3½ oz) unsalted butter
50 ml (1¾ fl oz) balsamic vinegar
2 teaspoons caster (superfine) sugar

Preheat the oven to 200°C (400°F/Gas 6).

Cut the eggplant in half and score the flesh in a diamond pattern, being careful not to pierce the skin. Rub the eggplant with sea salt and set aside for 20 minutes.

Rinse the eggplant well and pat dry with paper towels. Place on a greased baking tray, cover with foil, then bake for 20 minutes, or until tender. Set aside to cool. Scoop the flesh into a sieve and sit over a larger bowl. Refrigerate overnight to allow any excess liquid to drain off.

Preheat the oven to 70°C (150°F/Gas ¼). Cut the cherry tomatoes in half and place them, cut side up, on two baking trays lined with the rock salt. Oven-dry the tomatoes for 1½–2 hours. (If your oven doesn't go this low, turn it to the lowest temperature and cook for less time.)

Combine 1 egg, the egg yolks, olive oil and a pinch of sea salt in a food processor on low speed. Gradually add the flour and mix until the mixture comes together. If the dough is too wet, add a little extra flour; if it's too dry, add an extra egg. Transfer to a floured surface and knead until smooth. Wrap in plastic wrap and refrigerate for 3 hours.

Divide the dough into four portions. Pass through a pasta machine to form long, thin sheets, beginning from the highest to lowest setting. Lay the pasta on a floured surface.

Combine the eggplant, feta, parsley and chives in a bowl and season with sea salt and black pepper. Transfer the mixture to a piping (icing) bag. Pipe the filling lengthways down each pasta sheet, leaving a 2–3 cm (¾–1¼ inch) border on each side. Brush around the edges with the beaten egg, then fold over to enclose the filling. Using the handle of a spatula or the edge of your hand, make indents every 5 cm (2 inches), pressing down firmly on the pasta to seal the edges and form small pillows. Use a knife or pasta cutter to cut the agnolotti into individual pieces, trimming any excess. Store on a floured tray until required.

To make the burnt butter vinaigrette, melt the butter in a saucepan over medium heat. Once it begins to turn nut brown, remove from the heat and whisk in the balsamic vinegar and sugar. Season to taste and keep warm.

Cook the agnolotti, in batches, in a saucepan of boiling salted water for about 3 minutes, or until al dente. Drain.

Working in batches, heat a little olive oil in a heavy-based frying pan over medium heat. Sauté the agnolotti for 2–3 minutes, or until golden. Add the spinach and olives and toss until the spinach just begins to wilt.

To serve, divide the agnolotti, spinach and warm cherry tomatoes among bowls and spoon over the vinaigrette.

Potato gnocchi, pine mushrooms, cavolo nero, porcini butter, peas & pecorino

SERVES 6–8

1 kg (2 lb 4 oz) cavolo nero (Tuscan black cabbage) or silverbeet (Swiss chard)
100 ml (3½ fl oz) extra virgin olive oil
500 g (1 lb 2 oz) pine mushrooms, stems removed, gills scraped, sliced into 8 mm (⅜ inch) strips (use mixed exotic mushrooms, if unavailable)
1 quantity of potato gnocchi (Basics, page 238)
200 g (7 oz/1¼ cups) fresh shelled peas (use frozen if fresh unavailable), blanched
200 ml (7 fl oz) white chicken stock (Basics, page 228), boiling
sea salt and freshly ground black pepper
juice of 1 lemon
1 handful of flat-leaf (Italian) parsley leaves, finely chopped
freshly shaved pecorino cheese, to serve

PORCINI BUTTER

2 tablespoons extra virgin olive oil
4 French shallots (eschalots), sliced
4 garlic cloves, sliced
40 g (1½ oz) dried porcini mushrooms
340 g (11¾ oz) unsalted butter, softened
1 tablespoon Dijon mustard

To make the porcini butter, heat the extra virgin olive oil in a heavy-based saucepan over low heat. Sweat the eschalot and garlic until soft. Add the porcini mushrooms, 80 ml (2½ fl oz/⅓ cup) water and 40 g (1½ oz) of the butter and gently simmer for 3 minutes, or until the mushrooms are rehydrated and the liquid has reduced. Remove from the heat and cool to room temperature. Transfer to a food processor with the mustard and remaining butter and blend until smooth. Season with sea salt and black pepper. Refrigerate until needed. When ready to use, dice the butter.

Remove the stalks of the cavolo nero by holding the stalk in one hand, pinch the leaves either side then slide your fingers towards the tip. Blanch the leaves in a large saucepan of salted boiling water for 30 seconds. Refresh in iced water, drain, then squeeze to remove any excess moisture. Shred into 1 cm (½ inch) pieces, then set aside.

Working in two batches, heat half of the extra virgin olive oil in a large nonstick frying pan over high heat. Add half of the mushrooms and sauté for 1 minute, or until the mushrooms have coloured and are just cooked through. Add half of the gnocchi, allowing one handful per person, tossing gently so that they colour evenly and heat through. Repeat with the remaining oil, mushrooms and gnocchi, then return all of the gnocchi back to the pan.

Once the gnocchi is cooked, add the cavolo nero and peas to the pan. Add the chicken stock and bring to the boil, then reduce the heat to low and add the porcini butter, swirling the pan so the butter emulsifies with the chicken stock and coats the gnocchi. Season with sea salt, black pepper, lemon juice and half of the parsley.

To serve, divide the gnocchi among serving bowls, top with freshly shaved pecorino, scatter over the remaining parsley and finish with a grind of black pepper.

Blue cheese soufflé with a pear, hazelnut & truffle honey salad

SERVES 9—10

BLUE CHEESE SOUFFLÉ
unsalted butter, for greasing
plain (all-purpose) flour, for dusting
450 ml (16 fl oz) full-cream (whole) milk
1 small onion, sliced
a pinch of freshly ground nutmeg
2 teaspoons table salt
1½ teaspoons freshly ground black pepper
70 g (2½ oz) unsalted butter
70 g (2½ oz/½ cup) plain (all-purpose) flour
6 eggs, separated
110 g (3¾ oz) fully matured Gorgonzola Piccante cheese, cut into large cubes

PARMESAN GLAZE
125 ml (4 fl oz/½ cup) pouring (whipping) cream
60 g (2¼ oz) grated best-quality Italian parmesan cheese
2 egg yolks

PEAR, HAZELNUT & TRUFFLE HONEY SALAD
60 g (2¼ oz) mixed frisée (curly endive) and wild rocket (arugula) leaves
1 large handful of mixed herbs, such as flat-leaf (Italian) parsley, chervil and chive batons
3 ripe but firm pears, cored and thinly sliced
70 g (2½ oz/½ cup) hazelnuts, roasted, skinned and roughly chopped
150 g (5½ oz) truffle honey (see Note)

To make the soufflés, preheat the oven to 220°C (425°F/Gas 7). Grease nine or ten 185 ml (6 fl oz/¾ cup) capacity soufflé dishes with butter, then dust with flour, shaking to remove the excess. Put the milk, onion, nutmeg, salt and black pepper in a saucepan over low heat and bring slowly to the boil. Remove from the heat and set aside for 15 minutes for the flavours to infuse. Strain into a clean saucepan and bring back to a gentle simmer.

Melt the butter in a large saucepan over medium heat. Add the flour and mix well. Cook over low heat for 5—8 minutes, stirring with a wooden spoon. Gradually whisk in the warm milk, a little at a time, stirring continuously to avoid lumps forming. Continue until all the milk has been used, then reduce the heat to very low and cook for a further 5—8 minutes. Remove from the heat. Add the egg yolks and beat with a wooden spoon to achieve a smooth batter. Add the Gorgonzola and continue to beat, allowing the mixture to cool to room temperature.

Whisk the egg whites in an electric mixer until soft peaks form, then fold into the soufflé mixture. Divide among the soufflé dishes and place in a deep roasting tin. Pour in enough boiling water to come halfway up the sides of the dishes. Bake for 15 minutes, then reduce the heat to 180°C (350°F/Gas 4) and bake for a further 13 minutes. Remove from the oven and leave to cool for 15 minutes before turning out onto a baking tray lined with baking paper. The soufflés can be made several hours in advance.

To make the parmesan glaze, whisk together all of the ingredients. Preheat the grill (broiler) to medium.

Gently reheat the soufflés in a moderate oven for about 10 minutes, or until just heated through. Coat the top of each soufflé with several spoonfuls of the parmesan glaze, then place under the hot grill. Grill until golden — do not walk away!

To make the pear, hazelnut and truffle honey salad, toss the mixed leaves and herbs together in a bowl with the pear and hazelnuts.

To serve, place a soufflé on each serving plate. Arrange the salad around the soufflé, then drizzle with the truffle honey and finish with a grind of black pepper.

Note: Truffle honey is available from good delicatessens or food emporiums. Alternatively, stir a few drops of truffle oil into 125 g (4½ oz) honey to taste, being mindful that truffle oil is very strong in flavour.

Mozzarella pan-fried with prosciutto & rosemary

SERVES 6

3 x 200 g (7 oz) balls mozzarella cheese, quartered
12 very thin slices prosciutto
150 ml (5 fl oz) extra virgin olive oil
1 tablespoon rosemary leaves
toasted crusty Italian-style bread, to serve

RICH TOMATO SAUCE

2 tablespoons olive oil
3 French shallots (eschalots), sliced
4 garlic cloves, finely chopped
800 g (1 lb 12 oz) tinned chopped tomatoes, puréed
6 roma (plum) tomatoes, blanched, peeled, seeded and chopped (Glossary)
2 tablespoons mixed oregano and thyme leaves, chopped
sea salt and freshly ground black pepper
a pinch of caster (superfine) sugar, optional

To make the rich tomato sauce, heat the oil in a heavy-based saucepan over medium heat. Sauté the eschalots and garlic for 5 minutes, or until translucent. Add the puréed and roma tomatoes and the mixed herbs. Reduce the heat to low and simmer, stirring occasionally, for 30 minutes, or until the sauce thickens, taking care it doesn't burn. Season with sea salt and black pepper. If the sauce tastes too acidic, add a pinch of sugar. The sauce can be made ahead of time and stored in an airtight container in the refrigerator for up to 1 week.

Grind a little black pepper over each piece of mozzarella and wrap with a slice of prosciutto. Heat one-third of the extra virgin olive oil in a large nonstick frying pan over medium–high heat. Add the mozzarella pieces and cook for 30 seconds on each side, or until the prosciutto is crisp and well coloured and the cheese has softened but still holds its shape. Drain on paper towels. Return the pan to medium heat with the remaining extra virgin olive oil. Add the rosemary and lightly fry for 30 seconds, then drain on paper towels.

To serve, gently reheat the tomato sauce, then spoon a generous amount into serving bowls. Place two baked mozzarella slices in the centre and scatter over the rosemary leaves. Serve with the bread on the side.

Parmesan wafer stack with lobster, watercress & lime mayonnaise

SERVES 6

300 g (10½ oz/3 cups) grated best-quality Italian parmesan cheese
60 g (2¼ oz/2 cups) watercress sprigs
2 French shallots (eschalots), sliced
360–400 g (12¾–14 oz) cooked lobster, moreton bay bug or prawn (shrimp) meat, sliced 5 mm (¼ inch) thick
lime mayonnaise (Basics, page 232), to serve
2 tablespoons salted capers, rinsed and squeezed dry

Preheat the oven to 160°C (315°F/Gas 2–3).

To make the parmesan wafers, draw three circles on a sheet of baking paper, each with a 10 cm (4 inch) diameter and invert the paper onto a baking tray. Repeat with another sheet of baking paper and baking tray. Place small handfuls of the grated parmesan cheese on the paper to fill each circle in an even layer, then bake for 3–4 minutes, or until golden in colour. Cool the wafers on the trays for 1 minute, then transfer to wire racks to cool completely. Repeat this two more times with the remaining parmesan to make 18 wafers in total. Wafers can be made the day before and stored in an airtight container.

To serve, place a parmesan wafer in the centre of each serving plate. Combine the watercress and eschalot. Place a small handful over each wafer, then top with a little lobster meat. Drizzle with a little lime mayonnaise and scatter over a couple of capers. Top with another parmesan wafer, a layer of lobster, watercress and eschalot and a drizzle of mayonnaise and some capers. Finish with a third parmesan wafer on top. Repeat to make six stacks in total.

Note: This dish is quite simple in its composition, yet the richness of the lobster meat turns it into something quite indulgent. It will also work equally well with moreton bay bugs, prawns (shrimp) or fresh sand (blue) crab. Enjoy with a chilled glass of Champagne.

Seared scallops, jerusalem artichokes, parsley & radish salad with mandarin sauce

SERVES 6
juice of 4 lemons
200 g (7 oz) jerusalem artichokes
150 g (5½ oz) red radishes
1 large handful of flat-leaf (Italian) parsley leaves, chopped
60 ml (2 fl oz/¼ cup) extra virgin olive oil
olive oil
750 g (1 lb 10 oz) large scallops, roe removed
a knob of unsalted butter
juice of 1 lemon, extra

MANDARIN SAUCE
juice of 4 mandarins
200 ml (7 fl oz) fish stock (Basics, page 229)
200 ml (7 fl oz) pouring (whipping) cream
2 tablespoons Grand Marnier
80 g (2¾ oz) cold unsalted butter, diced
sea salt and freshly ground white pepper

To make the mandarin sauce, strain the mandarin juice into a small saucepan over medium heat. Add the fish stock, bring to the boil, then reduce the heat and simmer until reduced by half. Add the cream and Grand Marnier. Continue to cook until the sauce has reduced and is thick enough to coat the back of a spoon. Strain through a fine sieve into a clean saucepan. Over very low heat, whisk in the cold butter and season with sea salt and white pepper. Set aside and keep warm.

Add half of the lemon juice to a bowl of cold water to make acidulated water. Peel the jerusalem artichokes and immediately place into the acidulated water, as they will discolour quickly once cut. Drain.

Using a mandolin or very sharp knife, thinly slice the jerusalem artichokes and radishes into rounds, then slice into thin strips.

In a large bowl, combine the artichoke, radish, parsley, extra virgin olive oil and remaining lemon juice to taste. Season with sea salt and black pepper and mix to combine.

Heat a little olive oil in a large nonstick frying pan over high heat. Season the scallops with sea salt and black pepper. In batches, quickly sear the scallops in the hot pan on both sides until opaque — they should only take about 20–30 seconds each side. Remove the pan from the heat and add the butter and a squeeze of lemon juice.

Divide the scallops among serving plates. Place a small handful of the salad in the centre and drizzle over a little of the warm mandarin sauce.

Barbecue bug tails with a salad of green mango, chilli, coriander & lime

Palm sugar, lime juice and fish sauce make this classic Thai dressing. Use more or less lime juice or fish sauce to adjust the acid/salt balance as needed. This salad is so lively it can be used as an accompaniment to just about any white fish.

SERVES 6

600 g (1 lb 5 oz) raw moreton bay bug, lobster or prawns (shrimp) meat, cut into bite-sized pieces
12–18 bamboo skewers, soaked in water for 30 minutes
olive oil
sea salt and freshly ground black pepper
lime wedges, to serve

PALM SUGAR & LIME DRESSING

150 g (5½ oz) light palm sugar (jaggery), chopped
150 ml (5 fl oz) freshly squeezed lime juice
1–2 tablespoons fish sauce, to taste

GREEN MANGO SALAD

2 green mangoes or papayas, peeled, stones removed, cut into thin strips (see Note)
1 long red chilli, seeded, thinly sliced lengthways
3 French shallots (eschalots), thinly sliced
2 spring onions (scallions), thinly sliced diagonally
1 large handful of coriander (cilantro) sprigs
1 small handful of Thai basil leaves
60 g (2¼ oz) tatsoi, or similar Asian greens, trimmed

To make the palm sugar and lime dressing, put the palm sugar and lime juice in a saucepan over medium heat. Bring to the boil and simmer briefly until the palm sugar is completely dissolved. Remove from the heat and add enough fish sauce to taste. Set aside.

To make the green mango salad, combine all of the ingredients in a large bowl and toss through enough of the palm sugar and lime dressing to moisten.

Thread the bug meat evenly on to the skewers. Brush with a little olive oil and season with sea salt and black pepper. Heat a barbecue or chargrill pan to high heat. Cook the bug skewers, turning to cook all sides, until well coloured and just cooked through, about 2–3 minutes.

To serve, place a handful of salad on each serving plate. Arrange two to three bug skewers on the side and drizzle with a little extra dressing. Serve with lime wedges.

Note: Green mango is best eaten very thinly sliced — the best way to achieve this is to use a mandolin. If you do not have a mandolin, use a vegetable peeler instead — first peel the fruit into strips, then thinly slice the strips with a sharp knife.

Wet polenta, sand crab, chilli, garlic & basil

Despite its simplicity, this is perhaps the dish that gets the most praise in the restaurant. Make sure the polenta is wet (add more milk, if necessary) and don't burn the garlic. The richness of the polenta and the freshness of the crab makes this dish a winner.

SERVES 6

1 quantity wet polenta (Sides, page 157)
extra virgin olive oil, plus extra for drizzling
2 garlic cloves, finely chopped
a pinch of dried chilli flakes
350 g (12 oz) cooked sand (blue) crabmeat (see Note)
sea salt and freshly ground black pepper
juice of ½ lemon
1 small handful of basil leaves, chopped
1 red chilli, seeded and thinly sliced lengthways

Prepare the wet polenta as the recipe directs and keep warm.

Heat a little extra virgin olive oil in a large heavy-based frying pan over medium heat. Sauté the garlic and chilli flakes for 2–3 minutes, or until the garlic has softened. Add the crabmeat, stirring until it is warmed through. Season with sea salt and black pepper. Remove from the heat and quickly toss in the lemon juice to combine.

To serve, place a spoonful of wet polenta in the centre of each plate and spoon some crabmeat neatly over the top. Scatter over the basil and red chilli, then finish with a drizzle of extra virgin olive oil and a grind of black pepper.

Note: Sand crabs belong to the Portunidae family of swimming crabs, including blue swimmer crabs found in the United States, or the velvet crabs popular in Britain and Northern Europe.

Thai red curry of prawns with Asian salad & peanuts

There's something rewarding about making red curry paste from scratch. The power of roasted spices, the kick of chilli and the aroma of fresh kaffir lime leaves. It's also time consuming, so please feel no guilt in reaching for a jar of quality pre-made curry paste — I recommend Maesri brand.

SERVES 6

200 g (7 oz) red curry paste (Basics, page 236)
800 ml (28 fl oz) coconut milk
juice of 2 limes
2 tablespoons fish sauce
18 large raw prawns (shrimp), shelled and deveined, sliced in half lengthways
80 g (2¾ oz/½ cup) peanuts, roasted and roughly chopped, to serve

ASIAN SALAD

1 telegraph (long) cucumber
125 g (4½ oz) bean sprouts
6 red radishes, thinly sliced
1 long red chilli, seeded and thinly sliced lengthways
2 spring onions (scallions), thinly sliced diagonally
1 small handful of coriander (cilantro) leaves
1 small handful of mint leaves
1 small handful of Vietnamese mint leaves
30 g (1 oz/¼ cup) Asian fried shallots
sesame oil (optional)

To make the Asian salad, use a mandolin or vegetable peeler to shave the cucumber into ribbons on four sides down to the seeds. Discard the seeds and put the cucumber ribbons in a bowl with the remaining salad ingredients and a light drizzle of sesame oil, if using. Toss to combine and refrigerate until required.

Heat the curry paste in a large, nonstick saucepan over medium heat. Gradually add the coconut milk, stirring constantly, until well combined. Bring to a simmer, then add the lime juice and fish sauce, to taste. Stir through the prawns and simmer gently for about 1 minute, then remove from the heat.

To serve, divide the prawn curry among serving bowls. Arrange a large handful of salad on top and scatter over the peanuts.

Note: The rich and intense flavour of this curry makes it suitable for smaller servings as a starter. It also makes a terrific main course accompanied by bowls of steamed jasmine rice and Asian greens.

Steamed scallops, leeks, rice wine vinegar & soy

I love the beautifully random mosaic-like patterns that the rice wine vinegar and soy dressing forms when you spoon it onto the plate. To allow the aromatic oils to split from the soy sauce and rice wine vinegar don't mix them together too briskly.

SERVES 6
6 leeks
vegetable oil, for frying
sea salt
750 g (1 lb 10 oz) scallops, roe removed

RICE WINE VINEGAR & SOY DRESSING
170 ml (5½ fl oz/⅔ cup) light olive oil
100 ml (3½ fl oz) rice wine vinegar
60 ml (2 fl oz/¼ cup) soy sauce
2 tablespoons sesame oil
1 tablespoon honey
1 teaspoon finely grated fresh ginger

To make the rice wine vinegar and soy dressing, place all of the ingredients in a bowl and whisk gently to combine. Cover and refrigerate until required.

Cut one-third from the top of the leeks and discard. Cut the leeks in half lengthways and separate the strips, washing if necessary. Remove any inner layers or ones that are not white enough and reserve for garnish. Bring a small saucepan of water to the boil. Blanch the leek strips briefly, refresh in iced cold water, then drain well. Set aside.

Slice the reserved leek into thin strips, about 7 cm (2¾ inches) long. Heat some vegetable oil in a heavy-based saucepan over high heat and fry the sliced leek until crisp; be careful as it will burn very quickly. Drain on paper towels and season with sea salt.

Wrap each scallop in a strip of the blanched leek, finishing with the green part on the outside. Put the wrapped scallops in a steamer basket over a saucepan of simmering water and steam for 2–3 minutes, or until just cooked and opaque.

To serve, spoon enough dressing onto each plate so that it covers the base. Arrange the scallops in a circular pattern with a small handful of the fried leek in the centre as garnish.

Note: The scallops can be served as a canapé using disposable bamboo chopsticks that are attached at one end (available from Asian supermarkets). Prepare the scallops as directed, then carefully open each chopstick, without splitting them in two, and place a scallop between the chopsticks to hold them in place. Then steam as the recipe directs. Arrange the chopsticks on a serving platter, scatter over the fried leek and serve the dressing separately as a dipping sauce.

Seared prawns with a salad of melon, ginger, lime & mint

SERVES 6
olive oil
18 large raw prawns (shrimp), shelled and deveined, with tails intact
3 cm (1¼ inch) piece of ginger, thinly sliced
40 g (1½ oz) unsalted butter
sea salt and freshly ground black pepper
juice of 2 limes
55 g (2 oz/½ cup) Asian fried shallots (optional)
lime wedges, to serve

MELON SALAD
½ rockmelon, rind removed and seeded
½ honeydew melon, rind removed and seeded
2 long red chillies, seeded, thinly sliced lengthways
3 spring onions (scallions), thinly sliced diagonally
1 handful of mint leaves, torn

To make the melon salad, cut the rockmelon and honeydew melon into 2 cm (¾ inch) cubes. Combine with the remaining salad ingredients and set aside.

Meanwhile, heat a little olive oil in a heavy-based or nonstick frying pan over high heat. Cook the prawns in two batches, adding half of the ginger and half of the butter to each batch just before they are cooked (they should be well coloured but still opaque in the centre). Season with sea salt and black pepper, then remove from the heat.

Add the prawns and ginger to the melon salad. Drizzle the lime juice over the salad and gently toss to combine.

To serve, pile some salad and three prawns onto each plate, then drizzle over any remaining juices. Scatter over the Asian fried shallots, if using, and garnish with the lime wedges.

Note: I generally have an aversion to using fruit in savoury dishes, although there are of course some exceptions to the rule. The use of melons here work really well; the sweet juicy flesh of the rockmelon and honeydew paired with seafood and simple Asian flavours makes a stunning and memorable combination.

Shaved nashi pear & crab salad with peanuts, watercress & pomelo

SERVES 6
2 large pomelos or ruby grapefruit
450 g (1 lb) cooked sand (blue) crabmeat
160 g (5¾ oz/1 cup) peanuts, roasted and chopped
60 g (2¼ oz/2 cups) watercress sprigs
2 spring onions (scallions), thinly sliced diagonally
2 tablespoons sesame oil
1 tablespoon fish sauce
juice of 1 lime
6 nashi pears (see Note)

Peel the pomelos, then segment them over a mixing bowl to catch any juices. Roughly chop the flesh and set aside in another large mixing bowl. Scrape any juices into the first bowl.

Add the crabmeat to the chopped pomelo with the peanuts, watercress and spring onion.

To make the dressing, whisk the sesame oil, fish sauce and lime juice with the pomelo juice. Add enough of the dressing to moisten the salad.

Using a mandolin or sharp knife, shave the pears into thin slices and add to the salad.

To serve, pile the crab salad in serving bowls and drizzle with any remaining dressing.

Note: Nashi pears are round little pears, originally from Northern Asia, with a texture that is crisp yet juicy. They add a lightness and a consistent crunch to a salad, making them the perfect vehicle for the vibrant flavours of this seafood dish.

Seared prawns, sautéed potatoes, fennel, watercress, avocado, saffron & vanilla beurre blanc

This dish is dressed with beurre blanc, a tangy hot butter sauce. You can prepare it in advance and keep it warm in a thermos. It will taste just as good and be ready to go when you want to serve it.

SERVES 6

olive oil

4 large or 6 small yellow-fleshed potatoes, such as southern gold (pink-eye), steamed in their skins until tender, cooled and sliced into 1 cm (½ inch) discs

sea salt and freshly ground black pepper

18 large raw prawns (shrimp), shelled and deveined, with tails intact

90 g (3¼ oz/3 cups) watercress sprigs

2 fennel bulbs, outer leaves and core removed, thinly sliced or shaved

3 avocados, skin and stones removed, flesh sliced

juice of ½ lemon

extra virgin olive oil, for drizzling

1 quantity warm saffron and vanilla beurre blanc (Basics, page 231), to serve

Heat a little olive oil in a large heavy-based frying pan over medium heat. Sauté the potato slices, turning, so they colour on both sides. Season lightly with sea salt and black pepper, then set aside and keep warm.

Meanwhile, heat a little olive oil in a heavy-based frying pan over medium heat. Add the prawns and briefly sauté on both sides. Season with sea salt and black pepper, then increase the heat and continue to cook for 2–3 minutes, or until the prawns are just pink and opaque.

In a mixing bowl, gently toss together the watercress, fennel and avocado with the lemon juice, a drizzle of extra virgin olive oil, sea salt and black pepper.

To serve, arrange the warm potato slices on the base of each serving plate. Pile a large handful of the watercress salad over the top, then arrange three prawns around the salad. Drizzle with the saffron and vanilla beurre blanc.

Note: This dish can also make a great canapé or small appetiser served on a Chinese soup spoon. Simply omit the potato and avocado, slice the prawns into bite-sized pieces and top with a little shaved fennel and a spoonful of the saffron and vanilla beurre blanc.

Sugar-cured ocean trout, celeriac rémoulade, salted lemon & basil oil

My head chef Mathias is Swedish and fondly remembers making sugar-cured fish, or gravlax, with his father every Christmas. I asked him if he pulled the tiny bones out of the fish himself but he always asked the fishmonger to do it for him. I recommend you do the same.

SERVES 6
115 g (4 oz) caster (superfine) sugar
40 g (1½ oz/⅓ cup) sea salt
600 g (1 lb 5 oz) ocean trout, skinned and pin-boned (see Note)
1 quantity celeriac rémoulade (Basics, page 237)
60 g (2¼ oz/2 cups) watercress sprigs
½ salted lemon (Basics, page 237), flesh discarded, zest thinly sliced into strips

BASIL OIL
2 large handfuls of basil leaves
200 ml (7 fl oz) olive oil

You will need to begin preparing this recipe two days before you wish to serve it.

Combine the sugar and salt, rub over the ocean trout and place in a shallow plastic (or non-reactive) tray. Cover and refrigerate for 24 hours. Turn the trout, cover, and continue to cure for a further 24 hours.

To make the basil oil, blanch the basil in a large saucepan of boiling salted water. Drain. Refresh the basil in iced water, then drain again and place on paper towels, squeezing out any excess moisture. Put the basil and olive oil in a blender and blend until smooth. Strain the oil through a fine sieve or piece of muslin (cheesecloth), allowing as much of the oil to pass through as possible without forcing it through. Set aside. The basil oil can be stored in an airtight container in the refrigerator for up to 3 days.

Remove the cured trout from the tray and wipe dry with paper towels, removing any excess sugar and salt mix. Use a very sharp knife to cut the trout into thin slices.

To serve, arrange three slices of trout over the base of each serving plate. Place a good spoonful of celeriac rémoulade in the centre. Dress the watercress with a little of the basil oil, then scatter over the trout with the salted lemon. Drizzle some of the basil oil around the plate.

Note: A cross between a rainbow trout and the Canadian steelhead trout, ocean trout have a distinctive rosy orange flesh that tends to have a little more fat content, making it moist as well as enhancing its natural flavour. Atlantic salmon is the best substitute, if it is unavailable.

Seared scallops, saffron potatoes, tomato, fresh peas, pine nuts & basil ravigotte

SERVES 6

12 kipfler (fingerling) potatoes, peeled
a good pinch of saffron threads
800 ml (28 fl oz) white chicken stock (Basics, page 228)
olive oil
750 g (1 lb 10 oz) large scallops, roe removed
a knob of unsalted butter
juice of 1 lemon
155 g (5½ oz/1 cup) fresh shelled peas (use frozen, if fresh unavailable), blanched and refreshed
2 tomatoes, blanched, peeled, seeded (Glossary) and diced
40 g (1½ oz/¼ cup) pine nuts, toasted

BASIL RAVIGOTTE

3 large handfuls of basil leaves
200 ml (7 fl oz) olive oil
6 French shallots (eschalots), finely diced
30 g (1 oz/⅔ cup) finely snipped chives
juice of 1 lemon
sea salt and freshly ground black pepper

To make the basil ravigotte, blanch the basil in a saucepan of salted boiling water. Drain. Refresh the basil in iced water, then drain again and place on paper towels, squeezing out any excess moisture. Put the basil and olive oil in a blender and blend until smooth. Strain the oil into a bowl through a fine sieve or piece of muslin (cheesecloth), allowing as much of the oil to pass through as possible without forcing it through. Whisk in the eschalot, chives and lemon juice. Season with sea salt and black pepper. Store refrigerated in an airtight container.

Place the whole, peeled potatoes in a wide saucepan with the saffron and enough chicken stock to cover. Bring to the boil, then reduce the heat and cook for 8–10 minutes. Remove from the heat and set aside to let the potatoes cool completely in the stock. Once cool, remove the potatoes and reserve the stock. Slice the potatoes into 1 cm (½ inch) discs and set aside until needed.

Heat a little olive oil in a large nonstick frying pan over high heat. Season the scallops with sea salt and black pepper. In batches, quickly sear the scallops in the hot pan on both sides until opaque — they should only take about 20–30 seconds each side. Remove the pan from the heat and add the butter and lemon juice.

Meanwhile, gently reheat the potatoes in the reserved stock. Remove the warm potatoes using a slotted spoon and divide among serving bowls. In a bowl, combine the peas, tomato and pine nuts and spoon over the potatoes.

To serve, arrange the scallops over the potatoes and spoon over the basil ravigotte.

Prawn & chickpea fritters, tomato & coriander salsa

These crunchy deep-fried morsels are surprisingly light due to the whisked egg whites that get folded through the nutty chickpea flour batter. This batter can be prepared up to six hours ahead without the egg white; add the chopped prawn just before frying.

SERVES 6
200 g (7 oz/1¾ cups) chickpea (besan) flour
2 teaspoons baking powder
1½ teaspoons korma (mild) curry paste
12 raw prawns (shrimp), peeled, deveined and chopped
1 long red chilli, seeded and diced
½ small red onion, diced
1 tablespoon chopped coriander (cilantro) leaves
2 egg whites
vegetable oil, for deep-frying

TOMATO & CORIANDER SALSA
80 ml (2½ fl oz/⅓ cup) extra virgin olive oil
juice of 2 lemons
4 large tomatoes, diced
1 small red onion, finely diced
3 tablespoons chopped coriander (cilantro) leaves
1–2 teaspoons ground cumin, to taste
sea salt and freshly ground black pepper

Sift the chickpea flour and baking powder into a large bowl. Gradually add 200 ml (7 fl oz) warm water, beating well to combine. Whisk in the curry paste. This batter mixture can be made in advance and kept refrigerated for up to 6 hours before use.

Combine the prawn meat, chilli, onion and coriander and stir into the batter to combine.

In the bowl of an electric mixer, whisk the egg whites to firm peaks, then fold into the batter.

Fill a deep-fryer or large heavy-based saucepan one-third full of oil and heat to 180°C (350°F), or until a cube of bread dropped into the oil browns in 15 seconds. In batches, gently place spoonfuls of the fritter mixture into the hot oil. Cook for 2–3 minutes, turning to cook evenly. Remove from the hot oil using a slotted spoon and drain on paper towels. Set aside and keep warm. Repeat with the remaining batter to make 12–18 fritters in total.

Meanwhile, to make the tomato and coriander salsa, combine all the ingredients in a bowl and season with sea salt and black pepper. Set aside for 10 minutes to allow the flavours to infuse.

To serve, divide the salsa among serving plates and top with two or three of the fritters.

Bug wontons, kecap manis, coriander & Thai basil

SERVES 6

olive oil
3 French shallots (eschalots) or 1 small red onion, diced
2 red chillies, seeded and diced
3 cm (1¼ inch) piece of ginger, finely diced
3 garlic cloves, finely diced
800 g (1 lb 12 oz) uncooked moreton bay bug, lobster or raw prawn (shrimp) meat
1 large handful of coriander (cilantro) leaves, roughly chopped
3–4 tablespoons kecap manis
sea salt and freshly ground black pepper
18 round Shanghai (eggless) dumpling wrappers
1 egg, lightly beaten
1 large handful of coriander (cilantro) leaves, to serve
1 large handful of Thai basil leaves, to serve

DRESSING

125 ml (4 fl oz/½ cup) kecap manis
80 ml (2½ fl oz/⅓ cup) rice wine vinegar
1 teaspoon sesame oil

To make the dressing, whisk together the ingredients and refrigerate in an airtight container until required.

Heat a little oil in a heavy-based saucepan over medium heat, add the eschalot and sweat briefly with little or no colour. Add the chilli, ginger and garlic and continue to cook for several minutes, or until the mixture begins to soften. Remove from the heat and set aside.

Dice the bug meat into a small, uniform size. Heat a little olive oil in a nonstick frying pan over high heat. Toss the bug meat quickly in the hot pan, sealing on all sides, then transfer to a baking tray to cool — the bug meat should be slightly undercooked with a glossy appearance.

Once cool, add the bug meat to the eschalot mixture, then fold through the coriander and just enough kecap manis to lightly coat the mixture. Adjust the seasoning with sea salt and black pepper.

Lay the dumpling wrappers on a clean work surface. Place a heaped teaspoon of the bug filling in the centre of each wrapper. Brush the edges with the beaten egg, then fold over to make a half-moon shape. You can leave them this shape, or pull each end around, brush the ends with the egg, and pinch together to form a tortellini shape.

Steam the wontons in a steamer basket over a saucepan of boiling water or simply boil in salted water for 3–5 minutes, or until the pastry is cooked. Drain well.

To serve, arrange three bug wontons on each plate with a small handful of combined coriander and Thai basil leaves in the centre and the dressing drizzled over the top.

Pancetta-wrapped scallops, parsnip purée & curry vinaigrette

This is one of my all-time favourite dishes, not only because it tastes so good but because you can prepare the vinaigrette ahead of time, make the purée the day before and reheat it when you want to serve it, and even have the scallops wrapped in pancetta in the refrigerator waiting to be cooked. I make the parsnip chips in advance and keep them crisp by storing them in a container with silica crystals (Glossary).

SERVES 6

vegetable oil, for shallow-frying
1 parsnip, peeled
30 long, thin slices flat pancetta
750 g (1 lb 10 oz) large scallops, roe removed
olive oil
juice of ½ lemon
1 large handful of mixed salad leaves and herbs, such as watercress, parsley, chervil and chive batons

CURRY VINAIGRETTE
150 ml (5 fl oz) olive oil
2 French shallots (eschalots), finely chopped
2 teaspoons korma (mild) curry paste (see Note)
50 ml (1¾ fl oz) freshly squeezed lemon juice

PARSNIP PURÉE
750 g (1 lb 10 oz) parsnips, peeled
1 bay leaf
full-cream (whole) milk, to cover
sea salt and freshly ground black pepper
50 g (1¾ oz) unsalted butter, softened
55–80 ml (1¾–2½ fl oz) pouring (whipping) cream

To make the curry vinaigrette, heat 1 tablespoon of the olive oil in a small saucepan, gently sweat the eschalot until soft, then stir through the curry paste. In a food processor or blender, purée the eschalot mixture with 60 ml (2 fl oz/¼ cup) olive oil until smooth. Transfer to a bowl, whisk in the lemon juice, then the remaining olive oil. Refrigerate in an airtight container until required.

To make the parsnip purée, cut the parsnips into large, even-sized pieces. Put the parsnip in a deep saucepan with the bay leaf and just enough milk to cover. Season lightly with sea salt and black pepper. Bring to the boil, then reduce the heat and simmer just until the parsnip is tender. Use a slotted spoon to remove the parsnip and place in a food processor, reserving the milk. Purée, gradually adding the butter and cream. If the purée is still a little firm, add a little of the cooking milk. Adjust the seasoning. Keep warm.

Meanwhile, heat some vegetable oil in a shallow frying pan over high heat. Use a potato peeler to peel the parsnip into long thin strips. Drop into the pan and fry until golden. Drain on paper towels.

Lay the strips of pancetta on a clean work surface. Place a scallop on its side at one end of a strip of pancetta. Roll the scallop wrapping it with the pancetta until it is double-layered around the outside of the scallop. Repeat with the remaining pancetta and scallops.

Heat a little olive oil in a large nonstick frying pan over high heat. Fry the scallops, in batches, pancetta side down, turning several times to crisp the pancetta. Finally, cook the face of the scallop until golden, being careful not to overcook them. Add the lemon juice to finish.

To serve, place a spoonful of the warm parsnip purée in the centre of each plate. Arrange the scallops around the purée. Dress a few salad leaves with the curry vinaigrette. Place a handful of the dressed salad leaves on top with the parsnip crisps. Drizzle over a little of the vinaigrette.

Note: Use a good-quality curry paste to make this dressing. We prefer Sharwood's Korma (blue label) curry paste, available from most supermarkets or Asian food stores.

Roast quail, fresh figs, frisée, salted ricotta & mint with a honey & vanilla dressing

SERVES 6

6 whole quails, wings tucked under and legs tied
olive oil
100 g (3½ oz/3 cups) frisée (curly endive) leaves
1 head radicchio, leaves separated
1 small handful of mint leaves
30 g (1 oz/½ cup) chives, cut into batons
100 g (3½ oz) salted ricotta, shaved (see Note)
6 fresh figs, cut into quarters

HONEY & VANILLA DRESSING

100 g (3½ oz) good-quality honey
1 vanilla bean, split lengthways and seeds scraped
60 ml (2 fl oz/¼ cup) extra virgin olive oil
60 ml (2 fl oz/¼ cup) vegetable oil
1 tablespoon freshly squeezed lemon juice, to taste
sea salt and freshly ground black pepper

To make the honey and vanilla dressing, gently heat the honey in a small saucepan over medium heat. Add the vanilla bean and seeds, then remove from the heat. Set aside and allow the flavours to infuse. Once cool, transfer the infused honey to a small mixing bowl, discarding the vanilla bean. Whisk in the combined oils and lemon juice to taste, then season with sea salt and black pepper. The dressing can be made in advance and will keep for several days in an airtight container in the refrigerator.

Preheat the oven to 200°C (400°F/Gas 6). Brush the quails with olive oil and season with sea salt and black pepper. Place the quails, breast side up, on roasting trays lined with baking paper. Roast for 12–15 minutes, then remove from the oven and allow to rest for several minutes.

Meanwhile, gently toss the frisée, radicchio, mint and chives together in a bowl with enough of the honey and vanilla dressing to moisten. Fold through the salted ricotta.

To serve, arrange four fig quarters on each serving plate with a handful of the salad leaves. Arrange the quail alongside, then drizzle the remaining honey and vanilla dressing around the plate.

Note: *La Ricotta Salata*, meaning, 'ricotta salted', is a dry salted ricotta made from the whey of pasteurised sheep's milk. Aged for two to four months, the cheese has a dense, slightly spongy texture and a salty, milky flavour, similar to a dry Italian feta cheese.

Soy-braised beef cheek, Asian herb salad & fried shallots

Beef cheeks are totally underrated. In this recipe they are slow-cooked to become super sweet and wonderfully sticky. Beef cheeks are not normally stocked at butcher shops, so order them well in advance.

SERVES 6

1.2 kg (2 lb 12 oz) beef cheeks (use wagyu if available)
olive oil
sea salt and freshly ground black pepper
125 ml (4 fl oz/½ cup) soy sauce
125 ml (4 fl oz/½ cup) mirin
100 ml (3½ fl oz) fish sauce
50 g (1¾ oz) caster (superfine) sugar
3 garlic cloves, sliced
6 cm (2½ inch) piece of ginger, sliced
3 red chillies, roughly chopped
12 white peppercorns
cornflour (cornstarch) or arrowroot, for thickening
lime wedges, to serve

ASIAN HERB SALAD

1 telegraph (long) cucumber
125 g (4½ oz/1⅓ cups) bean sprouts
½ white radish (daikon), thinly sliced
6 red radishes, thinly sliced
1 long red chilli, seeded and thinly sliced lengthways
2 spring onions (scallions), thinly sliced diagonally
1 small handful of coriander (cilantro) leaves
1 small handful of mint leaves
1 small handful of Vietnamese mint leaves
1 small handful of Asian fried shallots

Preheat the oven to 180°C (350°F/Gas 4).

Trim and remove all the excess fat from the beef cheeks and cut into approximately 100 g (3½ oz) pieces. Heat a little olive oil in a large heavy-based frying pan over high heat. Season the beef cheeks with sea salt and black pepper, then seal on all sides until well coloured. Remove from the pan and transfer to a large, deep baking dish.

Put the remaining ingredients, except the cornflour and lime wedges, with 500 ml (17 fl oz/2 cups) water in a large saucepan and bring to the boil. Remove from the heat, then pour over the cheek, making sure there is enough liquid to cover, adding more water, if necessary. Cover with foil, then cook in the oven for 1½–2 hours, or until tender. Allow to cool in the liquid. The cheeks can be prepared in advance, stored in the cooking liquid and refrigerated.

Once cool, remove the beef cheeks from the liquid and cut each piece in half. Strain the liquid into a clean saucepan and place over medium heat. If the sauce is too thin, thicken using a little cornflour. Add the beef cheeks to the sauce to gently reheat.

To make the Asian herb salad, use a mandolin or vegetable peeler to shave the cucumber into ribbons on four sides down to the seeds. Discard the seeds, put the cucumber ribbons in a bowl and toss together with the remaining salad ingredients.

To serve, divide the beef cheeks among serving bowls, about 2–3 pieces per serve with a little of the sauce. Arrange the salad on top and drizzle the sauce over and around. Serve with lime wedges.

Note: This dish can also make a great canapé served on a Chinese soup spoon or similar. To serve as a canapé, only prepare a half quantity of this recipe, which will make around 25 spoons and omit the cucumber from the salad. Before reheating the beef cheeks in the reduced sauce, slice each cheek into bite-sized pieces. Serve the beef cheeks on the spoons topped with a little salad.

Moroccan spiced quail, carrot purée, feta & olives

SERVES 6

6 quails, butterflied and boned
olive oil
150 g (5½ oz/1 cup) pitted Ligurian olives
100 g (3½ oz/⅔ cup) crumbled feta cheese
1 large handful of coriander (cilantro) leaves
jus (Basics, page 230), warmed, to serve

CHERMOULA

1 tablespoon cumin seeds, toasted
1 tablespoon coriander seeds, toasted
2 teaspoons sweet paprika
2 teaspoons sea salt
1 teaspoon freshly ground black pepper
1 teaspoon cayenne pepper, or to taste
a good pinch of saffron threads (optional)

CARROT PURÉE

1 kg (2 lb 4 oz) carrots, peeled and chopped
1 cinnamon stick
2 bay leaves
4 garlic cloves
1.2 litres (44 fl oz) white chicken stock
  (Basics, page 228)
80 ml (2½ fl oz/⅓ cup) extra virgin olive oil
sea salt and freshly ground black pepper

To make the chermoula, place all of the ingredients in a mortar and pestle or use a spice grinder to grind to a fine powder. Set aside.

To make the carrot purée, put the carrot, cinnamon, bay leaves and garlic in a large saucepan with enough chicken stock to cover well. Bring to the boil, then reduce the heat and simmer until the carrot is tender. Strain and leave the garlic cloves with the carrot, discarding the remaining aromatics. Blend in a food processor until smooth, adding just enough extra virgin olive oil for flavour and consistency. Season with sea salt and black pepper, to taste. Keep warm.

Preheat the oven to 220°C (425°F/Gas 7). Heat a large, heavy-based, ovenproof frying pan over high heat. Brush the quails with olive oil and season with the chermoula. Place in the hot pan, skin side down first, and sear both sides until golden, then turn the quail over and transfer the pan to the oven. Roast for a further 5–6 minutes, then remove the pan from the oven and allow to rest for several minutes.

To serve, place a large spoonful of the warm carrot purée off-centre on each serving bowl. Scatter with the olives, feta and coriander. Rest the whole quail alongside the carrot purée and drizzle with a little warm jus.

Warm chicken salad with avocado, apple, celery & pecans

I thought we were reinventing the wheel when we were serving warm salads at Ménage à Trois in London in the 1980s. Then one of the chefs read a recipe in a French book for a 'warm duck salad with raspberry vinaigrette'. It was dated 1918!

SERVES 6–8
1 whole roast chicken (Mains, page 104)
3 celery stalks, diced
2 green apples, cored, quartered and cut into small dice
2 tablespoons chopped flat-leaf (Italian) parsley leaves
2 tablespoons snipped chives
75 g (2¾ oz/¾ cup) pecans, roasted
125 g (4½ oz/½ cup) mayonnaise (Basics, page 232)
3 tablespoons sour cream
sea salt and finely ground black pepper
2 avocados, skin and stones removed, flesh diced
1 head cos (romaine) lettuce, broken into leaves

Roast the chicken as directed on page 104. While still warm, remove the meat in large pieces and keep warm. If roasting the chicken in advance, remove the meat from the cold roast chicken, spread over a baking tray lined with baking paper, cover with foil, and reheat in a moderate oven.

In a large bowl, gently toss together the warm chicken, celery, apple, parsley, chives and pecans.

In a separate bowl, whisk together the mayonnaise and sour cream, adding a little hot water if necessary to thin to drizzling consistency. Season with sea salt and black pepper, to taste.

Add enough of the dressing to the salad to coat. Lastly, gently toss through the avocado.

To serve, line serving bowls with the cos leaves. Pile the salad into the centre, then arrange the chicken pieces over the top.

Note: Make up the salad just prior to serving, as the heat from the meat can wilt the delicate salad leaves. This salad also makes an ideal picnic lunch and will work well with a bought barbecued chicken. Simply combine all of the salad ingredients in a large container with the dressing stored in a separate container. Purchase the chicken en route to your destination and it will still be warm by the time you are ready to assemble and eat it!

Peking duck salad, seared scallops, ginger & peanuts

SERVES 6

1 Chinese roast duck, meat removed and broken into bite-sized pieces (see Notes)
1 red chilli, seeded and thinly sliced lengthways
3 cm (1¼ inch) piece of ginger, thinly sliced
1 tablespoon Asian fried shallots
30 g (1 oz) peanuts, roasted and roughly chopped
150 g (5½ oz) tatsoi or similar baby Asian greens, stems removed
2 spring onions (scallions), thinly sliced diagonally
1 large handful of coriander (cilantro) leaves
olive oil
500 g (1 lb 2 oz) large scallops, roe removed
sea salt and freshly ground black pepper
a knob of unsalted butter
juice of 1 lemon
1 tablespoon sesame seeds, toasted, to serve

DRESSING

100 g (3½ oz) palm sugar (jaggery), roughly chopped
50 ml (1¾ fl oz) Chinese black vinegar (see Notes)
130 ml (4½ fl oz) light soy sauce
50 ml (1¾ fl oz) plum sauce

To make the dressing, put the palm sugar and 50 ml (1¾ fl oz) water in a small saucepan over low heat, stirring until the sugar dissolves. Remove from the heat, whisk in the remaining ingredients and set aside.

Preheat the oven to 160°C (315°F/Gas 2–3). Lay the duck meat on a baking tray lined with baking paper, cover with foil, then place in the oven to gently reheat.

In a large bowl, combine the warmed duck meat with the chilli, ginger, Asian fried shallots, peanuts, tatsoi, spring onion and coriander, with enough dressing to moisten.

Meanwhile, heat a little olive oil in a large nonstick frying pan over high heat. Season the scallops with sea salt and black pepper. In batches, quickly sear the scallops in the hot pan on both sides until opaque — they should only take 20–30 seconds each side. Remove from the heat and add the butter and lemon juice.

To serve, divide the duck meat and salad among serving plates. Arrange the scallops around the salad, scatter over the toasted sesame seeds and drizzle with a little of the remaining dressing.

Notes: Chinese roast ducks are readily available from Chinatown or any Asian barbecue restaurant. They may ask if you want it chopped into pieces or left whole; I always opt for the latter as it's easier to remove the meat.

Chinese black vinegar is a dark complex vinegar made from glutinous rice and malt, similar to balsamic vinegar but based on grain rather than grapes. It is often used in Chinese stir-fries, braises and sauces.

Ibérico ham, burrata, rocket, vincotto, tomato fondue & toasted ciabatta

I often joke that my chefs become snobs when they work with me because they get used to using only the best ingredients. This dish is a classic example: great Spanish ham, good-quality extra virgin olive oil and burrata, a rich, creamy soft cheese.

SERVES 6

6 x 2 cm (¾ inch) thick slices ciabatta
good-quality extra virgin olive oil, for drizzling
6 burrata, brought to room temperature (see Note)
100 g (3½ oz) wild rocket (arugula) leaves
1 small handful of oregano leaves
vincotto (see Note, page 23), for drizzling
12–18 slices Ibérico or Serrano ham

TOMATO FONDUE

100 ml (3½ fl oz) extra virgin olive oil
2 large onions, sliced
5 garlic cloves, sliced
2 kg (4 lb 8 oz) ripe tomatoes, blanched, peeled, seeded and diced (Glossary)
100 ml (3½ fl oz) balsamic vinegar
100 g (3½ oz) soft brown sugar
sea salt and freshly ground black pepper

To make the tomato fondue, heat the extra virgin olive oil in a large saucepan over very low heat. Sweat the onion and garlic, without colour, until very soft. Add the tomato and continue to cook over low heat for 40 minutes. Add the balsamic vinegar and brown sugar; season with sea salt and black pepper and continue to cook for 10 minutes. Remove from the heat. Pass the mixture through a fine sieve, using a ladle to force the mixture through. Cool to room temperature, then store in an airtight container until required.

To serve, preheat the grill (broiler) to medium heat. Drizzle the ciabatta with a little extra virgin olive oil and toast on both sides under the hot grill.

Place a burrata in the centre of each serving plate. Scatter the rocket and oregano around the burrata and drizzle with a little extra virgin olive oil and vincotto. Drape the ham over the rocket around the burrata. Finish with a little drizzle of extra virgin olive oil and a grind of black pepper. Spread a generous amount of the tomato fondue over the toasted ciabatta and serve alongside. Any remaining tomato fondue can be stored in an airtight container in the refrigerator for several days.

Note: Burrata is a fresh Italian cow's milk cheese made from mozzarella and cream. It has a thin shell that envelops a tremendously smooth and creamy filling that is almost slightly sweet in flavour. It's worth trying to source a supplier if you can, otherwise substitute with fresh, best-quality buffalo mozzarella.

Roast quail with a salad of witlof, dates, hazelnuts & saffron dressing

SERVES 6

6 large quails, butterflied and boned
olive oil
2 white witlof (chicory/Belgian endive), leaves separated
1 red witlof (chicory/Belgian endive), leaves separated
100 g (3½ oz/3 cups) frisée (curly endive) leaves
1 small red onion, halved, thinly sliced
180 g (6½ oz/1 cup) fresh dates, pitted, chopped
70 g (2½ oz/½ cup) hazelnuts, roasted, skinned and roughly chopped

SAFFRON DRESSING

a pinch of saffron threads
30 ml (1 fl oz) white wine
60 ml (2 fl oz/¼ cup) white wine vinegar
1½ teaspoons honey
4 French shallots (eschalots), finely diced
1 garlic clove, finely diced
½ red chilli, seeded and finely diced
1½ tablespoons thyme leaves, roughly chopped
a pinch of ground coriander seeds
a pinch of ground fennel seeds
juice of 1 lemon
125 ml (4 fl oz/½ cup) extra virgin olive oil
50 ml (1¾ fl oz) vegetable oil
sea salt and freshly ground black pepper

To make the saffron dressing, heat the saffron threads in a small saucepan over low heat until lightly toasted. Add the wine, vinegar and honey, stirring to dissolve the honey, until just heated through — do not boil. Add the eschalot, garlic, chilli and thyme, stirring to combine. Remove from the heat and transfer to a large bowl. Set aside to allow the flavours to infuse until cool. Add the ground coriander and fennel seeds. Whisk in the lemon juice and combined oils. Season with sea salt and black pepper. Refrigerate in an airtight container until required.

Preheat the oven to 220°C (425°F/Gas 7).

Heat a large, heavy-based ovenproof frying pan over high heat. Brush the quails with olive oil and season with sea salt and black pepper. Place in the hot pan, skin side down first, and sear both sides until golden, then turn the quail over and transfer the pan to the oven. Roast for a further 5–6 minutes, then remove the pan from the oven and allow to rest while assembling the salad.

In a large bowl, toss together the witlof, frisée, red onion, dates and hazelnuts with enough saffron dressing to moisten.

To serve, divide the salad evenly among serving plates. Carve each quail into two leg and two breast pieces and arrange alongside. Drizzle with a little extra saffron dressing to finish.

Asian-style barbecued pork & lychee salad

SERVES 6

1 telegraph (long) cucumber
1 tablespoon thinly sliced fresh ginger
1 red chilli, seeded and thinly sliced lengthways
2 spring onions (scallions), thinly sliced
125 g (4½ oz) baby corn, thinly sliced
140 g (5 oz/1½ cups) bean sprouts
1 large handful of coriander (cilantro) leaves
1 large handful of Vietnamese mint leaves
1 large handful of Thai basil leaves
350 g (12 oz) piece Chinese barbecued pork, thinly sliced (see Note)
30 lychees, peeled and seeded

DRESSING

90 g (3¼ oz/¼ cup) honey
60 ml (2 fl oz/¼ cup) soy sauce
3 teaspoons freshly squeezed lime juice
1 teaspoon fish sauce
sesame oil, to taste

To make the dressing, whisk together the honey and soy sauce in a small bowl. Add the lime juice, fish sauce and a drizzle of sesame oil. Check the seasoning — you may need to adjust with a little extra lime juice or fish sauce. Set aside until needed.

Use a mandolin or vegetable peeler to shave the cucumber into ribbons on four sides down to the seeds. Discard the seeds and put the cucumber ribbons in a bowl with the ginger, chilli, spring onion, baby corn, bean sprouts, coriander, Vietnamese mint and Thai basil. Add the pork and lychees and enough dressing to moisten.

To serve, divide the salad among serving plates and drizzle with a little extra dressing.

Note: The best place to shop for barbecue pork is in busy Chinese restaurants that may also have duck hanging from hooks in the window. If you want nice thin slices, buy your piece of pork whole and use a sharp knife at home, otherwise the chef will give you a pork hatchet job — literally!

Roast quail, carrot & cumin salad with a coriander & mint dressing

SERVES 6

6 large quail, butterflied and boned
olive oil

CORIANDER & MINT DRESSING
250 g (9 oz/1 cup) Greek-style yoghurt
2 French shallots (eschalots), cut into quarters
juice of 1 lemon
a pinch of ground toasted cumin seeds
a pinch of dried chilli flakes
2 large handfuls of mint leaves
2 large handfuls of coriander (cilantro) leaves
sea salt and freshly ground black pepper

CARROT & CUMIN SALAD
100 ml (3½ fl oz) olive oil
1 tablespoon cumin seeds
1 tablespoon black mustard seeds
3 large carrots, peeled and grated
grated zest of 1 orange
1 tablespoon white wine vinegar
1 handful of coriander (cilantro) leaves

To make the coriander and mint dressing, put the yoghurt in a fine sieve over a bowl. Set aside to rest for at least 1 hour to remove the excess water. Put the eschalot and lemon juice in a food processor and blend to form a smooth paste. Add the cumin, chilli flakes, mint and coriander and season with sea salt and black pepper. Blend until smooth. Transfer the mixture to a bowl, stir in the yoghurt, adjusting the seasoning as required. Cover and refrigerate until needed.

To make the carrot and cumin salad, heat the olive oil, cumin and mustard seeds in a large saucepan over medium heat. When the seeds begin to pop, add the carrot and orange zest. Cook for a few minutes, stirring well, until the carrot just begins to soften. Add the white wine vinegar and season with sea salt and black pepper. Set aside to cool.

Preheat the oven to 220°C (425°F/Gas 7).

Heat a large, heavy-based, ovenproof frying pan over high heat. Brush the quails with olive oil and season with sea salt and black pepper. Place in the hot pan, skin side down first, and sear both sides until golden, then turn the quails over and transfer the pan to the oven. Roast for 5–6 minutes further, then remove the pan from the oven and allow to rest for several minutes.

To serve, toss the coriander leaves through the carrot and cumin salad, then divide among serving plates. Spoon the coriander and mint dressing around the salad and rest the quail on top. Finish with a drizzle of olive oil.

Duck liver crostini with fried duck egg

This dish is a rich but enticing way to kick off a meal, particularly with a glass of savoury pinot noir. For a lighter touch you can use chicken livers and substitute the duck eggs for quail eggs, which are available through boutique markets and good butchers.

SERVES 6

olive oil
2 garlic cloves, chopped
2 French shallots (eshalots), finely diced
250 ml (9 fl oz/1 cup) good-quality port
125 ml (4 fl oz/½ cup) good-quality red wine
400 ml (14 fl oz) jus (Basics, page 230)
sea salt and freshly ground black pepper
1 kg (2 lb 4 oz) duck livers, cleaned and trimmed
125 ml (4 fl oz/½ cup) white chicken stock (Basics, page 228) or water
1 handful of flat-leaf (Italian) parsley leaves, roughly chopped, plus extra to garnish
3 tablespoons salted baby capers, rinsed
clarified butter (Basics, page 230), melted
6 duck eggs
6 slices ciabatta, toasted, to serve

Heat a little olive oil in a saucepan over medium heat. Add the garlic and eschalot and sauté, with little or no colour, until soft. Deglaze the pan with the port and red wine. Reduce the heat and simmer until the liquid reduces to about 80 ml (2½ fl oz/⅓ cup). Add the jus, bring back to the boil, then remove from the heat. Season with sea salt and black pepper, to taste. Set aside.

Heat a little olive oil in a large heavy-based frying pan over high heat. Add the duck livers and quickly seal on both sides. Add the reduced sauce, thinning with a little chicken stock, if necessary.

Reduce the heat and simmer briefly until the livers are pink in the centre, then stir through the parsley and capers to combine.

Meanwhile, heat a heavy-based or nonstick frying pan over medium heat. Brush the pan with clarified butter, then crack the eggs into the pan and fry until cooked with the yolk still soft — do not turn.

To serve, place a slice of toasted ciabatta on each serving plate. Spoon over the duck livers and some sauce and serve with the fried egg alongside. Finish with a grind of black pepper.

Note: Livers are best eaten just pink and not overdone. To avoid overcooking them, cook to medium-rare, then remove from the heat and leave to rest in the hot sauce for 1–2 minutes before serving.

Carpaccio of beef, horseradish cream & chorizo oil

SERVES 6
300 g (10½ oz) good-quality eye-fillet of beef
3 large red radishes
60 g (2¼ oz/2 cups) watercress sprigs

HORSERADISH CREAM
100 g (3½ oz) horseradish cream sauce (see Notes)
juice of 1 lemon
1 tablespoon grated fresh horseradish
125 ml (4 fl oz/½ cup) pouring (whipping) cream, softly whipped
sea salt and freshly ground black pepper

CHORIZO OIL
200 ml (7 fl oz) olive oil
1 fresh chorizo sausage, sliced diagonally

Wrap the beef in plastic wrap and freeze for several hours, or until firm.

To make the horseradish cream, combine the horseradish cream sauce, lemon juice and fresh horseradish. Fold in the whipped cream. Season with sea salt and black pepper. Refrigerate in an airtight container until required.

To make the chorizo oil, heat the olive oil in a heavy-based frying pan over medium heat. Add the chorizo and cook for 5 minutes, turning once. Remove from the heat and set aside to cool. Blend the oil and chorizo in a food processor, strain, and set aside.

Use a very sharp carving knife to slice the frozen beef very thinly. Arrange the carpaccio in a symmetrical pattern on serving plates. Using the back of a teaspoon, rub a little of the chorizo oil over the carpaccio.

Using a mandolin or sharp knife, very thinly slice the radishes. Scatter the radish slices over the carpaccio and drizzle with the horseradish cream. (If the cream is too thick, use a little hot water to thin to pouring consistency.)

Top with a handful of watercress and finish with a grind of black pepper.

Notes: To create an eye-catching dish that is surprisingly light and refreshing make sure you cut the thinnest slices of beef that you can — they should be paper thin. Freezing the beef makes it easier to cut. If your knife skills give you slices that are too thick, place them between slices of lightly oiled plastic wrap and gently pound them out with a meat mallet.

Horseradish cream sauce is a bottled condiment made with fresh horseradish, vinegar and cream. It is available from good delicatessens and food providores.

Roast quail, frisée, Manchego, salted almonds & quince dressing

SERVES 6

6 quails, butterflied and boned
olive oil

QUINCE DRESSING

2 teaspoons quince paste
30 ml (1 fl oz) sherry vinegar
sea salt and freshly ground black pepper
125 ml (4 fl oz/½ cup) extra virgin olive oil

SALAD

150 g (5½ oz) frisée (curly endive)
1 head radicchio, leaves separated
30 g (1 oz) whole unblanched almonds, roasted and salted
100 g (3½ oz) Manchego cheese, shaved thinly (see Notes)
1 small handful basil leaves

To make the quince dressing, place the quince paste in a bowl and whisk in the sherry vinegar until smooth. Season with sea salt and freshly ground black pepper, then gradually whisk in the extra virgin olive oil. You may need to thin the dressing with a dash of hot water. Set aside.

Preheat the oven to 220°C (425°F/Gas 7).

Heat a heavy-based ovenproof frying pan over high heat. Brush the quails with olive oil and season with sea salt and black pepper. Place in the hot pan, skin side down first, and sear until golden underneath, then turn the quail over and transfer the pan to the oven. Roast for 5–6 minutes, then remove the pan from the oven and allow to rest briefly.

To make the salad, combine all the ingredients with enough of the quince dressing to moisten.

To serve, place a handful of the salad in the centre of each serving plate. Cut the quail in half and arrange over the top of the salad.

Note: This light salad with a fruity sweet and sour dressing topped with a little golden quail makes the perfect starter.

Manchego is Spain's best-known cheese. It is made from sheep's milk and is available from most good delicatessens.

Mains

Seafood
Poultry & Meat

Rare-seared tuna, zucchini, pecorino, salted lemon, olives & salsa verde

SERVES 6

4 large zucchini (courgettes)
2 French shallots (eschalots), finely diced
1 garlic clove, crushed
1 salted lemon (Basics, page 237), flesh discarded, zest thinly sliced into strips
1 handful of flat-leaf (Italian) parsley leaves
juice of ½ lemon
extra virgin olive oil
sea salt and freshly ground black pepper
60 g (2¼ oz/⅔ cup) finely shaved pecorino cheese
100 g (3½ oz) pitted black olives, such as Ligurian or kalamata, cut into quarters
1 quantity salsa verde (Basics, page 232)
6 x 140 g (5 oz) sashimi-grade tuna steaks (see Note)

Use a mandolin or vegetable peeler to shave the zucchini into ribbons, then thinly slice lengthways. In a bowl, combine the zucchini, eschalot, garlic, salted lemon, parsley, lemon juice and a splash of extra virgin olive oil. Season lightly with sea salt and black pepper. Place a pile in the centre of each serving plate. Sprinkle over the pecorino, then scatter with the olives. Spoon a little of the salsa verde around each plate.

Brush both sides of the tuna steaks with some of the extra virgin olive oil and season with sea salt and black pepper. Heat a large nonstick frying pan over high heat. Sear the tuna for 10–15 seconds each side — it should be well coloured but still raw in the centre. Immediately remove the pan from the heat, as the tuna will continue to cook once removed from the direct heat.

To serve, arrange the tuna steaks over the zucchini salad.

Note: Top-quality tuna is often referred to as sashimi-grade, purely because in Japanese cuisine it is eaten raw, therefore must be of superior quality. Even when it is cooked, tuna is best eaten rare, medium-rare at the most, to ensure it remains moist and velvety smooth. Overcooked tuna can be dry and tough.

Steamed whiting fillets with iceberg lettuce & anchovy mayonnaise

Whiting are superb little white fish that are sweet, soft and delicate. Steaming them retains their beautiful texture and flavour. I love using the little sand whiting fillets we get in Brisbane but equally appreciate the King George whiting from South Australia, which are slightly larger so you may consider serving a smaller portion.

SERVES 6

2 heads iceberg lettuce, outer leaves removed
2 anchovy fillets, chopped
250 g (9 oz/1 cup) mayonnaise (Basics, page 232)
2 tablespoons salted capers, rinsed and squeezed dry
2 hard-boiled eggs, peeled and grated
35 g (1¼ oz/⅓ cup) freshly grated Italian parmesan cheese
2 spring onions (scallions), chopped
1 kg (2 lb 4 oz) boneless whiting fillets, skin on, scaled and pin-boned
sea salt and freshly ground black pepper

Slice the iceberg lettuce into wedges and arrange on plates. Fold the anchovy through the mayonnaise, adding a little hot water if necessary to achieve pouring consistency. Drizzle the mayonnaise over the lettuce. Scatter over the capers, grated egg, parmesan and spring onion.

Put the whiting fillets in a steamer basket over a saucepan of boiling water or on a rack inside a wok filled with boiling water. Season with sea salt and black pepper, cover with a tight-fitting lid, and steam for 5 minutes, or until the whiting is cooked through.

To serve, arrange the whiting fillets alongside the lettuce and finish with a grind of black pepper.

Note: I love the complexity, texture and the juicy crunch that the iceberg lettuce adds to what is otherwise a simple dish. You could use baby cos (romaine) and achieve a similar effect, but avoid using soft, small-leafed lettuces.

Seared ocean trout, colcannon, sauce matelote & horseradish crème fraîche

SERVES 6

60 g (2¼ oz) piece of fresh horseradish
300 g (10½ oz) crème fraîche
6 x 180 g (6½ oz) ocean trout or salmon fillets, skin on, scaled and pin-boned
100 g (3½ oz/3⅓ cups) watercress sprigs, to serve

COLCANNON

1.2 kg (2 lb 12 oz) pink-skinned waxy potatoes, such as desirée, peeled and diced
250 ml (9 fl oz/1 cup) full-cream (whole) milk, plus a little extra to reheat
125 ml (4 fl oz/½ cup) pouring (whipping) cream
125 g (4½ oz) unsalted butter, diced
sea salt and freshly ground black pepper
vegetable oil
½ large cabbage, shredded
olive oil
300 g (10½ oz) smoked bacon, diced

SAUCE MATELOTE

2 tablespoons olive oil
1 brown onion, chopped
1 leek, white part only, sliced
1 carrot, chopped
1 fennel bulb, chopped
4 garlic cloves, chopped
2 thyme sprigs
1 kg (2 lb 4 oz) ocean trout or salmon bones, head and tail removed
300 ml (10½ fl oz) red wine
500 ml (17 fl oz/2 cups) jus (Basics, page 230)
150 ml (5 fl oz) fish stock (Basics, page 229)
4 roma (plum) tomatoes, roughly chopped
2 tablespoons tomato paste (concentrated purée)
1 tablespoon good-quality red wine vinegar
1–2 teaspoons caster (superfine) sugar, to taste
20 g (¾ oz) cold unsalted butter, chopped

To make the sauce matelote, heat the olive oil in a large heavy-based saucepan over medium heat, add the vegetables, garlic and thyme and sauté for several minutes until the onion has softened. Add the trout bones, stirring, then deglaze the pan with the red wine. Simmer until the wine has reduced by half. Add the jus, fish stock, tomato and tomato paste, bring back to the boil, then reduce the heat and simmer for 30 minutes. Remove from the heat. Strain through a fine sieve placed over a bowl, discarding the solids. Season to taste with the red wine vinegar and sugar. Cool, then store in the refrigerator until required.

To make the colcannon, boil the potato in a saucepan of salted water until tender, drain, then pass through a mouli or mash by hand. Put the milk, cream and butter in a saucepan, bring to the boil, then stir into the potato to achieve a smooth consistency. Season to taste. Set aside.

Heat some vegetable oil in a saucepan or wok over high heat. Add the cabbage, in batches, to the hot oil, and fry until it just begins to colour. Remove with a slotted spoon and drain on paper towels. Set aside.

Heat a little olive oil in a heavy-based frying pan over medium heat. Cook the bacon until crisp. Drain on paper towels. Set aside.

Peel the horseradish, then finely grate into a bowl with the crème fraîche and mix gently to combine. Refrigerate until required.

Season the ocean trout skins with sea salt and black pepper. Heat a large, heavy-based or nonstick frying pan over high heat and add a little olive oil. Sear the trout, skin side down, until the skin is crisp and well coloured. Reduce the heat to medium, turn the trout, then cook for a further 3–5 minutes for medium-rare.

Meanwhile, add the cabbage and bacon to the mashed potato over medium heat. Gradually add a little extra milk, stirring, until the colcannon is heated through.

Gently reheat the sauce matelote in a saucepan over low heat. Bring to a gentle simmer then whisk in the butter, piece by piece, until the sauce appears thick and glossy.

To serve, place a generous spoonful of the colcannon in the centre of each serving plate. Lay the ocean trout over the mash and top with a handful of watercress sprigs and a spoonful of horseradish crème fraîche. Drizzle the hot matelote sauce around the plate.

Whole rainbow trout baked in sea salt with salsa verde

Break open the salt crust and you've got the juiciest, sweetest fish imaginable and surprisingly, not salty, as the fish doesn't absorb the salt, it just steams in its own juices inside the crust. This is wonderful on its own with some vegetables or salad, or as part of a shared banquet-style menu, and always good served with salsa verde.

SERVES 6

2 x 500 g (1 lb 2 oz) whole rainbow trout, skin on, scaled
freshly ground black pepper
3–4 rosemary or basil sprigs
1 lemon, sliced
1.5 kg (3 lb 5 oz) grey salt, such as Sel Gris, or damp grey salt (see Note)
1 quantity salsa verde (Basics, page 232), to serve

Preheat the oven to 200°C (400°F/Gas 6).

Season the cavity of the rainbow trout with black pepper, then fill with the rosemary or basil sprigs and the lemon slices. Moisten a generous amount of grey salt with a little water. Pack a thick layer of the moistened salt onto a large baking tray. Place the trout on the tray, pressing into the salt. Pack the remaining salt over and around to completely cover the trout. Bake for 20–25 minutes, or until a fork gently pierced into the trout is very warm or hot. Remove from the oven and set aside to rest for 10 minutes.

To serve, crack the salt crust on the trout and pull it away from the fish. Carefully peel off the skin, then, using a fork, lift off large pieces of trout, avoiding any bones, and place on serving plates.

Serve with generous spoonfuls of salsa verde.

Note: Sel Gris, or grey salt, is organic sea salt from the coastal area of Guérande in Brittany, France. The salt is moist and unrefined, its grey colour a result of the salt flats where it is collected by hand. It is lower in sodium than processed salt but higher in flavour making it ideal for cooking. In this recipe, the natural moisture of the salt also helps to keep the 'crust' intact and seal in the natural flavours of the trout.

Roast blue-eye trevalla, saffron potatoes, baby leeks & peas

SERVES 6

12 kipfler (fingerling) potatoes, scrubbed
   and cut into quarters
a good pinch of saffron
800 ml (28 fl oz) fish stock (Basics, page 229)
6 baby leeks, white part only, cut into
   2 cm (¾ inch) pieces
230 g (8½ oz) fresh shelled peas
   (use frozen if fresh unavailable)
50 g (1¾ oz) cold unsalted butter, diced
10 cherry tomatoes, cut into quarters
sea salt and freshly ground black pepper
juice of ½ lemon
2 tablespoons snipped chives
6 x 180 g (6½ oz) blue-eye trevalla, barramundi or other
   white fish fillets, skin on, scaled and pin-boned
olive oil

Preheat the oven to 180°C (350°F/Gas 4).

Put the potato in a large saucepan with the saffron and fish stock — there should be sufficient stock to just cover the potato. Bring to the boil, then reduce the heat and gently simmer for 8–10 minutes, or until tender.

When the potato is tender, add the leek, increase the heat and cook for 8–10 minutes, allowing the stock to reduce slightly. Add the peas and cook for 2 minutes, then add the diced butter and gently stir the vegetables in the pan — the stock should be glossy and have thickened slightly. Add the cherry tomato and season with sea salt and black pepper. Stir through the lemon juice and chives. Remove from the heat and keep warm.

Use a sharp knife to score the skin of the fish diagonally several times. Heat a large heavy-based or nonstick frying pan over high heat and add a little olive oil. Season the fish with sea salt and black pepper, then place, skin side down, in the pan. Sear for several minutes until the skin is crisp and well coloured — a sheet of baking paper placed over the fish, topped with a small skillet or pan will help to achieve a nice crisp skin. Remove the pan from the heat.

Carefully turn the fillets, then transfer to a baking tray and cook in the oven for 8–10 minutes, or until the fish is just cooked but still moist.

To serve, spoon the potato mixture into a shallow serving bowl and rest the fish carefully on top.

Barramundi, pan-fried potatoes, leeks & vanilla beurre blanc

SERVES 6

6 x 180 g (6½ oz) barramundi, blue-eye trevalla or other white fish fillets, skin removed and pin-boned
sea salt and freshly ground black pepper
plain (all-purpose) flour, for dusting
olive oil
12 yellow-fleshed potatoes, such as southern gold (pink-eye), steamed in their skins, cut in half
40 g (1½ oz) unsalted butter
2 leeks, white part only, sliced
1 quantity warm vanilla beurre blanc (Basics, page 231)

Preheat the oven to 180°C (350°F/Gas 4).

Season the fish fillets with sea salt and black pepper, then dust them lightly with flour, shaking to remove any excess. Heat a heavy-based or nonstick frying pan over high heat, add a little olive oil and sear the fish on one side until golden. Remove the pan from the heat. Carefully turn the fillets, then transfer to a baking tray and cook in the oven for 8–10 minutes, or until the fish is just cooked but still moist.

Heat a little olive oil in a heavy-based frying pan. Sauté the potatoes, cut side down, until they are well coloured and heated through.

Heat the butter in a separate heavy-based saucepan over medium heat. Sauté the leek until softened. Remove from the heat and keep warm.

To serve, arrange the potato on each serving plate, top with the sautéed leek and a fillet of fish. Drizzle over the warm vanilla beurre blanc.

Note: For a long time wild barramundi was heralded as supreme over the farmed variety. However with fish levels ever-decreasing, farmed barramundi is a far more sustainable option, not only for the environment but for consistency, availability and price, and therefore overall quality.

Grilled swordfish with warm kipfler potato salad & salsa verde

SERVES 6

12 kipfler (fingerling) potatoes, peeled and halved lengthways
125 ml (4 fl oz/½ cup) extra virgin olive oil
1 tablespoon wholegrain mustard
2 tablespoons red wine vinegar
grated zest and juice of 1 lemon
sea salt and freshly ground black pepper
olive oil
40 g (1½ oz/¼ cup) salted capers, rinsed and squeezed dry
6 x 180 g (6½ oz) swordfish fillets, skin removed
155 g (5½ oz/1 cup) pitted kalamata olives
55 g (2 oz/½ cup) small gherkins (cornichons), roughly chopped
1 French shallot (eschalot), finely diced
1 handful of basil leaves, torn
1 quantity salsa verde (Basics, page 232)

Cook the potatoes in salted boiling water until tender. Drain well, then transfer to a large bowl. Whisk together the extra virgin olive oil, mustard, vinegar, lemon zest and juice and season with sea salt and black pepper. While the potato is still warm, pour over the dressing, tossing to combine, then set aside for several minutes for the flavours to infuse. Keep warm.

In a heavy-based frying pan, heat a good splash of olive oil until very hot, but not smoking. Add the capers and fry until crisp. Remove from the pan using a slotted spoon. Drain on paper towels. Set aside to cool.

Meanwhile, in a separate heavy-based chargrill pan over high heat, add a little olive oil. Season the swordfish with sea salt and black pepper. Sear the swordfish until well coloured, then turn and continue to cook for 6–8 minutes — the fish should be moist and opaque in the centre.

To serve, add the olives, gherkins, eschalot and basil to the potatoes and divide among serving plates. Rest the swordfish alongside the salad, scatter with fried capers and top with a spoonful of salsa verde.

Note: Swordfish is one of the world's great firm-fleshed fish, but cook it too long and it can get too firm. I like to apply enough heat to sear the outside and cook the centre until just opaque, then remove the fish from the pan and let the residual heat gently finish the cooking. However, you be the judge to how you like yours.

Roast snapper, jerusalem artichokes, pine mushrooms & sorrel

Pine mushrooms make this dish really shine. Unfortunately, the season for them is limited to the cooler months. Whatever you do don't substitute them with everyday Swiss browns, whites or portobellos. Try the imported king browns or oyster mushrooms instead, available from good greengrocers and Asian food stores.

SERVES 6

juice of 2 lemons
400 g (14 oz) jerusalem artichokes
6 x 180 g (6½ oz) snapper fillets or other firm white fish fillets, skin on, scaled and pin-boned
olive oil
sea salt and freshly ground black pepper
400 g (14 oz) pine mushrooms, sliced
4 garlic cloves, thinly sliced
150 g (5½ oz) English spinach, stems removed
80 g (2¾ oz) sorrel leaves, thinly sliced
1 quantity warm beurre blanc (Basics, page 231)

Add the lemon juice to a bowl of cold water to make acidulated water. Peel the jerusalem artichokes and immediately place into the acidulated water as they will discolour quickly once cut. Drain the jerusalem artichokes and cook whole in a steamer basket over a saucepan of simmering water for 5–8 minutes, or until just tender when pierced with a small knife. Cool slightly, then slice into 5 mm (¼ inch) thick slices.

Preheat the oven to 180°C (350°F/Gas 4). Use a sharp knife to score the skin of the fish diagonally several times. Heat a large ovenproof frying pan over high heat and add a little olive oil. Season the fish with sea salt and black pepper, then place, skin side down, in the pan. Sear for several minutes until the skin is crisp and well coloured — a sheet of baking paper placed over the fish, topped with a small skillet or pan, will help to achieve a nice crisp skin. Remove the pan from the heat. Carefully turn the fillets, transfer to a baking tray and bake for 8–10 minutes, or until the fish is just cooked through but still moist.

Heat some olive oil in a large heavy-based frying pan over medium heat. Add the sliced artichokes and pine mushrooms and sauté for several minutes until well coloured. Season with sea salt and black pepper.

Heat some olive oil in a separate large heavy-based frying pan over low heat. Add the garlic and sauté for 1–2 minutes, without colour. Increase the heat to medium, add the spinach and sauté briefly until just wilted. Season with sea salt and black pepper, then drain on paper towels.

To serve, divide the spinach among serving plates. Arrange the artichokes and mushrooms over the spinach and top with a fish fillet. Stir the sorrel through the beurre blanc and lightly spoon over and around the plate.

Barramundi with a salad of globe artichokes, broad beans & lemon beurre blanc

SERVES 6
rock salt
400 g (14 oz) cherry tomatoes, cut in half
juice of 2 lemons
8–10 globe artichokes
½ garlic bulb, roughly chopped
3–4 thyme sprigs
olive oil
sea salt and freshly ground black pepper
100 g (3½ oz) green beans, trimmed
300 g (10½ oz) broad (fava) beans, shelled
6 x 180 g (6½ oz) barramundi, blue-eye trevalla or other white fish fillets, skin on, scaled and pin-boned
a knob of unsalted butter
juice of ½ lemon
155 g (5½ oz/1 cup) pitted kalamata olives
1 handful of mint leaves
good-quality balsamic vinegar
1 quantity warm lemon beurre blanc (Basics, page 231)

Spread a layer of rock salt on a baking tray. Lay the cherry tomatoes over the salt and leave in a warm part of the kitchen for about 4 hours to dry them out (you can also do this in a very low oven, but make sure you keep the oven door open).

Preheat the oven to 180°C (350°F/Gas 4).

Add the lemon juice to a bowl of cold water to make acidulated water. Prepare the artichokes by carefully pulling away the tough, dark green outer leaves. Cut off the tips, then use a peeler or paring knife to peel or shave the outer layer of fibres from the stem and base of the vegetable. Remove the choke, if any, by cutting and spooning out with a teaspoon. Put the artichokes immediately into the acidulated water as they will discolour quickly once cut. Drain, then pat dry with paper towels.

Wrap the artichokes in a large sheet of foil with the garlic, thyme, a good splash of olive oil and seasoned with sea salt and black pepper. Place on a baking tray, then roast in the oven for 30–40 minutes, or until soft.

Blanch the beans and broad beans separately in a saucepan of boiling salted water until tender. Drain and refresh in iced water. Peel the second skin from the broad beans.

Use a sharp knife to score the skin of the fish diagonally several times. Heat a large heavy-based or nonstick frying pan over high heat and add a little olive oil. Season the fish with sea salt and black pepper, then place skin side down in the pan. Sear for several minutes, or until the skin is crisp and well coloured — a sheet of baking paper placed over the fish, topped with a small skillet or pan, will help to achieve a nice crisp skin. Remove the pan from the heat. Carefully turn the fillets, add the butter and lemon juice, then transfer to a baking tray and cook in the oven for 8–10 minutes, basting at regular intervals, until the fish is just cooked but still moist.

Meanwhile, put the broad beans, green beans, olives and mint in a bowl. Moisten with a good splash of olive oil and balsamic vinegar and season with sea salt and black pepper.

To serve, reheat the artichokes if necessary, then arrange in the centre of serving plates. Place a handful of the bean salad over the artichokes and top with a fish fillet. Drizzle the lemon beurre blanc over and around.

Barbecue seafood skewers with papaya, lemongrass, lime & chilli salad
(*pictured page 92*)

SERVES 6

12 bamboo skewers, soaked in water for 30 minutes
500 g (1 lb 2 oz) salmon or ocean trout fillets, skin removed, pin-boned and cubed
500 g (1 lb 2 oz) white fish fillets, skin removed, pin-boned and cubed
24 large scallops, roe removed
24 large raw prawns (shrimp), shelled and deveined, with tails intact
lime wedges, to serve

MARINADE

125 ml (4 fl oz/½ cup) olive oil
a pinch of dried chilli flakes
grated zest of 1 lemon
2 garlic cloves, thinly sliced
2 makrut (kaffir lime) leaves, thinly sliced

SALAD

1 red papaya, peeled, seeded and diced
½ lemongrass stem, white part only, very finely diced
1 red chilli, seeded and very finely diced
5 makrut (kaffir lime) leaves, very thinly sliced
1 handful of mint leaves, torn
1 tablespoon fish sauce
2 tablespoons freshly squeezed lime juice
2 tablespoons grated palm sugar (jaggery)

....

Thread the seafood onto the skewers, alternating with the salmon, white fish, scallops and prawns. Lay the seafood skewers flat in a shallow baking tray.

To make the marinade, combine all of the ingredients in a bowl. Pour over the seafood skewers, turning so they are well coated on all sides, then cover and refrigerate for 3 hours.

To make the salad, combine the red papaya, lemongrass, chilli, makrut leaves and mint in a large bowl. In a separate bowl, whisk together the fish sauce, lime juice and palm sugar. Pour enough dressing over the salad to moisten.

Heat a barbecue or chargrill pan to high heat. Sear the seafood skewers on the hot grill for 1 minute each side, or until cooked.

To serve, divide the salad among serving plates and place the seafood skewers alongside. Serve with lime wedges.

Note: These seafood skewers also work well served on their own as part of a barbecue banquet or as an appetiser. Drizzle them with an Asian-inspired sauce or dressing (the papaya salad dressing here would work beautifully), serve them with lime mayonnaise (Basics, page 232) to dip or with a squeeze of lemon or lime juice.

Barbecue seafood skewers with papaya, lemongrass, lime & chilli salad

Atlantic salmon in brik pastry with betel leaves, eggplant, lime & coconut

Atlantic salmon in brik pastry with betel leaves, eggplant, lime & coconut

Betel leaves epitomise the lively cutting taste of Asian street food and are slowly being embraced by Australian chefs. At e'cco we've been using them for years and suggest you look for them in Asian food stores, perhaps even in the freezer section. Brik (or malsouqa pastry) is a bit like filo pastry and can be found at Middle Eastern or speciality food stores. You could also use spring roll pastry, which is available from most Asian food stores.

(pictured page 93)

SERVES 6–8

LIME & COCONUT SAUCE
30 g (1 oz) fresh turmeric, roughly chopped
70 g (2½ oz) fresh ginger, roughly chopped
20 g (¾ oz) galangal, roughly chopped
2 French shallots (eschalots), roughly chopped
1 long red chilli, seeded and roughly chopped
2 garlic cloves, roughly chopped
1 tablespoon shrimp paste
½ lemongrass stem, white part only, roughly chopped
1½ tablespoons vegetable oil

150 ml (5 fl oz) Shaoxing rice wine
1 large roma (plum) tomato, roughly diced
2 makrut (kaffir lime) leaves
2 fresh curry leaves
400 ml (14 fl oz) fish stock (Basics, page 229)
875 ml (30 fl oz/3½ cups) coconut milk
a small pinch of saffron threads
juice of ½ lime, or to taste
fish sauce, to taste
½ tablespoon grated palm sugar (jaggery), or to taste

To make the lime and coconut sauce, put the turmeric, ginger, galangal, eschalot, chilli, garlic, shrimp paste and lemongrass in a food processor. With the machine running, drizzle in the oil to form a smooth paste. Transfer the paste to a large heavy-based saucepan over medium heat. Sauté for 5 minutes, or until the paste splits from the oil, scraping the bottom of the pan often. Deglaze the pan with the Shaoxing rice wine, then add the tomato, makrut and curry leaves. Bring to the boil, then reduce the heat and simmer until reduced by half, scraping the bottom of the pan frequently. Add the fish stock, bring back to the boil, then reduce the heat and simmer until reduced by two-thirds. Add the coconut milk and saffron and bring back to the boil, then reduce the heat to low and simmer for 20 minutes. Remove from the heat. Add the lime juice, fish sauce and palm sugar to taste. Pass the sauce through a very fine sieve or muslin (cheesecloth). Store the sauce refrigerated in an airtight container until required.

To prepare the salmon, lay the pastry sheets on a clean work surface. Top each salmon portion, spine side up, with a betel leaf. Invert each salmon portion onto the pastry, then season with sea salt and black pepper. Trim the pastry and betel leaf flush down the length of the salmon. Bring the top and bottom of the pastry together over the salmon, so that it overlaps by at least 1 cm (½ inch), and seal together using a little water. The salmon can be prepared in advance and refrigerated on trays lined with baking paper until required.

Preheat the oven to 190°C (375°F/Gas 5).

Heat the olive oil in a nonstick frying pan over medium heat. Add the salmon, betel leaf side down, and cook for 2–3 minutes until the pastry is crisp and golden. Turn the salmon gently, being careful not to damage the pastry, and cook for a further 2–3 minutes, or until the pastry is light golden. Transfer the salmon carefully to a baking tray and cook in the oven for a further 2–3 minutes, if necessary, for medium-rare. Rest for 5 minutes before serving.

SALMON IN BRIK PASTRY

4 x 25 cm (10 inch) brik pastry or square spring roll pastry sheets

8 x 180 g (6½ oz) Atlantic salmon fillets, skin removed and pin-boned

8 large betel leaves or 3 makrut (kaffir lime) leaves, thinly sliced

sea salt and freshly ground black pepper

2½ tablespoons olive oil

DASHI EGGPLANT

1 tablespoon dashi powder (see Note)

1 large eggplant (aubergine), peeled, cut into 1.5 cm (⅝ inch) cubes

200 g (7 oz) snow pea (mangetout) sprouts

3 long red chillies, seeded and thinly sliced lengthways

2 spring onions (scallions), thinly sliced diagonally

1 handful of coriander (cilantro) leaves

140 g (5 oz/1½ cups) bean shoots

Meanwhile, to make the dashi eggplant, combine the dashi powder and 800 ml (28 fl oz) hot water in a saucepan over medium heat, stirring well to combine. Bring to the boil, then reduce the heat to a simmer. Add the eggplant and cook gently for 3 minutes, stirring occasionally, until the eggplant is tender, opaque in colour and just cooked through. The dashi stock should almost all be absorbed by the eggplant. Add the snow pea sprouts, chilli, spring onion, coriander and bean shoots and wilt slightly. Remove from the heat. Adjust the seasoning.

To serve, gently reheat the sauce in a saucepan over low heat. Remove from the heat and blend briefly with a hand-held blender or whisk to lighten and aerate the sauce. Divide the eggplant mixture among serving bowls and rest the salmon on top. Spoon the sauce around the plate.

Note: Dashi is Japanese stock used as a base for soups and dressings. It is generally sold as a powder. Check the packet instructions as they may vary among brands.

Pan-fried whiting, curry-spiced cauliflower, wild rocket, raisins & flaked almonds

You can't overestimate the difference freshly toasted and ground spices make to a dish. By buying spices in small quantities and freshly toasting and grinding them, you can make a meal really sing.

SERVES 6
350 g (12 oz) cauliflower, cut into small florets
olive oil
1 teaspoon unsalted butter
30 g (1 oz/⅓ cup) flaked almonds, toasted
2 tablespoons raisins
60 g (2¼ oz/1¾ cups) wild rocket (arugula) leaves
juice of ½ lemon
extra virgin olive oil
plain (all-purpose) flour, for dusting
sea salt and freshly ground black pepper
1 kg (2 lb 4 oz) whiting fillets, skin on, scaled and pin-boned (allow 3–4 fillets per serve)
a pinch of sumac

SPICE MIX
1 teaspoon coriander seeds
1 teaspoon cumin seeds
1 teaspoon fennel seeds
3 cardamom pods
⅓ teaspoon ground turmeric

CAULIFLOWER PURÉE
750 g (1 lb 10 oz) cauliflower, stems removed, chopped
1 bay leaf
full-cream (whole) milk, enough to cover
sea salt and freshly ground white pepper
50 g (1¾ oz) unsalted butter
80 ml (2½ fl oz/⅓ cup) pouring (whipping) cream

To make the spice mix, toast the coriander, cumin, fennel seeds and cardamom pods in a dry frying pan over medium heat until fragrant. Transfer the seeds to a mortar and pestle, discarding the pods of the cardamom, then grind together (or use a spice grinder) to make a fine powder. Combine with the turmeric.

To make the cauliflower purée, put the cauliflower in a deep saucepan with the bay leaf and enough milk to just cover. Season lightly with sea salt and white pepper. Bring to the boil, then reduce the heat and simmer until the cauliflower is tender when tested with a knife. Gently heat the butter and cream in a small saucepan. Drain the cauliflower pieces, reserving the cooking milk. Place the cauliflower in a food processor and purée, gradually adding the combined butter and cream. If the purée is a little thick add a little of the cooking milk. Season with sea salt and white pepper; set aside and keep warm.

Blanch the cauliflower florets in salted boiling water for 1–2 minutes, then plunge into iced water to cool. Drain well.

Heat a little olive oil and the butter in a nonstick frying pan over medium heat. Sauté the cauliflower florets for 1–2 minutes. Once slightly coloured, add the spice mix. Transfer to a bowl and toss gently with the almonds, raisins and rocket. Dress with a squeeze of lemon juice and some extra virgin olive oil. Season to taste.

Season some flour with a little sea salt and black pepper. Dust the whiting fillets in the flour, shaking to remove any excess. Heat a little olive oil on a barbecue flatplate or in a nonstick frying pan over medium heat. Cook the whiting, skin side down, for 1–2 minutes, turning once, then quickly remove from the heat.

To serve, spoon the warm cauliflower purée into the centre of each serving plate and form into a circle. Place the warm spiced cauliflower salad in the centre and lay the whiting fillets over the top. Finish with a drizzle of extra virgin olive oil and a sprinkle of sumac.

Eye fillet of beef, pommes allumettes, crisp pancetta & horseradish cream

SERVES 6

1.2 kg (2 lb 11 oz) pink-skinned waxy potatoes, such as desiree, peeled
400 ml (14 fl oz) light olive oil
olive oil
6 x 200 g (7 oz) best-quality beef eye-fillets
100 g (3½ oz/3⅓ cups) watercress sprigs
2 spring onions (scallions), thinly sliced
18 thin slices flat pancetta, grilled
jus (Basics, page 230), warmed, to serve

HORSERADISH CREAM

300 ml (10½ fl oz) pouring (whipping) cream
50 g (1¾ oz) fresh horseradish, finely grated
a squeeze of lemon juice
sea salt and freshly ground black pepper

To make the horseradish cream, whisk together the cream, horseradish and lemon juice, to taste, until soft peaks form. Season with sea salt and black pepper. Refrigerate in an airtight container until ready to serve. It will keep for up to 3 days.

Cut the potatoes into allumettes (matchsticks), about 7 cm (2¾ inches) long and 6 mm (¼ inch) thick. Put the allumettes into a large bowl, rinse with cold water, drain, then rinse again to remove any excess starch. Drain well and pat dry with paper towels.

Preheat the oven to 220°C (425°F/Gas 7).

Heat half of the light olive oil in a large nonstick frying pan over medium heat. As the oil just begins to smoke, carefully add half of the allumettes, spreading them out in a single layer. Cook for 1–2 minutes, or until golden, then gently turn using a spatula being careful they don't break. Continue to cook the potatoes for 4–5 minutes, turning occasionally, until golden on all sides and cooked through. Drain on paper towels. Keep warm and repeat with the remaining oil and allumettes until all are cooked. Keep warm.

Meanwhile, heat a little olive oil in a large heavy-based ovenproof frying pan over high heat. Season the eye-fillets with sea salt and black pepper, then seal in the hot pan for 2–3 minutes each side. Transfer to the oven and cook for a further 5–6 minutes or until pink (medium). Remove from the oven and set aside to rest for 5 minutes.

Season the warm allumettes, then gently toss together with the watercress, spring onion and a drizzle of olive oil.

To serve, divide the allumettes and watercress salad among serving plates. Arrange four slices of pancetta over the allumettes, then top with a fillet of beef. Place a spoonful of horseradish cream on the beef and drizzle the hot jus around the plate.

Chicken breast wrapped in Parma ham with salsa Romesco

SERVES 6

1.5 kg (3 lb 5 oz) chicken breast fillets
100 ml (3½ fl oz) extra virgin olive oil
1 garlic clove, crushed
2 tablespoons chopped thyme leaves
30 thin slices Parma ham or prosciutto
olive oil
sea salt and freshly ground black pepper
1 quantity salsa Romesco (Basics, page 235)

Remove the chicken tenderloins where it joins the breast, removing the sinew. Set aside. Remove any fat and sinew from the chicken breast, then carve on an angle into three even-sized thin, wide pieces. If the pieces are thick, lay them between two sheets of plastic wrap and use a meat mallet or rolling pin to lightly tap into 1 cm (½ inch) thick escalopes (see Glossary). Put the chicken tenderloins and breast pieces in a shallow non-reactive tray. Whisk together the extra virgin olive oil, garlic and thyme, then pour over the chicken, tossing the chicken through the oil so they are well coated. Cover and refrigerate for 1 hour to marinate.

Lay two large sheets of plastic wrap on a flat work surface. Lay the Parma ham horizontally in long strips across both sheets of the plastic wrap, slightly overlapping, allowing a 2–3 cm (¾–1¼ inch) border around the outside. Lay the chicken pieces evenly over the Parma ham, laying them vertically across the bottom edge of the ham and working your way up. Starting from the bottom edge, roll the chicken and ham into a roulade — tightly like a scroll — pulling away the plastic wrap as you go. Once completely rolled, wrap the roulade tightly in a large sheet of plastic wrap, then twist the ends tightly like a lolly (candy) wrapper. Pop any air bubbles that appear in the plastic, then roll in another sheet of plastic wrap (this will ensure even cooking). Repeat with the remaining chicken and ham to make another tightly wrapped roulade.

Bring a large saucepan of water to the boil. Poach the chicken roulades for 8 minutes, then remove from the heat. Set aside to rest for 10 minutes. Remove the plastic wrap from the warm chicken roulades and pat dry with paper towels.

Heat some olive oil in a large nonstick frying pan over medium heat. Add the chicken roulades, season with sea salt and black pepper, and cook for several minutes, turning frequently so that it colours evenly. Remove from the heat and allow to rest for 5 minutes.

To serve, use a sharp knife to carve each chicken roulade into nine even-sized pieces, being careful not to tear the ham. Arrange three slices on the base of each serving plate with a spoonful of salsa Romesco alongside. Serve accompanied with a side dish of braised fennel, pine nuts, raisins, wild rocket, Persian feta and vincotto (Sides, page 171) and roast kipflers with artichokes, olives and lemon (Sides, page 159), or your favourite side dishes.

Duck breast, pumpkin purée, balsamic braised red cabbage & candied walnuts

SERVES 6

6 x 240 g (8½ oz) duck breasts, trimmed
olive oil
100 g (3½ oz/1 cup) candied walnuts (Basics, page 239)
jus (Basics, page 230), warmed, to serve

PUMPKIN PURÉE

1.5 kg (3 lb 5 oz) jap or kent pumpkin (winter squash)
100 g (3½ oz) unsalted butter
4 garlic cloves
sea salt and freshly ground black pepper
100–150 ml (3½–5 fl oz) pouring (whipping) cream

BALSAMIC BRAISED RED CABBAGE

250 ml (9 fl oz/1 cup) good-quality balsamic vinegar
250ml (9 fl oz/1 cup) red wine
150 g (5½ oz) soft brown sugar
1 small red cabbage, outer leaves and core removed, shredded

Preheat the oven to 180°C (350°F/Gas 4).

To make the pumpkin purée, cut the pumpkin in half horizontally through the middle. Use a large metal spoon to scoop out the seeds and pith. Put half the butter and 2 garlic cloves in the cavity of each half, season with sea salt and black pepper, then wrap tightly in foil. Place on a baking tray and bake for 1 hour, or until very soft. Remove from the oven. Carefully open the foil and leave the pumpkin to cool slightly; discard the garlic. Scoop the flesh into a sieve and let stand for 10 minutes for any excess liquid to drain off. Transfer the pumpkin to a food processor, season with sea salt and black pepper and blend until very smooth, adjusting the consistency with the cream, as needed. Refrigerate until required.

To make the balsamic braised red cabbage, put the balsamic vinegar, red wine and sugar in a large heavy-based saucepan over medium–high heat. Add the cabbage and cook for 8–10 minutes, or until the cabbage begins to soften and the liquid has reduced by half. Reduce the heat to low and continue to cook, stirring often, until no liquid remains and the cabbage is completely cooked and shiny. Season to taste with sea salt and black pepper. Remove from the heat and set aside.

Score the skin of the duck breast with a sharp knife and season with sea salt and black pepper. Heat a little olive oil in a large heavy-based frying pan over medium heat and place the duck, skin side down, in the pan. Cook slowly to render down the fat, draining off any excess. Increase the heat and cook for 3–4 minutes, then turn over and cook for a further 3–4 minutes. Remove from the heat and rest the duck breast for several minutes.

Meanwhile, gently reheat the pumpkin purée and red cabbage, if necessary.

To serve, place a spoonful of the pumpkin purée to one side of each serving plate, with a large spoonful of the braised red cabbage alongside. Slice each duck breast into five or six slices and arrange over the cabbage. Scatter over the candied walnuts and drizzle a little of the warmed jus around the plate.

Rack of lamb with herb-mustard crust & a salad of Ligurian olives, parsley & onion

SERVES 6

10 slices stale white bread, crusts removed
3 handfuls of flat-leaf (Italian) parsley leaves, chopped
sea salt and freshly ground black pepper
50 g (1¾ oz) unsalted butter
2 French shallots (eschalots), diced
2 garlic cloves, crushed
grated zest of 1 lemon
2 teaspoons Dijon mustard, plus extra
6 x four-finger lamb racks, trimmed
olive oil
80 g (2¾ oz/½ cup) Ligurian olives, pitted
½ red onion, thinly sliced
1 quantity red wine vinaigarette (Basics, page 233)

Put the bread in a food processor and process until it resembles coarse crumbs. Mix the crumbs with one-third of the parsley, some sea salt and black pepper. Melt the butter over medium heat, then add the eschalot, garlic, lemon zest and mustard and cook for 2–3 minutes. Pour enough of the butter mixture over the breadcrumbs to moisten — it should hold together when pressed with your fingers. The crust mixture can be made in advance and stored in an airtight container in the refrigerator for up to 2 days.

Preheat the oven to 200°C (400°F/Gas 6). Brush the lamb racks with a little olive oil and season with sea salt and black pepper. Heat a heavy-based frying pan over high heat, add the lamb racks and sear on all sides until well coloured. Remove from the heat.

Put the lamb racks on a baking tray. Brush the top of the lamb racks with a little of the extra mustard. Pack the herb crust onto the lamb, pressing gently but making sure it is firm enough so that the crust holds in place. Roast for about 15–20 minutes, or until pink (medium). Remove from the oven and set aside to rest for 10 minutes.

To serve, toss the remaining parsley, olives and onion in enough red wine vinaigrette to moisten. Slice the lamb racks in half and arrange on serving plates with a handful of salad to one side. Serve with a bowl of steamed, buttered new season potatoes on the side.

Sichuan pork belly, black bean broth & Asian greens

SERVES 6

4 tablespoons Sichuan peppercorns (Glossary)
½ cinnamon stick
1 star anise
100 g (3½ oz/¾ cup) sea salt
a pinch of dried chilli flakes
1.2–1.5 kg (2 lb 12 oz–3 lb 5 oz) boneless pork belly

ASIAN GREENS
30 g (1 oz) salted black beans, soaked in water for 1 hour
olive oil
2 red chillies, thinly sliced
3 cm (1¼ inch) piece of ginger, thinly sliced
4 spring onions (scallions), thinly sliced
100 g (3½ oz) shiitake mushrooms, thinly sliced
300 g (10½ oz) bok choy (pak choy), cut into 5 cm (2 inch) pieces
300 g (10½ oz) choy sum, cut into 5 cm (2 inch) pieces
100 g (3½ oz) bean shoots

BLACK BEAN BROTH
30 g (1 oz) salted black beans (Glossary), soaked in water for 1 hour
2 tablespoons olive oil
2 tablespoons sesame oil
4 French shallots (eschalots), thinly sliced
2 garlic cloves, thinly sliced
3 cm (1¼ inch) piece of ginger, finely chopped
1 red chilli, seeded and finely chopped
750 ml (26 fl oz/3 cups) white chicken stock (Basics, page 228)
80 ml (2½ fl oz/⅓ cup) rice wine vinegar
80 ml (2½ fl oz/⅓ cup) soy sauce
2 tablespoons honey
70 g (2½ oz) caster (superfine) sugar
½ teaspoon fish sauce

....

Heat a heavy-based frying pan over medium heat. Roast the Sichuan peppercorns, cinnamon stick and star anise in the hot pan for several minutes until fragrant. Using a mortar and pestle or in a spice grinder, grind the spices to a fine powder. Add the sea salt and chilli flakes and mix through.

Using a sharp knife, score the skin of the pork belly in a diamond pattern all over. Rub the spice mix over the pork belly, using just enough to cover. Reserve any remaining spice mix for another use. Cover and refrigerate the pork belly overnight for the flavours to develop.

To make the black bean broth, drain the black beans and set aside. Heat the olive and sesame oils in a deep heavy-based saucepan over low-medium heat. Lightly sauté the eschalot, garlic, ginger and chilli, with little or no colour, until the eschalot is soft and translucent. Add the stock, rice wine vinegar, soy sauce, honey, sugar, fish sauce and black beans, bring to the boil, then reduce the heat and simmer for 30 minutes. Strain, discarding the black beans and aromatics. Set aside.

Preheat the oven to 250°C (500°F/Gas 9). Put a little water in the base of a large roasting tray. Sit the pork, skin side up, on a wire rack inside the tray. Bake for 15 minutes. Reduce the temperature to 170°C (325°F/Gas 3) and continue to cook for 1 hour, or until the pork is tender and the juices run clear when pierced with a knife.

Meanwhile, to make the Asian greens, drain the black beans and set aside. Heat a little olive oil in a large heavy-based frying pan over medium heat. Lightly sauté the chilli, ginger and spring onion, then add the shiitake mushrooms and cook for 2 minutes. Add 500 ml (17 fl oz/2 cups) of the black bean broth. Bring to the boil, reduce the heat, then add the black beans, bok choy and choy sum. Simmer briefly until the greens are tender. Lastly add the bean shoots.

To serve, divide the vegetables and broth among serving bowls. Carve the pork belly into thin slices, allowing three or four slices per person. Arrange the pork slices over the vegetables.

Roast chicken, baby carrots, eschalots, salted lemon & pine nuts

SERVES 6

2 garlic bulbs, unpeeled, cut in half
3–4 thyme sprigs
2 lemons, cut into quarters
2 x 1.6 kg (3 lb 8 oz) whole chickens
olive oil
sea salt and freshly ground black pepper
60 g (2¼ oz) unsalted butter
500 g (1 lb 2 oz) French shallots (eschalots)
1 salted lemon (Basics, page 237), flesh discarded and zest cut into strips
80 g (2¾ oz/½ cup) pine nuts, toasted
2 tablespoons chopped flat-leaf (Italian) parsley leaves
18 baby carrots, peeled and trimmed
300 g (10½ oz) sugarsnap peas, trimmed

DRESSING

125 ml (4 fl oz/½ cup) jus (Basics, page 230), warmed
1 tablespoon wholegrain mustard
60 ml (2 fl oz/¼ cup) sherry vinegar
250 ml (9 fl oz/1 cup) extra virgin olive oil

Preheat the oven to 200°C (400°F/Gas 6). Combine the garlic and thyme with the lemon quarters and divide between the cavity of each chicken. Rub the skins all over with olive oil, then season with sea salt and black pepper. Sit the chickens on a baking tray and roast for 1 hour–1 hour 20 minutes, or until cooked. Rest for 10 minutes.

Meanwhile, heat the butter and a little olive oil in a nonstick ovenproof frying pan over medium heat. Add the eschalot, season with sea salt and black pepper and sauté for several minutes, or until golden, stirring to achieve an even colour. Cover the pan with a lid or foil, transfer to the oven and roast for 15 minutes, or until just tender. Remove from the oven, set aside and keep warm.

To make the dressing, whisk together the jus, mustard and sherry vinegar until well combined. Gradually whisk in the extra virgin olive oil, then season with sea salt and black pepper. Set aside.

Put the salted lemon, pine nuts and parsley in a bowl and moisten with a little of the dressing.

Cook the carrots in a large saucepan of salted boiling water for 2–3 minutes. During the last minute of cooking add the sugarsnap peas. Cook until tender, then drain.

To serve, carve the chickens into pieces and arrange on serving plates. Spoon over the vegetables, then drizzle over the warm dressing.

Note: Any left-over roast chicken meat can be used in the salad with avocado, apple, celery and pecans (see page 64). You can also substitute slow-cooked rabbit meat with roast chicken meat, in the risotto of slow-cooked rabbit, peas and mascarpone (see page 135).

Roast pork belly, caramelised pear purée, potato fondant, silverbeet & pomegranate jus

(pictured page 108)

SERVES 6

1½ tablespoons fennel seeds
¾ tablespoon dried chilli flakes
30 g (1 oz) sea salt
1.2 kg (2 lb 10 oz) boneless pork belly
250 ml (9 fl oz/1 cup) jus (Basics, page 230)
1 pomegranate
extra virgin olive oil
150 g (5½ oz) young silverbeet (Swiss chard), stems removed, chopped
sea salt and freshly ground black pepper

CARAMELISED PEAR PURÉE

400 g (14 oz) caster (superfine) sugar
750 g (1 lb 10 oz) pears, peeled, cored and cut into quarters
175 g (6 oz) unsalted butter, diced and softened

Combine the fennel seeds, chilli flakes and sea salt. Using a sharp knife, score the skin of the pork belly. Rub the spice mix over the pork belly so it is completely covered. Sit the pork on a baking tray, cover with plastic wrap, then refrigerate for at least 12 hours for the pork to cure.

To make the caramelised pear purée, put the sugar and 100 ml (3½ fl oz) water in a large, deep frying pan over medium heat, stirring until the sugar has dissolved. Bring to the boil and boil without stirring until the syrup turns a dark caramel colour. Immediately remove from the heat and very carefully, as hot caramel spits, add the pear. Return the pan to low heat and cook, tossing the pears in the caramel for 10–15 minutes, or until soft. Remove from the heat. Transfer the pear and caramel to a food processor, then gradually add the butter and blend until smooth. Cool completely before storing in an airtight container and refrigerating until required.

Preheat the oven to 200°C (400°F/Gas 6). Put a little water in the base of a large roasting tray. Sit the pork belly, skin side up, on a wire rack inside the tray. Roast the pork belly for 1½–2 hours, or until the juices run clear when pierced with a knife or the centre of the pork reaches 60°C (140°F) when probed with a meat thermometer. If the skin isn't crisp enough, cook for a further 5 minutes under a hot grill (broiler) being careful it doesn't burn. Rest the pork for 20 minutes before serving (see Note).

Meanwhile, to make the potato fondants, trim the ends of the potatoes so they sit flat upright, then cut into rounds using a sharp 5–6 cm (2–2½ inch) pastry cutter. Press the butter into the base of a heavy-based saucepan, push the potatoes into the butter, then add the chicken stock. Cook over low–medium heat for 10–12 minutes, or until the butter and stock begin to boil rapidly, shaking the pan gently to prevent the potatoes from sticking. Reduce the heat and bring to a simmer. Cook for a further 20–25 minutes, turning halfway through the cooking time once they've coloured. Remove from the heat and stand in a warm place for 10 minutes.

Gently lift the potatoes from the cooking liquid onto a baking tray, then transfer to a moderate oven for 5–8 minutes to warm through while the pork is resting.

POTATO FONDANTS
6 large waxy potatoes, such as sebago or desiree potatoes, unpeeled, scrubbed
300 g (10½ oz) unsalted butter, diced
200 ml (7 fl oz) white chicken stock (Basics, page 228)

Bring the jus to a gentle simmer, then remove from the heat. Remove the seeds from the pomegranate, discarding any white membrane. Put the seeds in a large bowl and pour over the hot jus. Set aside and keep warm.

Heat a heavy-based frying pan over high heat. Add a little extra virgin olive oil and the silverbeet. Season with sea salt and black pepper and toss briefly until just wilted.

Gently reheat the pear purée in a saucepan over low heat to warm through.

To serve, divide the silverbeet among serving plates. Place a potato fondant and a spoonful of pear purée alongside. Carve the pork and arrange two to three slices over the silverbeet. Spoon the pomegranate jus around the plate.

Note: The pork belly is best rested for 20 minutes before carving to ensure it remains moist and easier to carve. It is often easier to carve the pork belly skin side down.

Roast pork belly, caramelised pear purée, potato fondant, silverbeet & pomegranate jus

Slow-cooked duck, roast kipflers, caramelised onions & bacon

Slow-cooked duck, roast kipflers, caramelised onions & bacon

The French call it confit — I love duck cooked this way. A few things are going on here. The salt draws the liquid from the flesh while the flesh absorbs the aromatics from the herbs and spices, and the gentle cooking makes the duck succulent. Goose or duck fat can be purchased from good delicatessens. Vive le confit!
(pictured page 109)

SERVES 6

10 kipfler (fingerling) potatoes, unpeeled, scrubbed and cut into quarters lengthways
2 teaspoons thyme leaves
olive oil
200 g (7 oz) bacon lardons (Glossary)
1 tablespoon chopped flat-leaf (Italian) parsley leaves
18 asparagus spears or 350 g (12 oz) green beans, trimmed
a knob of unsalted butter
jus (Basics, page 230), warmed, to serve

SLOW-COOKED DUCK

6 x 300 g (10½ oz) duck thigh and leg portions
2 thyme sprigs
zest of 1 lemon, removed in strips
zest of 1 orange, removed in strips
6 garlic cloves, unpeeled, lightly crushed
3 star anise
sea salt
500 g (1 lb 2 oz/2 cups) duck or goose fat
  or 500 ml (17 fl oz/2 cups) light olive oil

To make the slow-cooked duck legs, prepare the duck portions by removing each thigh bone, then run a sharp knife around the bone just below the knuckle of each leg to allow the meat to shrink down during cooking. Put the duck in a shallow baking dish and scatter with the thyme, zest, garlic, star anise and a generous amount of sea salt. Rub the mixture thoroughly into the duck, then cover and refrigerate for 24 hours.

Remove the duck from the marinade, discarding the aromatics, and rinse in a bowl of cold water, changing the water several times. Drain the duck, then pat dry with paper towels.

Preheat the oven to 130°C (250°F/Gas 1). Place the duck in a roasting tray that fits them snugly. Heat the fat in a large saucepan until liquefied, then pour over the duck in the tray. Place in the oven and cook for 2–2½ hours, or until tender. Allow to cool, then put the duck in a container and cover with the cooking fat to seal and preserve it. The duck can be stored in the fat in the refrigerator for up to 2 weeks.

To make the caramelised onions, heat the oil and butter in a wide, shallow heavy-based frying pan over medium heat. Add the onion and cook for 30–40 minutes, stirring often. Add the vinegar and sugar and cook for a further 15–20 minutes, or until the onion is dark in colour and jam-like in consistency. Season with sea salt and black pepper and allow to cool. The onions can be prepared a day or two in advance and refrigerated.

Preheat the oven to 200°C (400°F/Gas 6). Grease and line a baking tray with baking paper. Put the potato in a large bowl and toss together with the thyme leaves, a drizzle of olive oil, sea salt and black pepper. Spread the potatoes in the prepared tray and roast for 30 minutes, or until tender and golden.

Meanwhile, put the duck legs on a paper-lined baking tray, skin side up, and place in the oven for about 12–15 minutes, or until warmed through and the skin is crisp. Remove from the oven and keep warm, resting on paper towels to absorb any excess fat.

CARAMELISED ONIONS
1 tablespoon olive oil
20 g (¾ oz) unsalted butter
5 onions, thinly sliced
2 tablespoons balsamic vinegar
30 g (1 oz) soft brown sugar
sea salt and freshly ground black pepper

Meanwhile, heat a little olive oil in a large heavy-based frying pan over medium heat. Add the bacon and gently fry for 2–3 minutes. Add the potato, then the caramelised onions, gently tossing together. Fold through the parsley.

Blanch the asparagus in salted boiling water until tender, drain, then toss in a bowl with the butter, a little sea salt and black pepper.

To serve, spoon the potato into the centre of each serving plate. Top with the asparagus, then with the duck. Spoon the warm jus over and around.

Note: Confit is a great technique to master (one of the classics) but these days it is not uncommon to see duck confit sold in good delicatessens. These store-bought versions are a good alternative when preparation time is limited.

Pork loin with prunes, sage, sautéed apples & hazelnuts

SERVES 6

165 g (5¾ oz/¾ cup) pitted prunes, roughly chopped
100 ml (3½ fl oz) brandy
1.5 kg (3 lb 5 oz) boneless pork loin, skin on
1 handful of sage leaves
sea salt and freshly ground black pepper
olive oil
2 garlic bulbs
2 onions
2 carrots
2 leeks
2 celery stalks
300 g (10½ oz) cavolo nero (Tuscan black cabbage) or silverbeet (Swiss chard)
3 garlic cloves, thinly sliced
1 teaspoon dried chilli flakes
1 tablespoon fennel seeds, toasted and crushed
jus (Basics, page 230), warmed, to serve

SAUTÉED APPLES & HAZELNUTS

50 g (1¾ oz) unsalted butter
4 green apples, peeled, cored and cut into wedges
2 tablespoons caster (superfine) sugar
70 g (2½ oz/½ cup) hazelnuts, roasted and skinned
80 ml (2½ fl oz/⅓ cup) sherry

Put the prunes in a mixing bowl. Bring the brandy to the boil in a saucepan over high heat, then pour over the prunes. Set aside to soak for 15 minutes. Drain.

Score the skin of the pork loin with a sharp knife and place it, skin side down, on a work surface. Make a 3 cm (1¼ inch) deep slit in the flesh where the loin meets the belly. Stuff the soaked prunes and most of the sage leaves in the incision and season well with sea salt and black pepper. Roll the loin up tightly and secure with kitchen string at 3 cm (1¼ inch) intervals. Rub the pork skin with a little olive oil and sea salt.

Preheat the oven to 220°C (425°F/Gas 7).

Roughly chop the garlic bulbs, onions, carrots, leeks and celery and spread over the base of a baking tray with a little water. Put the pork loin on the vegetables and roast for 15 minutes. Reduce the oven temperature to 170°C (325°F/Gas 3) and continue to roast for 30–40 minutes. The pork is cooked when the juices run clear when pierced with a knife or when it reaches 60°C (140°F) when probed with a meat thermometer. Remove the pork from the oven and set aside to rest for 10 minutes. Discard the vegetables.

Meanwhile, blanch the cavolo nero in salted boiling water until tender (do not refresh) — you may need to do this in batches. Lay on wire racks and refrigerate to cool. When cold, wring out any excess moisture, roughly chop, then set aside.

To make the sautéed apples and hazelnuts, melt the butter in a large, heavy-based frying pan over medium-high heat. Add the apples and quickly sauté on all sides until they soften slightly and begin to colour. Sprinkle with the sugar and add the hazelnuts, tossing well to combine. Add the sherry and cook for 2 minutes. Chop the remaining sage leaves and stir through. Remove from the heat, set aside and keep warm.

Heat a little olive oil in a heavy-based frying pan over medium heat. Add the garlic, chilli and fennel seeds, cook briefly, then add the cavolo nero and continue to cook until heated through. Season with sea salt and black pepper.

To serve, arrange the cavolo nero in the centre of a large serving platter or individual serving plates. Carve the pork loin into thick slices and lay over the cavolo nero. Spoon the sautéed apples and hazelnuts on the side. Drizzle the warm jus over and around.

Lamb tagine with couscous & harissa

SERVES 6

LAMB TAGINE
800 g (1 lb 12 oz) lamb leg or shoulder, diced
olive oil
3 onions, sliced
4 garlic cloves, sliced
600 ml (21 fl oz) tomato juice
600 ml (21 fl oz) white chicken stock (Basics, page 228)
1 cinnamon stick, broken
150 g (5½ oz/1 cup) whole blanched almonds
sea salt and freshly ground black pepper
4 tomatoes, blanched, peeled, seeded (Glossary) and chopped
60 g (2¼ oz/½ cup) raisins
2 tablespoons honey
12 small new potatoes, cut in half
1 large handful of coriander (cilantro) leaves, roughly chopped
½ quantity harissa (Basics, page 236)

MARINADE
60 ml (2 fl oz/¼ cup) olive oil
a pinch of saffron threads
1 teaspoon ground ginger
1 teaspoon ground paprika
1 teaspoon ground cinnamon
grated zest of 1 lemon
a pinch of freshly ground black pepper

COUSCOUS
370 g (13 oz/2 cups) couscous
500 ml (17 fl oz/2 cups) white chicken stock (Basics, page 228) or water, boiling
a knob of unsalted butter
juice of ½ lemon
½ salted lemon (Basics, page 237), flesh discarded and zest finely diced
1 handful of flat-leaf (Italian) parsley leaves, chopped

....

Combine all of the marinade ingredients and mix well. Put the lamb in a non-reactive shallow tray and pour over the marinade to coat. Cover and refrigerate overnight.

Preheat the oven to 180°C (350°F/Gas 4).

Heat a little olive oil in a heavy-based frying pan over high heat. Seal the lamb, in batches, and set aside. Reduce the heat to medium, add the onion and garlic to the pan and cook for several minutes, or until the onion is translucent. Add the tomato juice and chicken stock, stirring to loosen any sediment. Return the lamb to the pan with the cinnamon stick and almonds. Season with sea salt and black pepper. Bring to the boil, then remove from the heat. Transfer to a tagine pot or earthenware dish and cook in the oven for 1½ hours, or until the lamb is tender.

Remove the lamb from the tagine using a slotted spoon. Set aside and keep warm. Add the tomato, raisins, honey and potato to the tagine and cook for 15–20 minutes, or until the potato is tender and the sauce has thickened. Return the lamb to the tagine to heat through.

Meanwhile, to make the couscous, put the couscous in a large bowl. Pour over the boiling stock or water, stir briefly, then cover with plastic wrap and set aside for the couscous to steam for 10–15 minutes. Use a fork to separate the grains, then add the butter, lemon juice, salted lemon and parsley and season with sea salt and black pepper, stirring well to combine.

To serve, spoon the tagine into serving dishes with the couscous and scatter over the coriander. Serve the harissa separately on the side.

....

Note: A tagine is a Moroccan terracotta cooking dish with a conical lid that traps the aromas of the food as it slowly cooks. When the tagine is served at the table the lid is lifted and a theatrical pillar of steam rises from the table. Tagine pots are relatively inexpensive and available from good food stores but a good cast-iron pot works just as well.

Soy-poached chicken, hokkien noodles, ginger & spring onion

SERVES 6

400 ml (14 fl oz) good-quality soy sauce
3 cm (1¼ inch) piece of ginger, roughly chopped,
   plus 3 cm (1¼ inch) extra, thinly sliced
½ red chilli, roughly chopped, plus 2 extra, seeded
   and thinly sliced lengthways
3 skinless chicken breast fillets
500 g (1 lb 2 oz) hokkien (egg) noodles
2 tablespoons chopped coriander (cilantro) leaves
4 spring onions (scallions), thinly sliced diagonally

Put the soy sauce, chopped ginger, chilli and 400 ml (14 fl oz) water in a large saucepan over medium heat and bring to a simmer. Add the chicken breasts and gently poach for 8–10 minutes, or until cooked. Remove from the heat. Cool the chicken in the poaching liquid.

Remove the chicken from the poaching liquid and set aside. Strain the liquid into a clean saucepan, discarding the aromatics, and bring to the boil. Remove from the heat.

Meanwhile, cook the hokkien noodles in salted boiling water until tender. Drain well.

Mix together the coriander, spring onion, extra ginger and chilli in a bowl.

To serve, divide the noodles among large serving bowls. Slice each chicken breast into six slices, then arrange over the noodles. Pour over the warm poaching liquid then top with a handful of the ginger and spring onion mixture.

Note: Gently cooked in a wonderfully aromatic soy stock, this chicken breast is easy to carve but some people really like the taste of food cooked on the bone so you could use thigh. It's also a good method for cooking a whole chicken — just increase the cooking time to 20 minutes and remember to allow it to cool in the liquid.

Escalope of veal with Marsala, beans & pancetta

SERVES 6

1 garlic bulb, cloves separated, unpeeled
olive oil
700 g (1 lb 9 oz) veal fillet, trimmed
sea salt and freshly ground black pepper
plain (all-purpose) flour
unsalted butter
200 g (7 oz) small green beans, trimmed
60 g (2¼ oz/½ cup) walnuts, roughly chopped
125 ml (4 fl oz/½ cup) pouring (whipping) cream
a good splash of Marsala (sweet Italian wine) or similar
1 large handful of sage leaves
12 slices flat pancetta, grilled until crisp

Preheat the oven to 160°C (315°F/Gas 2–3).

Put the garlic cloves on a sheet of foil, drizzle liberally with olive oil and fold up loosely. Place on a baking tray and roast for 30–40 minutes, or until tender. Set aside and keep warm.

Cut the veal into 5 mm (¼ inch) thick medallions. Lay the veal medallions between two sheets of plastic wrap. Using a meat mallet or rolling pin, lightly tap the medallions into escalopes, about 8 cm (3¼ inches) in diameter. Season with sea salt and black pepper, then dust with flour, shaking to remove any excess.

Heat a little olive oil or butter in a nonstick or heavy-based frying pan over high heat. Fry the veal escalopes on both sides until just golden — do not overcook. Remove from the heat. Keep warm.

Meanwhile, blanch the beans in a saucepan of boiling salted water. Drain. Heat a good knob of butter in a saucepan over medium heat. Add the walnuts and toss until the butter begins to turn nut brown. Add the beans and continue to cook briefly. Add the cream and Marsala, bring to the boil, then remove from the heat. Check the seasoning.

Heat a little olive oil in a small saucepan, add the sage leaves and fry until crisp. Remove with a slotted spoon and drain on paper towels.

To serve, arrange three or four veal escalopes on each serving plate. Arrange the beans and walnuts in the centre and drizzle over the warm cream. Scatter over the roast garlic and the sage leaves and top with the crisp pancetta.

Lamb cutlets, scorched tomatoes, sumac croutons, Persian feta, sugarsnap peas & olives

SERVES 6

2 tablespoons extra virgin olive oil
2 cups chopped sourdough bread
1 tablespoon sumac
6 four-finger lamb racks, trimmed
olive oil
sea salt and freshly ground black pepper
100 g (3½ oz) sugarsnap peas, trimmed
200 g (7 oz) cherry tomatoes
100 ml (3½ fl oz) balsamic dressing (Basics, page 233)
200 g (7 oz) yellow pear tomatoes (see Note)
30 g (1 oz/1 cup) baby watercress sprigs
175 g (6 oz/1 cup) pitted black manzanilla olives
250 g (9 oz) marinated Persian feta (see Note, page 171)
jus (Basics, page 230), warmed, to serve

Preheat the oven to 160°C (315°F/Gas 2–3). Heat the extra virgin olive oil in a large heavy-based frying pan over medium heat. Add the sourdough pieces and cook for several minutes, tossing frequently, until the bread begins to colour. Remove from the heat. Scatter over the sumac and toss well. Spread the sourdough in the base of a baking tray and bake for 5 minutes, or until crisp and golden, though not dry. Remove from the oven and cool completely. The croutons can be made in advance and stored in an airtight container until required.

Increase the oven temperature to 200°C (400°F/Gas 6). Brush the lamb racks with olive oil and season with sea salt and black pepper. Heat a wide, heavy-based frying pan over high heat and seal the lamb on all sides until well coloured. Transfer the lamb to a roasting tray and roast for about 15–20 minutes, or until pink (medium). Remove from the oven and rest for 5 minutes.

Meanwhile, blanch the sugarsnap peas in a saucepan of boiling salted water. Drain, refresh in iced water, then drain again.

Heat a large heavy-based frying pan over high heat. Add the cherry tomatoes and cook for 2–3 minutes, tossing constantly, until the tomatoes begin to blacken. Add 1½ tablespoons of the balsamic dressing and continue to cook until the skins have blistered. Remove from the heat and set aside. Return the pan to the heat and repeat with the yellow pear tomatoes and another 1½ tablespoons of balsamic dressing.

In a large mixing bowl, gently combine the watercress and olives with a little of the balsamic dressing to moisten.

To serve, divide the watercress and olives among serving plates. Arrange the croutons, sugarsnap peas, tomatoes and small spoonfuls of feta around the salad. Carve each lamb rack into four cutlets and arrange next to the salad, then drizzle over the warm jus.

Note: Yellow pear tomatoes tend to have a higher moisture content than red cherry tomatoes and will cook faster, so it's best to either cook them in separate frying pans, or in two batches. Use all cherry tomatoes if yellow pear tomatoes are unavailable.

Open spatchcock pie, eschalots, peas, mushrooms, tarragon & brandy cream

(*pictured page 122*)

SERVES 6

BRAISED SPATCHCOCK

6 whole spatchcock, butterflied and boned
50 ml (1¾ fl oz) olive oil
50 g (1¾ oz) unsalted butter
1.5 litres (52 fl oz) white chicken stock
 (Basics, page 228)
500 g (1 lb 2 oz) duck fat or 500 ml (17 fl oz/2 cups)
 light olive oil
½ garlic bulb, cloves separated, unpeeled
3 thyme sprigs
3–4 black peppercorns
1 fresh bay leaf

BRANDY CREAM

350 ml (12 fl oz) white wine
350 ml (12 fl oz) brandy
1 litre (35 fl oz/4 cups) white chicken stock
 (Basics, page 228)
3 French shallots (eschalots), sliced
3 garlic cloves, sliced
3–4 thyme sprigs
10 g (¼ oz/1 cup) dried porcini mushrooms
3–4 white peppercorns
650 ml (22½ fl oz) pouring (whipping) cream
sea salt and freshly ground black pepper

Preheat the oven to 180°C (350°F/Gas 4).

Prepare the spatchcock by separating the breasts from the thigh-and-leg portions. Cover and refrigerate the breast portions until required. Remove the thigh bone from the leg if necessary. Score the skin and flesh of the leg then run a sharp knife around the bone just below the knuckle of each leg to allow the meat to shrink down during cooking.

Heat the olive oil in a large nonstick frying pan over medium-high heat. Add the spatchcock, skin side down, and sear for several minutes, then add the butter. As the butter begins to foam, turn the legs and continue to cook until well coloured and golden. You may need to do this in two batches. Remove the legs from the pan and place in a large roasting tray. Strain the fat from the pan, then return the pan to high heat and deglaze using a little chicken stock. Pour the pan juices, chicken stock and remaining ingredients over the spatchcock. Put the roasting tray over medium heat and bring the braising stock to a gentle simmer, skimming any impurities that rise to the surface. Cover with foil, then bake for 30 minutes. Remove from the oven, then allow the legs to cool in the braising stock. Once cool, remove the meat, discarding the skin and bones. Set aside.

To make the brandy cream, put the wine and brandy in a large heavy-based saucepan and bring to the boil. Carefully tilt the pan and, using a match, ignite the liquid to burn off the alcohol. Once the flame goes out, reduce the heat to low and simmer until the liquid reduces by three-quarters. Add the chicken stock, eschalot, garlic, thyme, porcini mushrooms and white peppercorns. Bring to the boil, then reduce the heat and simmer until reduced by two-thirds. Remove from the heat. Strain through a fine sieve into a clean saucepan over low-medium heat. Add the cream, bring to a gentle boil, then reduce the heat and simmer for 30 minutes, or until the sauce has thickened slightly. Season with sea salt and black pepper, then remove from the heat. Strain the sauce again through a fine sieve, then set aside and keep warm. If making the sauce in advance, place a sheet of baking paper directly on the surface to prevent a skin forming, then allow to cool completely before refrigerating.

To make the pie, preheat the oven to 190°C (375°F/Gas 5). Roll the pastry out on a lightly floured work surface to make a 26 x 38 cm (10½ x 15 inch) rectangle. Use a pastry cutter to cut out six circles, each with a 10 cm (4 inch) diameter.

TO MAKE THE PIE

375 g (13 oz) block store-bought butter puff pastry
plain (all-purpose) flour, for dusting
1 egg yolk
160 g (5¾ oz) unsalted butter
60 ml (2 fl oz/¼ cup) olive oil
200 g (7 oz) French shallots (eschalots)
400 g (14 oz) Swiss brown button mushrooms
155 g (5½ oz/1 cup) fresh shelled peas
   (use frozen if fresh unavailable), blanched
1 tablespoon finely chopped tarragon leaves
2 tablespoons snipped chives

Put the pastry discs on baking trays lined with baking paper. Dock the pastry with a fork. Lightly whisk the egg yolk with a dash of cold water and brush over the tops of the pastry. Season lightly. Place a wire rack over the tray, ensuring the rack extends beyond the lip of the tray — this will ensure the pastry rises to the same height as well as being neat and flat. Bake for 8 minutes, then reduce the oven temperature to 160°C (315°F/Gas 2–3) and bake for 6 minutes. Transfer to a wire rack to cool. Increase the oven temperature to 200°C (400°F/Gas 6).

Heat 60 g (2¼ oz) of the butter and 2 tablespoons of the olive oil in a nonstick ovenproof frying pan over medium heat. Add the eschalot, season with sea salt and black pepper and sauté for several minutes until golden, stirring to achieve an even colour. Cover the pan with a lid or foil, transfer to the oven and roast for 15 minutes, or until just tender. Remove from the heat, set aside and keep warm.

Meanwhile, heat some olive oil in a large heavy-based frying pan over high heat. Season the spatchcock breasts, then seal, skin side down, in the hot pan. Turn, then transfer to the oven and roast for 3–4 minutes. Remove from the oven, add the remaining butter to the pan, then set aside to rest for 5 minutes.

Heat the remaining olive oil in a large heavy-based saucepan over medium heat. Sauté the mushrooms for several minutes until they begin to soften. Add the braised leg meat, roasted eschalots, peas and brandy cream and simmer gently for 5 minutes, or until the ingredients are well heated and the sauce has reduced to coating consistency. Check the seasoning, then fold through the tarragon and chives.

Gently reheat the pastry lids.

To serve, ladle the braised spatchcock mixture into shallow serving bowls. Carve the breasts in half, arrange over the top of the 'filling' and rest the pastry alongside.

Eye-fillet of beef, truffled kipfler potatoes, buttered spinach, sauce soubise & crisp sweetbreads
Opposite: Open spatchcock pie, eschalots, peas, mushrooms, tarragon & brandy cream

Eye-fillet of beef, truffled kipfler potatoes, buttered spinach, sauce soubise & crisp sweetbreads

This perfectly cooked beef is a pure savoury decadence, rich potatoes redolent with truffles and accompanied by a beautifully rich onion sauce (soubise). Although by no means compulsory, the little sweetbreads add a rich yet crisp texture to the dish. Order them well in advance from your butcher.

(pictured page 123)

SERVES 6

9 kipfler (fingerling) potatoes, unpeeled, scrubbed
1 tablespoon black truffle paste (see Note)
½ teaspoon truffle oil
extra virgin olive oil
sea salt and freshly ground black pepper
180–200 g (6½–7 oz) veal sweetbreads (Glossary)
1 onion, sliced
3–4 thyme sprigs
5 black peppercorns
250 ml (9 fl oz/1 cup) full-cream (whole) milk
250 ml (9 fl oz/1 cup) white chicken stock (Basics, page 228)

6 x 200 g (7 oz) good-quality beef eye-fillets
olive oil
unsalted butter
plain (all-purpose) flour
400 g (14 oz) baby spinach leaves
jus (Basics, page 230), warmed, to serve

Boil or steam the potatoes in their skins until tender. While still warm, peel and cut in half lengthways, then gently toss through the black truffle paste, truffle oil and enough extra virgin olive oil to coat. Season with sea salt and black pepper. Cool, then cover and refrigerate overnight.

Rinse the sweetbreads under cold water for several minutes. Soak overnight in cold salted water — use 100 g (3½ oz/¾ cup) salt for every 1 litre (35 fl oz/4 cups) water.

Remove the sweetbreads from the water and gently rinse in fresh cold water. Put the sweetbreads, onion, thyme and peppercorns in a saucepan and completely cover with the milk and chicken stock. Over low heat, bring to just before a simmer, then remove from the heat and set aside to cool completely. Strain the sweetbreads, discarding the cooking liquid and aromatics. Clean the outer membrane from the sweetbreads, then cut into 1 cm (½ inch) pieces.

To make the sauce soubise, melt the butter in a heavy-based saucepan over medium heat. Add the onion and sauté, without colour, until it just begins to soften. Add the eschalot and continue to cook for 2 minutes. Season with sea salt and black pepper, add the stock and diced butter and continue cooking until tender. Transfer to a food processor and purée until smooth. Check the seasoning, then strain through a fine sieve. Set aside and keep warm.

Preheat the oven to 220°C (425°F/Gas 7).

Brush the eye-fillets with olive oil and season with sea salt and black pepper. Heat a large heavy-based ovenproof frying pan over high heat and seal the beef in the hot pan for 2–3 minutes each side. Transfer to the oven and cook for 5–6 minutes, or until pink (medium). Remove from the oven and set aside to rest for 5 minutes.

Spread the potatoes over a baking tray lined with baking paper and warm through in the hot oven for several minutes.

SAUCE SOUBISE
a knob of unsalted butter
350 g (12 oz) onions, sliced
350 g (12 oz) French shallots (eschalots), sliced
200 ml (7 fl oz) white chicken stock (Basics, page 228)
150 g (5½ oz) unsalted butter, diced

Meanwhile, heat a good knob of unsalted butter in a small heavy-based frying pan over medium heat. Lightly dust the sweetbreads with flour. Once the butter begins to foam, add the sweetbreads and cook until crisp. Drain on paper towels.

In a separate frying pan, melt a good knob of butter over medium-high heat. As it begins to foam, add the baby spinach and season with sea salt and black pepper. Gently toss until the spinach just begins to wilt. Remove from the heat and drain on paper towels.

To serve, place a spoonful of sauce soubise in the centre of each serving plate, using the back of the spoon to spread it into a circle. Place the wilted spinach in the centre of the soubise, with three potato halves around the outside.

Place the beef on the spinach. Dot the sweetbreads around the plate and drizzle the warm jus over and around.

Note: Black truffle paste is available from selected delicatessens and food emporiums. We prefer to use the Elle Esse brand.

Pork neck with chilli & lime

SERVES 6
1.5 kg (3 lb 5 oz) pork neck
60 ml (2 fl oz/¼ cup) sweet chilli sauce
grated zest and juice of 1 lime
600 g (1 lb 5 oz) bok choy (pak choy), halved if large
1 large red chilli, seeded and thinly sliced lengthways, to serve

MARINADE
1 large handful of coriander (cilantro) leaves, roughly chopped
3 garlic cloves, crushed
freshly ground black pepper
100 ml (3½ fl oz) oyster sauce
100 ml (3½ fl oz) vegetable oil
2 teaspoons dark soy sauce
grated zest and juice of 1 lime
2 teaspoons fish sauce
1 teaspoon dried chilli flakes

Trim any fat from the pork neck and place in a shallow tray. Combine the ingredients for the marinade and rub over the pork. Cover and refrigerate overnight.

Preheat the oven to 180°C (350°F/Gas 4).

Remove the pork from the marinade and pat dry with paper towels. Sit the pork on a wire rack inside a roasting tray and roast for 1½ hours — the pork is cooked when the juices run clear or when the centre of the pork neck reaches 60°C (140°F) when probed with a meat thermometer. Remove the pork from the oven, reserving the pan juices. Wrap the pork in foil and set aside to rest for 15 minutes.

In a bowl, whisk together the sweet chilli sauce, lime zest, lime juice and reserved pan juices.

Meanwhile, steam or blanch the bok choy in a saucepan of boiling salted water until tender. Drain.

To serve, carve the pork neck into thick slices and arrange two to three slices to one side of each serving plate. Arrange the bok choy alongside the sliced pork neck and drizzle with the chilli and lime sauce. Garnish with the sliced red chilli.

Note: Marinated with dark Asian flavours, this sweet cut of pork has a nice little kick from the chilli and a sweetly sharp sauce. Pork neck is sometimes called pork scotch fillet and not all butchers carry it all the time, so order it a few days ahead.

Rare-roasted venison, balsamic beetroot, ruby chard & smoked eggplant

SERVES 6

2–3 large beetroot (beets), washed and cut into 1.5 cm (⅝ inch) thick slices
½ garlic bulb, unpeeled
3–4 thyme sprigs
olive oil
500 ml (17 fl oz/2 cups) good-quality balsamic vinegar
150 g (5½ oz) caster (superfine) sugar
6 x 160 g (5¾ oz) venison striploins
200 g (7 oz) ruby chard (red Swiss chard) or young silverbeet (Swiss chard), stems removed
jus (Basics, page 230), warmed, to serve

SMOKED EGGPLANT

1 large eggplant (aubergine)
3 garlic cloves, finely chopped
200 g (7 oz) Greek-style yoghurt
juice of 1 lemon
60 ml (2 fl oz/¼ cup) olive oil
sea salt and freshly ground black pepper

To make the smoked eggplant, put the eggplant over a naked flame for 5 minutes on each side to blacken the skin. Alternatively, grill under a hot grill (broiler), turning occasionally until blackened. The eggplant will begin to soften. Remove from the heat and cool.

Once the eggplant has cooled completely, peel, leaving a little skin on. Put the eggplant in a food processor with the garlic, yoghurt, lemon juice and olive oil. Season with sea salt and black pepper. Store in a sealed container in the refrigerator until required.

Preheat the oven to 180°C (350°F/Gas 4).

Put the beetroot slices, garlic and thyme in a large bowl and toss together with a good drizzle of olive oil, sea salt and black pepper. Spread over a nonstick baking tray, splash with a little cold water, then cover with foil. Roast for 15–20 minutes, or until the beetroot is tender. Allow to cool. Use a 6–8 cm (2½–3¼ inch) round cutter to cut the beetroot into rounds. Set aside and keep warm.

Put the balsamic vinegar and sugar in a saucepan over medium heat, stirring until the sugar dissolves. Bring to the boil, then reduce the heat and simmer until reduced by half. Set aside.

Increase the oven temperature to 220°C (425°F/Gas 7). To cook the venison, heat a little olive oil in a heavy-based ovenproof frying pan over high heat, seal the venison on all sides until well coloured, then roast in the oven for 5 minutes for rare. Remove from the oven and set aside to rest for 5 minutes.

Meanwhile, heat a heavy-based frying pan over high heat. Add a little olive oil and the ruby chard. Season with sea salt and black pepper and toss briefly until just wilted.

To serve, put the beetroot slices and balsamic reduction in a nonstick frying pan over medium heat until warmed through. Arrange the beetroot and ruby chard on serving plates, slice the venison and place on top, with a spoonful of smoked eggplant to one side. Drizzle a little hot jus over and around.

Palliard of chicken with a mixed leaf salad

Beautiful tender grilled chicken always goes well with a green salad. I love using baby greens, perhaps some rocket, watercress or colourful oak leaf lettuce and throwing over some soft herbs from the garden. Just picked parsley, chervil, a little marjoram or even some tarragon, then dressed with a vinaigrette gently lifted through by hand.

SERVES 6

6 chicken breast fillets
80 ml (2½ fl oz/⅓ cup) extra virgin olive oil
4 garlic cloves, crushed
grated zest of 1 lemon
1 handful of flat-leaf (Italian) parsley leaves, roughly chopped
sea salt and freshly ground black pepper
150–200 g (5½–7 oz) mixed salad leaves, such as baby spinach, rocket (arugula), mesclun or watercress sprigs
balsamic dressing (Basics, page 233)
lemon wedges, to serve

Cut the chicken breasts in half horizontally without cutting all the way through. Open the breasts out and lay between two pieces of plastic wrap. Using a meat mallet or rolling pin, lightly tap the chicken to an even thickness of about 5 mm (¼ inch) all over.

Whisk together the extra virgin olive oil, garlic, lemon zest and parsley, season with sea salt and black pepper, then brush over both sides of the chicken. Heat a chargrill pan or barbecue to high heat. Cook the chicken for about 2–3 minutes each side. Remove from the heat.

To serve, toss the salad leaves with enough balsamic dressing to moisten. Place the chicken on serving plates with a lemon wedge and a handful of salad leaves alongside.

Note: Because the chicken has been flattened to thin pieces, make sure you put them in a hot pan and only just cook enough on each side to achieve a good colour — this will be enough to cook the chicken through while still remaining moist. Rest briefly before serving.

Braised lamb shanks, red wine risotto & roast garlic

SERVES 6

LAMB SHANKS
plain (all-purpose) flour
sea salt and freshly ground black pepper
6 lamb shanks
125 ml (4 fl oz/½ cup) olive oil
1 onion, diced into 1 cm (½ inch) pieces
1 carrot, diced into 1 cm (½ inch) pieces
1 celery stalk, diced into 1 cm (½ inch) pieces
1 leek, white part only, cut in half lengthways
5 garlic cloves, unpeeled, lightly crushed
3–4 rosemary sprigs
3–4 thyme sprigs
60 g (2¼ oz/¼ cup) tomato paste (concentrated purée)
400 ml (14 fl oz) red wine
1–2 litres (35–70 fl oz) beef stock (Basics, page 229)

ROAST GARLIC
2 large or 3 garlic bulbs, cloves separated, unpeeled
olive oil

RED WINE RISOTTO
2 tablespoons olive oil
50 g (1¾ oz) unsalted butter
4 French shallots (eschalots), diced
2 garlic cloves, crushed
500 g (1 lb 2 oz/2¼ cups) risotto (arborio) rice
750 ml (26 fl oz/3 cups) red wine, boiling
1–1.25 litres (35–45 fl oz) white chicken stock (Basics, page 228), boiling
50 g (1¾ oz/½ cup) freshly grated Italian parmesan cheese
3 tablespoons finely chopped flat-leaf (Italian) parsley leaves

Preheat the oven to 160°C (315°F/Gas 2–3).

Season the flour with sea salt and black pepper and lightly coat the lamb shanks with the flour, shaking off any excess.

Heat the olive oil in a large, heavy-based frying pan and seal the shanks well on all sides, transferring them to a large flameproof casserole dish as they brown. Add the diced vegetables, leek, garlic and herbs to the pan and cook for 5–6 minutes, or until golden. Stir in the tomato paste and cook for 5 minutes, then spoon over the meat in the dish. Add the wine, stirring well to deglaze, then pour the mixture over the meat. Add enough stock to cover and bring to the boil. Cover the dish with a lid or foil, then transfer to the oven and bake for 1–1½ hours, or until the meat is tender and pulls away from the bone. Remove from the oven and allow to cool in the stock.

To roast the garlic, put the cloves on a sheet of foil, drizzle liberally with olive oil and fold up loosely. Place on a baking tray and roast for 30 minutes, or until tender. Set aside.

Carefully remove the lamb shanks from the stock. Strain the stock into a heavy-based saucepan, discarding the vegetables. Boil, uncovered, until reduced to a rich, glossy sauce. Return the lamb shanks to the sauce and keep warm.

To make the red wine risotto, heat the oil and half the butter in a heavy-based saucepan over low-medium heat. Add the eschalot and garlic and sauté for 8–10 minutes, or until the eschalot is soft. Add the rice and stir to coat in the oil. Reduce the heat to low, add 250 ml (9 fl oz/1 cup) of the boiling red wine and stir briefly. Allow the risotto to cook until the wine is almost completely absorbed by the rice before adding another cup of wine. Continue to cook in this way, stirring frequently. Once all the wine has been added, begin to add the boiling stock 1 cup at a time. Continue to gradually add the stock, stirring frequently, until the rice is almost cooked. Stir through the parmesan, remaining butter and parsley. Season with sea salt and black pepper and ensure the risotto isn't too wet — if it is, increase the heat so the excess liquid evaporates.

To serve, spoon the risotto into shallow serving bowls. Sit a lamb shank in the centre of the risotto, drizzle over a little of the cooking liquid and scatter over the roast garlic.

Note: Any left-over meat can be stored in the cooking liquid in an airtight container in the refrigerator for 3 days.

Braised beef cheeks, Paris mash, baby carrots, asparagus & fresh horseradish

SERVES 6

1.8 kg (4 lb) beef cheek (use wagyu if available or oyster blade if beef cheeks unavailable)
olive oil
sea salt and freshly ground black pepper
135 g (4¾ oz/1 cup) diced leek
155 g (5½ oz/1 cup) diced carrot
140 g (5 oz/1 cup) diced celery
3 garlic cloves, sliced
1 bay leaf
6–8 thyme sprigs
325 ml (11 fl oz) full-bodied red wine
2 litres (70 fl oz) beef stock (Basics, page 229)
12 baby carrots, peeled
12 white asparagus spears, trimmed
a knob of unsalted butter
1 quantity Paris mash (Sides, page 156), warm
60 g (2¼ oz) fresh horseradish, to serve

Trim and remove all excess fat from the beef cheek and cut into approximately 150 g (5½ oz) pieces. Heat a little olive oil in a large heavy-based frying pan over high heat. Season the beef cheek with sea salt and black pepper, then seal on all sides. Remove from the pan and set aside.

Return the pan to medium heat, add a little extra olive oil and briefly sauté the leek, carrot, celery, garlic, bay leaf and half of the thyme sprigs. Add the red wine, bring to the boil, then simmer until reduced by half.

Add the beef stock and sealed beef cheek. Bring back to the boil, then reduce the heat to a very gentle simmer and cook for approximately 2–2½ hours, or until the meat is tender. Leave to cool in the cooking liquid.

Once cool, remove the beef cheek from the liquid and refrigerate until required. Strain the cooking liquid into a clean saucepan, discarding the vegetables and herbs. Bring to the boil, then simmer until reduced to a sauce.

Preheat the oven to 180°C (350°F/Gas 4).

Meanwhile, toss the baby carrots with a little olive oil, the remaining thyme, sea salt and black pepper. Spread over a baking tray lined with baking paper and roast for 20 minutes, or until tender. Keep warm.

Steam or blanch the asparagus in a large saucepan of salted boiling water until tender. Drain, then toss with the butter and season with sea salt and black pepper. Keep warm.

To serve, reheat the beef cheek in the reduced cooking liquid. Place a large spoonful of Paris mash on each serving plate and top with two pieces of beef. Arrange the carrots and asparagus on top, drizzle with a little of the cooking sauce and grate over the fresh horseradish.

Duck breast, brussels sprouts, baby onions, bacon lardons & sauce diable

SERVES 6

12 pickling onions, unpeeled, cut in half lengthways
15 brussels sprouts, outer leaves removed, cut in half
6 x 240 g (8½ oz) duck breasts, trimmed
sea salt and freshly ground black pepper
80 g (2¾ oz/½ cup) bacon lardons (Glossary)

SAUCE DIABLE

olive oil
2 French shallots (eschalots), thinly sliced
1 garlic clove, sliced
80 g (2¾ oz/½ cup) bacon lardons (Glossary)
100 ml (3½ fl oz) white wine vinegar
60 ml (2 fl oz/¼ cup) white wine
1 tablespoon white peppercorns, crushed
100 ml (3½ fl oz) white chicken stock (Basics, page 228)
300 ml (10½ fl oz) beef stock (Basics, page 229)

To make the sauce diable, heat a little olive oil in a heavy-based saucepan over medium heat. Sauté the eschalot, garlic and bacon lardons until the mixture begins to caramelise. Remove from the heat and drain off any excess oil, then return to the heat and add the white wine vinegar, wine and peppercorns. Bring to the boil, then reduce the heat and simmer until reduced by two-thirds. Add the chicken and beef stock, bring back to the boil, then simmer for a further 15 minutes, skimming off any impurities that may rise to the surface. Remove from the heat. Strain the sauce through a fine sieve, discarding the aromatics and bacon lardons. Set aside.

Preheat the oven to 180°C (350°/Gas 4).

Grease and line a baking tray with baking paper. Spread the onions, cut side down, on the tray and bake for 20 minutes, or until tender. Set aside to cool. Once cool, peel and discard the skins.

Meanwhile, blanch the brussels sprouts in salted boiling water for 3–4 minutes, or until tender. Drain and set aside.

Score the skin of each duck breast with a sharp knife and season with sea salt and black pepper. Heat a little olive oil in a heavy-based frying pan over medium heat and place the duck, skin side down, in the pan. Cook slowly to render down the fat, draining off any excess. Increase the heat to medium-high and cook for 3–4 minutes, then turn over and continue to cook for a further 3–4 minutes. Set aside the duck breasts to rest.

Drain the excess fat from the pan and return to medium heat. Add the bacon lardons and cook for 3–4 minutes. Add the brussels sprouts and cook for several minutes, turning occasionally until they have warmed through and the bacon is well coloured. Fold through the onion to warm. Remove from the heat.

To serve, gently reheat the sauce diable. Divide the brussels sprouts, bacon and onion among serving plates. Slice each duck breast into five or six slices and arrange over the brussels sprouts. Drizzle the sauce diable over and around the duck.

Risotto of slow-cooked rabbit, peas & mascarpone

SERVES 6

4 rabbit hindquarters, thighbone removed (ask your butcher to do this)
4 thyme sprigs
2 rosemary sprigs
zest of 1 lemon, removed in strips
2 teaspoons black peppercorns
sea salt
500 g (1 lb 2 oz/2 cups) duck or goose fat or 500 m(17 fl oz/2 cups) light olive oil
2 tablespoons olive oil
80 g (2¾ oz) unsalted butter
4 French shallots (eschalots), diced
2 garlic cloves, finely chopped
440 g (15½ oz/2 cups) risotto rice (Glossary)
1.5 litres (52 fl oz) white chicken stock (Basics, page 228), boiling
250 g (9 oz/1⅔ cups) fresh shelled peas (use frozen if fresh unavailable), blanched
80 g (2¾ oz/¾ cup) freshly grated Italian parmesan cheese
freshly ground black pepper
100 g (3½ oz) mascarpone

Put the rabbit legs in a shallow dish and sprinkle with the thyme, rosemary, lemon zest, black peppercorns and a generous amount of sea salt. Rub the mixture all over the rabbit legs, then cover with plastic wrap and refrigerate for 24 hours.

Remove the rabbit from the marinade, discarding the aromatics and rinse in a bowl of cold water, changing the water several times. Drain and pat dry with paper towels and place in a baking dish.

Preheat the oven to 170°C (325°/Gas 3). Heat the fat in a saucepan until liquefied and hot, then pour directly over the rabbit, ensuring the legs are completely covered. Place a sheet of baking paper over the oil. Transfer the dish to the oven and slowly roast for 1½–2 hours, or until tender. Allow to cool, then put the rabbit legs in a container and cover with the cooking fat to seal and preserve them. The rabbit can be stored in the fat in the refrigerator for up to 2 weeks.

When you are ready to make the risotto, remove the rabbit legs from the cooking fat and scrape off any excess fat. Shred the meat from the bone and set aside.

Heat the olive oil and half of the butter in a heavy-based saucepan over low–medium heat. Add the eschalot and garlic and gently sweat until the eschalot is translucent. Add the rice and stir until it is coated in the oil. Reduce the heat to low, add 250 ml (9 fl oz/1 cup) of boiling stock and stir. Allow the risotto to cook until the stock is almost completely absorbed by the rice before adding another cup of stock. Continue to gradually add stock and cook in this way, stirring frequently, until the rice is almost cooked.

Add the peas and rabbit meat and cook briefly to heat through. Stir in the parmesan cheese and remaining butter. Season with sea salt and black pepper, to taste. Stir through the mascarpone and spoon the risotto into shallow bowls, to serve.

Note: If rabbit is unavailable or not to your taste, substitute with roast chicken meat (page 104).

Sides

Crisp cabbage salad with feta, mint & chilli

SERVES 6

½ savoy cabbage
100 g (3½ oz/1 cup) thinly sliced snow peas (mangetout)
120 g (4¼ oz/¾ cup) crumbled feta cheese
1 red chilli, seeded and finely diced
sea salt and freshly ground black pepper
2 tablespoons good-quality white wine vinegar
80 ml (2½ fl oz/⅓ cup) extra virgin olive oil
1 large handful of mint leaves, roughly torn

Remove the outer leaves from the cabbage to give 6 small or 3 large cups, discarding any that are wilted or torn. Set aside. Very finely shred the inner cabbage leaves and add to a large mixing bowl with the snow peas, tossing well to combine.

Add the feta and chilli to the bowl, season with sea salt and black pepper, and dress with the vinegar and extra virgin olive oil. Set aside for 10 minutes, tossing occasionally, to allow the flavours to infuse. Add the mint leaves just before serving.

Divide the cabbage salad among the reserved cabbage leaf 'cups', or alternatively, serve in a large serving bowl.

Salad of shaved jerusalem artichokes, rocket, orange & feta

SERVES 6
juice of 2 lemons
10 jerusalem artichokes
100 g (3½ oz/2¾ cups) rocket (arugula) leaves
4 oranges, peeled and sliced
½ red onion, sliced
150 g (5½ oz/1 cup) crumbled feta cheese
100 g (3½ oz/1 cup) pecans

BURNT ORANGE VINAIGRETTE
600 ml (21 fl oz) freshly squeezed orange juice
80 ml (2½ fl oz/⅓ cup) extra virgin olive oil
sea salt and freshly ground black pepper
caster (superfine) sugar, to taste

To make the burnt orange vinaigrette, put the orange juice in a heavy-based saucepan over medium heat. Bring to the boil, then reduce the heat and simmer until reduced by one-third. Remove from the heat and cool slightly before whisking in just enough of the extra virgin olive oil, to taste. Season with sea salt and black pepper. Depending on the oranges used, if the vinaigrette is very sharp, you may also need to whisk in a good pinch of sugar.

To make the salad, add the lemon juice to a bowl of cold water to make acidulated water. Peel the jerusalem artichokes and immediately place into the acidulated water as they will discolour quickly once peeled. Drain.

Using a mandolin or very sharp knife, thinly slice the artichokes. Drain, then pat dry with paper towels.

To serve, toss together the jerusalem artichokes, rocket, orange slices, onion, feta and pecans with enough burnt orange vinaigrette to moisten. Divide among serving plates or pile onto a large serving plate or bowl.

Salad of apple, fennel, frisée, pancetta & ricotta

SERVES 6

250 g (9 oz) thinly sliced flat pancetta
3 red or green apples, skin on, core removed, cut in half
4 baby fennel, outer leaves and core removed
100 g (3½ oz) frisée (curly endive)
200 g (7 oz) fresh ricotta cheese

HONEY MUSTARD DRESSING

2 tablespoons full-flavoured honey
2 teaspoons wholegrain mustard
50 ml (1¾ fl oz) freshly squeezed lemon juice
100 ml (3½ fl oz) olive oil
sea salt and freshly ground black pepper

To make the honey mustard dressing, combine the honey, mustard and lemon juice in a small bowl. Gradually whisk in the olive oil, then season with sea salt and black pepper. Set aside.

Cook the pancetta under a preheated hot grill (broiler) for 5–6 minutes, or until crisp. Drain on paper towels and set aside.

Using a mandolin or very sharp knife, thinly slice the apple and fennel. In a bowl, combine the apple, fennel, frisée and grilled pancetta with just enough dressing to moisten.

To serve, divide the salad among serving bowls. Place several teaspoons of ricotta over and around the salad. Finish with a good grind of black pepper.

Shaved baby beetroot, goat's cheese & hazelnut salad

SERVES 6

12 mixed red and golden baby beetroot (beets), peeled, stalks trimmed, small inner leaves reserved for garnish (see Note)
100 g (3½ oz/¾ cup) hazelnuts, roasted, skinned and roughly chopped
250 g (9 oz) goat's curd
sea salt and freshly ground black pepper
extra virgin olive oil, for drizzling
crusty bread or grissini, to serve

Use a mandolin or sharp knife to thinly shave the beetroot into rounds and arrange over the base of each serving plate, using a mixture of the red and golden beetroot.

Scatter over the reserved beetroot leaves and hazelnuts, then dot with teaspoons of the goat's curd. Season with sea salt and black pepper, and drizzle with a little extra virgin olive oil. Serve with the warm crusty bread.

Note: If baby beetroot isn't available, place 4–6 unpeeled large whole beetroot in enough boiling water to cover. Add 100 g (3½ oz) soft brown sugar and 50 ml (1¾ fl oz) white vinegar. Boil until just tender, drain, then allow to cool. Once cool, peel the beetroots and cut into wedges. Use as the recipe directs.

Tomato salad with salted ricotta & basil

(*pictured page 147*)

SERVES 6

1.2 kg (2 lb 12 oz) vine-ripened tomatoes, core removed
150 g (5½ oz) baby roma (plum) tomatoes
150 g (5½ oz) yellow teardrop tomatoes
2 tablespoons good-quality balsamic vinegar
100 ml (3½ fl oz) extra virgin olive oil
sea salt and freshly ground black pepper
1 large handful of basil leaves
100 g (3½ oz) salted ricotta (see Note, page 58)

Slice the vine-ripened tomatoes and arrange over the base of a large flat serving plate. Cut the baby roma and teardrop tomatoes in half and dot around the plate.

Whisk together the balsamic vinegar and extra virgin olive oil. Season with sea salt and black pepper.

To serve, drizzle the dressing liberally over the tomatoes. Tear the basil leaves and scatter over the tomatoes. Shave the salted ricotta over the top and finish with a good grind of black pepper.

Marinated eggplant with labneh & balsamic

(*pictured page 146*)

SERVES 6
1 large eggplant (aubergine)
olive oil
sea salt and freshly ground black pepper
60 ml (2 fl oz/¼ cup) good-quality balsamic vinegar
1 handful of flat-leaf (Italian) parsley leaves
extra virgin olive oil
200 g (7 oz) labneh in oil drained (see Note)

Cut the top off the eggplant and slice lengthways into long strips about 8 mm (⅜ inch) thick. Brush with olive oil and season with sea salt and black pepper. Heat a barbecue or chargrill pan and grill the eggplant on both sides until well coloured and softened.

Put the eggplant in a bowl with the balsamic vinegar. Set aside for 30–40 minutes for the flavours to develop, turning occasionally. The eggplant can be prepared in advance and can be stored in an airtight container with the vinegar and refrigerated for 1–2 days.

To serve, drain off the excess balsamic vinegar from the eggplant and reserve the vinegar. In a bowl, mix together the eggplant, parsley and a good drizzle of extra virgin olive oil, then spoon over the labneh. Finish with a good grind of black pepper and a little reserved balsamic, if necessary.

Note: Labneh is an eastern Mediterranean cheese made from strained yoghurt. Yoghurt is strained through muslin (cheesecloth) to remove the whey, giving it a consistency between yoghurt and cheese, while preserving the yoghurt's distinctive sour flavour. Labneh can be purchased from most good delicatessens, usually bottled in oil, or you could try making your own.

Clockwise from top left: Marinated eggplant with labneh & balsamic; Saganaki & lemon; Tomato salad with salted ricotta & basil; Spiced pumpkin, spinach & harissa salad.

Saganaki & lemon

(pictured page 147)

SERVES 6

100 g (3½ oz/2¾ cups) wild rocket (arugula) leaves
good-quality balsamic vinegar
extra virgin olive oil
350 g (12 oz) kefalograviera (Glossary) or haloumi cheese
plain (all-purpose) flour
olive oil
lemon wedges, to serve
freshly ground black pepper

Arrange the rocket in the centre of each serving plate or a large platter and drizzle with a little balsamic vinegar and extra virgin olive oil.

Slice the cheese into 6 cm (2½ inch) long slices about 5 mm (¼ inch) thick, then dust with flour, shaking to remove any excess.

Heat a little olive oil in a heavy-based frying pan until very hot. Add the cheese, turning once to fry each side. Once the cheese is golden in colour and slightly soft in the centre, remove from the heat and drain on paper towels.

Arrange the cheese slices over the rocket. Garnish with lemon wedges and finish with a good grind of black pepper. Serve immediately.

Note: Saganaki can be served as an appetiser or individual side dish with the rocket and lemon, or simply serve slices on their own as an accompaniment with lemon wedges for squeezing over.

Spiced pumpkin, spinach & harissa salad
(*pictured page 146*)

SERVES 6

1 butternut pumpkin (winter squash), peeled (optional) and seeded
extra virgin olive oil
2 teaspoons cumin seeds, toasted and ground
sea salt and freshly ground black pepper
60 g (2¼ oz/1⅓ cups) baby spinach leaves
80 g (2¾ oz/½ cup) harissa (Basics, page 236)
olive oil

Preheat the oven to 200°C (400°F/Gas 6).
    Cut the pumpkin into large pieces and place on a baking tray lined with baking paper. Drizzle the pumpkin with a little extra virgin olive oil and sprinkle with the cumin, sea salt and black pepper. Roast for 20 minutes, or until tender.
    To serve, put the warm pumpkin in a large bowl with the spinach, a few good spoonfuls of harissa and a drizzle of olive oil. Lightly toss together and arrange on a serving plate.

Roasted fennel, kipfler potatoes & pancetta

SERVES 6

10–12 kipfler (fingerling) potatoes, scrubbed, cut in half lengthways
4 fennel bulbs, outer leaves removed, cut into half lengthways
1 tablespoon thyme leaves
1 garlic bulb, cloves separated, unpeeled
olive oil
sea salt and freshly ground black pepper
200 g (7 oz) pancetta, diced

Preheat the oven to 180°C (350°F/Gas 4).

In a large bowl, toss the potato, fennel, thyme and garlic with some olive oil, sea salt and black pepper. Spread over a baking tray and roast for 30–40 minutes, or until the potato and fennel are tender and golden in colour.

Meanwhile, cook the pancetta in a heavy-based frying pan over medium heat for 5–6 minutes, or until crisp. Drain on paper towels.

To serve, arrange the potato on a serving platter and top with the fennel, garlic and crisp pancetta.

Warm potato salad with lemon & grain mustard

SERVES 6–8

12–18 baby new potatoes, scrubbed
extra virgin olive oil
juice of 1–2 lemons
sea salt and freshly ground black pepper
1 heaped tablespoon good-quality wholegrain mustard
3 tablespoons snipped chives
1 handful of flat-leaf (Italian) parsley leaves
6–8 thin slices bacon, grilled until crisp (optional)

Steam or boil the potatoes in a large saucepan of boiling salted water until tender. Drain. Cut the potatoes in half while still warm and place in a large bowl. Drizzle over a little extra virgin olive oil and lemon juice and season with sea salt and black pepper. Set aside for the potatoes to absorb the flavours.

When ready to serve, gently reheat the potatoes in a moderate oven, then fold through the mustard, chives and parsley. Transfer to a large serving bowl and crumble over the crisp bacon, if using.

Salad of grilled figs, radicchio & Gorgonzola

SERVES 6
6 large or 9 small fresh figs
olive oil
1 head radicchio, outer leaves removed, leaves separated
100 g (3½ oz/2¾ cups) wild rocket (arugula) leaves
1 handful of basil leaves
12 thin slices prosciutto
100 g (3½ oz) Gorgonzola Dolcelatte
    or similar-style blue cheese, sliced
extra virgin olive oil
vincotto (see Note, page 23) or balsamic vinegar
freshly ground black pepper

Using your hands, tear each fig gently in half. Drizzle with a little olive oil and place under a hot grill (broiler) until golden brown and heated through.

Arrange the radicchio leaves, rocket and basil on a serving plate. Place the grilled fig halves on top, drape the prosciutto over, then scatter the Gorgonzola over the salad.

To serve, drizzle with a little extra virgin olive oil and vincotto, and finish with a grind of black pepper.

Pan-fried asparagus with Ligurian olives, garlic & chilli

SERVES 6
extra virgin olive oil
24 asparagus spears, trimmed and peeled if very thick
sea salt and freshly ground black pepper
3 garlic cloves, thinly sliced
1 red chilli, seeded and thinly sliced lengthways
unsalted butter
160 g (5¾ oz/1 cup) Ligurian olives

Working in two batches, heat a little extra virgin olive oil in a heavy-based frying pan over medium heat. Add half of the asparagus, season with sea salt and black pepper and toss until the asparagus just begins to colour. Remove from the pan and repeat with the remaining asparagus, returning all of the asparagus to the pan once cooked.

Add the garlic, chilli and a good knob of butter to the pan. Continue to cook briefly, then add the olives, tossing to warm through.

Paris mash

SERVES 6

1 kg (2 lb 4 oz) pink-skinned, waxy potatoes, such as desiree, washed, unpeeled
300 ml (10½ fl oz) pouring (whipping) cream
100 g (3½ oz) unsalted butter, diced
sea salt and freshly ground white pepper

Cook the potatoes in a saucepan of boiling salted water until tender. Drain and set aside until just cool enough to handle — do not allow the potatoes to cool too much as they will be too hard to pass through the mouli.

Peel the skins from the potatoes then pass through a mouli, or mash by hand.

Put the cream and butter in a saucepan, bring to the boil, then gradually stir this mixture into the potato using a wooden spoon, until the potato has a light, smooth consistency. Season with sea salt and white pepper.

Polenta

SERVES 6
1 litre (35 fl oz/4 cups) full-cream (whole) milk
½ onion
3–4 thyme sprigs
1 rosemary sprig
2 bay leaves
4 garlic cloves, cut in half
130 g (4¾ oz) polenta
60 g (2¼ oz/⅔ cup) freshly grated Italian parmesan cheese
1 tablespoon unsalted butter
sea salt and freshly ground black pepper

Put the milk, onion, herbs and garlic in a saucepan and bring almost to the boil. Put the polenta in a large, heavy-based saucepan, strain the infused milk into the polenta and whisk until combined.

Stir constantly over medium heat until the mixture returns to the boil. Reduce the heat to very low and cook, stirring often, for 20–30 minutes, or until the polenta is cooked and has thickened — it should have a smooth consistency.

Just before you are ready to serve, fold in the parmesan and butter and season to taste with sea salt and black pepper. You can continue to keep it warm over a double-boiler, until ready to use (see Note).

Polenta can also be cooked over a double-boiler, covered with a lid or foil. You will need to cook it for 1–1½ hours, whisking occasionally.

Note: Polenta is best served immediately, however, if you need to prepare it in advance, cook the polenta as above, omitting the parmesan, butter, salt and pepper. Allow to cool, then cover and refrigerate until needed. To reheat, put 125 ml (4 fl oz/½ cup) milk in a saucepan over medium heat and gradually whisk in the cold polenta. Heat through over medium heat, then stir in the parmesan, butter and seasoning.

Variation: To make grilled polenta, prepare the wet polenta as the recipe directs, except increase the polenta to 160 g (5¾ oz) and omit the parmesan cheese and butter. Press the cooked wet polenta into a 20 x 30 cm (8 x 12 inch) greased baking dish to about 1 cm (½ inch) thick all over. Allow to cool.

Preheat a grill (broiler) or a barbecue hotplate to high. Cut the cooled polenta into triangles and brush with melted butter or olive oil. Grill or barbecue the polenta until golden on both sides and warmed through. Serve hot, with red pepper jam (Basics, page 235) or as the recipe directs.

Roast baby beetroot with blue cheese, walnuts & chervil
(*pictured page 160*)

SERVES 6

12–15 red and golden baby beetroot (beets), washed, stalks trimmed, unpeeled
½ garlic bulb, unpeeled, roughly chopped
3–4 thyme sprigs
olive oil
sea salt and freshly ground black pepper
150 g (5½ oz) Gorgonzola Dolcelatte, or similar-style blue cheese
70 g (2½ oz) walnuts, roasted and roughly chopped
2 tablespoons good-quality balsamic vinegar
150 ml (5 fl oz) extra virgin olive oil
1 handful of chervil sprigs

Preheat the oven to 180°C (350°F/Gas 4).

Put the unpeeled whole baby beetroot in a large bowl with the garlic and thyme. Toss together with a good drizzle of olive oil, sea salt and black pepper. Spread over a nonstick baking tray, splash with a little water and cover with foil. Roast for 45–50 minutes, or until the beetroot are tender when pierced with a knife. Once cool, peel and cut the beetroot in half.

To serve, place the beetroot on a serving plate. Crumble pieces of the blue cheese on the beetroot and top with the walnuts. Drizzle over the balsamic vinegar and extra virgin olive oil, scatter over the chervil and finish with a good grind of black pepper.

Roast kipflers with artichokes, olives & lemon
(*pictured page 160*)

SERVES 6

10 kipfler (fingerling) potatoes, scrubbed, cut in half lengthways
60 ml (2 fl oz/¼ cup) olive oil
4 garlic cloves, unpeeled
3–4 thyme sprigs
sea salt and freshly ground black pepper
300 g (10½ oz) good-quality bottled Italian artichokes, preferably with stems attached, drained
juice of ½ lemon
2 tablespoons chopped flat-leaf (Italian) parsley leaves
80 g (2¾ oz/½ cup) pitted kalamata olives, halved

Preheat the oven to 160°C (315°F/Gas 2–3). Line a baking tray with baking paper.

In a bowl, toss together the potato, olive oil, garlic and thyme. Season with sea salt and black pepper. Spread over the prepared tray and roast for 40 minutes, or until just tender. Add the artichokes to the tray and return to the oven for a further 10–15 minutes.

In a large bowl, combine the lemon juice, parsley and olives. Add the potato and artichokes and gently toss to combine. Transfer to a large dish, to serve.

Clockwise from top left: Roast kipflers with artichokes, olives & lemon; Baby carrots with cumin, orange & thyme; Roast baby beetroot with blue cheese, walnuts & chervil.

Baby carrots with cumin, orange & thyme

SERVES 6
2 tablespoons olive oil
24–30 baby carrots, trimmed and scrubbed
1 teaspoon cumin seeds, roasted and coarsely ground
2 teaspoons thyme leaves, chopped
sea salt and freshly ground black pepper
60 g (2¼ oz) unsalted butter
500 ml (17 fl oz/2 cups) freshly squeezed orange juice, strained

Heat the olive oil in a large heavy-based frying pan over medium heat. Add the carrots, tossing the pan frequently to allow the carrots to colour evenly. Season with the ground cumin, thyme, sea salt and black pepper.

Add the butter and orange juice to the pan, bring to the boil, then reduce the heat and simmer for 3–4 minutes, turning the carrots occasionally, until they are tender and the liquid has reduced. Transfer to a large serving plate and serve immediately.

Steamed greens with salted lemon, white anchovies & toasted almonds

SERVES 6

350 g (12 oz) broccolini
250 g (9 oz) green beans, trimmed
250 g (9 oz) sugarsnap peas, trimmed
50 ml (1¾ fl oz) extra virgin olive oil
sea salt and freshly ground black pepper
45 g (1½ oz/½ cup) flaked almonds, toasted
16 white anchovies, sliced in half lengthways (see Note)
1 salted lemon (Basics, page 237), flesh discarded, zest thinly sliced into strips
¼ cup snipped chives

Steam or blanch the broccolini, beans and sugarsnap peas in separate batches in a large saucepan of salted boiling water for 1–2 minutes, or until tender. Drain well. Drizzle with the extra virgin olive oil and season lightly with sea salt and black pepper. Arrange the greens in a large serving dish, then scatter over the almonds, anchovies, salted lemon zest and chives.

Note: White anchovies are fresh anchovy fillets that have been marinated in white vinegar. The flavour is quite mild and sweet and the texture firm to the bite, making them a lovely alternative to regular anchovies.

Shaved kipfler potatoes, green beans, eschalots, parmesan & truffle cream

SERVES 6

12–15 kipfler (fingerling) potatoes, scrubbed
150 g (5½ oz) green beans, trimmed
2 French shallots (eschalots), finely sliced
50 g (1¾ oz/½ cup) shaved Italian parmesan cheese
60 g (2¼ oz/2 cups) watercress sprigs

TRUFFLE CREAM

250 g (9 oz/1 cup) mayonnaise (Basics, page 232)
1 tablespoon black truffle paste (see Note, page 125)
juice of 1–2 lemons
sea salt and freshly ground black pepper

To make the truffle cream, put the mayonnaise in a mixing bowl. Whisk in the truffle paste and enough lemon juice to taste — you may need to thin the truffle cream with a little hot water to achieve a dressing consistency. Season with sea salt and black pepper and refrigerate until required.

Using a mandolin or sharp knife, very thinly slice the potatoes lengthways. Blanch the potato slices in a saucepan of boiling salted water for 2 minutes. Drain well, then plunge immediately in iced water to refresh. Drain again. Lay the potato slices on paper towels to absorb any excess moisture. Transfer the potato slices to a mixing bowl.

Meanwhile, steam or blanch the beans in a saucepan of salted boiling water for 1 minute. Drain. Refresh in iced water, then drain again. Slice the beans lengthways using a sharp knife or bean slicer. Place the beans in a bowl along with the potato slices, eschalot, parmesan and watercress. Add just enough truffle cream to coat the salad.

Note: This salad can be served as a separate side dish but also makes a simple main course plated individually with a thick cut of good-quality eye-fillet steak or with fillets of grilled white fish.

Roast pumpkin, wild rocket, pine nuts, honey & cumin dressing

SERVES 6

1 kg (2 lb 4 oz) jap or kent pumpkin (winter squash), seeded and sliced into 6 wedges
100 ml (3½ fl oz) olive oil
2 teaspoons cumin seeds, toasted and ground
60 g (2¼ oz/1¾ cups) wild rocket (arugula) leaves
40 g (1½ oz/¼ cup) pine nuts, toasted

HONEY & CUMIN DRESSING

175 g (6 oz/½ cup) honey
3 teaspoons cumin seeds, toasted and ground
juice of ½ lemon
80 ml (2½ fl oz/⅓ cup) vegetable oil
80 ml (2½ fl oz/⅓ cup) extra virgin olive oil
sea salt and freshly ground black pepper

To make the honey and cumin dressing, heat the honey in a small saucepan over low heat. Add the cumin, then remove from the heat. Transfer to a small mixing bowl, then whisk in the remaining ingredients. Season to taste with sea salt and black pepper.

Preheat the oven to 180°C (350°F/Gas 4). Grease and line two baking trays with baking paper.

In a bowl, toss the pumpkin with the olive oil, cumin and some sea salt and black pepper. Arrange in a single layer on the prepared trays and bake for 25–30 minutes, or until the pumpkin is tender and slightly caramelised.

To serve, arrange the pumpkin in a serving bowl. Gently toss the rocket and pine nuts with enough dressing to moisten and scatter over the pumpkin. Drizzle a little extra dressing over the top.

Pommes écrasées
(*pictured page 169*)

SERVES 6–8
6 large pink-skinned waxy potatoes, such as desiree, scrubbed
rock salt (optional)
sea salt and freshly ground black pepper
a knob of unsalted butter
1 small handful of flat-leaf (Italian) parsley leaves, chopped

Preheat the oven to 180°C (350°F/Gas 4).

Bake the potatoes on a wire rack or on a baking tray lined with rock salt for 45–50 minutes, or until tender when pierced with a knife. Set aside until cool enough to handle.

Scoop out the potato flesh and discard the skins. Season the potato with sea salt and black pepper, then fold through the butter and parsley so that some texture remains. Keep warm or gently reheat in the oven to serve.

Roast parsnip, rocket, lemon, honey & thyme
(*pictured page 169*)

SERVES 6

1 kg (2 lb 4 oz) parsnips
1 garlic bulb, cloves separated, unpeeled, lightly crushed
10 thyme sprigs
100 ml (3½ fl oz) extra virgin olive oil
60 g (2¼ oz/1¾ cups) rocket (arugula) leaves
1 small red onion, thinly sliced

LEMON, THYME & HONEY DRESSING

175 g (6 oz/½ cup) honey
10 thyme sprigs
juice of ½ lemon
70 ml (2¼ fl oz) olive oil
70 ml (2¼ fl oz) vegetable oil
sea salt and freshly ground black pepper

To make the lemon, thyme and honey dressing, heat the honey and thyme in a small non-reactive saucepan over low heat until it just begins to simmer. Remove from the heat. Set aside to cool to room temperature and to allow the flavours to infuse.

Transfer the honey to a mixing bowl, discarding the thyme. Slowly whisk in the lemon juice, and olive and vegetable oils. Season with sea salt and black pepper. Refrigerate in an airtight container until required.

Preheat the oven to 180°C (350°F/Gas 4). Grease and line two baking trays with baking paper.

Peel and trim the parsnips, removing the tops and tails if too thin, then halve lengthways or quarter if large. Put into a large bowl with the garlic and thyme sprigs, then toss with the extra virgin olive oil until well coated. Season with sea salt and black pepper. Spread the parsnip on the prepared trays in an even layer. Roast for 10 minutes, turn, then continue to cook for a further 10 minutes, or until the parsnip is tender and golden in colour.

To serve, arrange the parsnip on a serving dish. Dress the rocket and red onion with enough of the honey dressing to moisten, then scatter over the parsnip.

Sautéed brussels sprouts, pancetta & garlic

SERVES 6

650 g (1 lb 7 oz) brussels sprouts
2 tablespoons olive oil
2 garlic cloves, thinly sliced
a pinch of dried chilli flakes
125 ml (4 fl oz/½ cup) white wine
sea salt and freshly ground black pepper
40 g (1½ oz) unsalted butter, diced
juice of ¼ lemon
12 thin slices flat pancetta, grilled

Remove any loose or damaged leaves from the stem of the brussels sprouts, then cut out the core using a small sharp paring knife. Carefully separate the leaves. If the leaves don't come apart easily at the centre, simply cut into quarters.

Heat the olive oil in a large nonstick frying pan over medium heat, add the garlic, chilli flakes and brussels sprouts. Toss together for 2 minutes, then add the white wine. Season well with sea salt and black pepper. Reduce the heat to a simmer, cover loosely, and cook for about 5–8 minutes. Add the butter and toss through the brussels sprouts. Finish with a squeeze of lemon juice.

To serve, spoon into a large serving bowl and pour over the cooking juices. Top with the grilled pancetta.

From top to bottom: Sautéed brussels sprouts, pancetta & garlic; Pommes écrasées; Roast parsnip, rocket, lemon, honey & thyme.

Braised fennel, pine nuts, raisins, wild rocket, Persian feta & vincotto

SERVES 6
60 g (2¼ oz/½ cup) raisins
125 ml (4 fl oz/½ cup) white wine vinegar
olive oil
4 large fennel bulbs, outer leaves removed, chopped
sea salt and freshly ground black pepper
2 garlic cloves, chopped
1 tablespoon chopped thyme leaves
625 ml (21½ fl oz/2½ cups) boiling water
60 g (2¼ oz/1¾ cups) wild rocket (arugula) leaves
40 g (1½ oz/¼ cup) pine nuts, toasted
extra virgin olive oil
vincotto (see Note, page 23)
100 g (3½ oz) marinated Persian feta (see Note)

Put the raisins in a small saucepan over medium heat and pour in enough white wine vinegar to just cover. Bring to the boil, then reduce the heat and simmer until the raisins are soft and the liquid has almost fully evaporated. Remove from the heat and allow to cool.

Heat a good splash of olive oil in a heavy-based frying pan over medium heat. Add the fennel, season with sea salt and black pepper and cook for 15–20 minutes, or until the fennel begins to colour. Add the garlic and thyme and continue to cook for several minutes. Add the boiling water, reduce the heat and simmer for 15 minutes, or until the fennel becomes very soft. You may need to add a little extra water to keep it moist during cooking, though there should be no excess liquid once the fennel is fully cooked. Remove from the heat.

To serve, gently toss the rocket, pine nuts and raisins with a drizzle of extra virgin olive oil and vincotto. Season lightly with sea salt and black pepper. Add the warm fennel and toss to combine then arrange on a serving plate. Dot with the Persian feta and finish with a grind of black pepper.

Note: Persian feta is not really from Persia. It is simply the name given to this very soft, creamy, smooth-textured feta cheese that is marinated in oil and often a blend of herbs and other aromatics. It is a rich, luxuriant cheese, much like its name suggests.

Desserts

Pear & hazelnut clafoutis with pear crisps & honey cream

SERVES 6
vanilla bean ice cream (Basics, page 241), to serve

CLAFOUTIS BATTER
280 g (10 oz) self-raising flour
2 teaspoons baking powder
420 g (15 oz) caster (superfine) sugar
165 g (5¾ oz/1½ cups) ground hazelnuts
250 ml (9 fl oz/1 cup) vegetable oil
600 ml (21 fl oz) full-cream (whole) milk
8 eggs

POACHED PEARS
750 g (1 lb 10 oz/3¼ cups) caster (superfine) sugar
3 beurre bosc pears
zest of 1 lemon, removed in strips
1 cinnamon stick

PEAR CRISPS
2 beurre bosc pears
lemon juice
caster (superfine) sugar, for dusting

HONEY CREAM
300 ml (10½ fl oz) thick (double/heavy) cream
2 tablespoons icing (confectioners') sugar
½ tablespoon honey

To make the clafoutis batter, sift the flour and baking powder into a large mixing bowl. Stir through the sugar and ground hazelnuts.

In a separate mixing bowl, whisk together the oil, milk and eggs. Add to the dry ingredients, mixing to form a smooth batter. Cover and refrigerate overnight for the batter to rest.

To make the pear crisps, preheat the oven to 70°C (150°F/Gas ¼), or as low as your oven will go. Grease and line two baking trays with baking paper. Use a mandolin or slicer to shave the pears into very thin slices, slicing across the bottom of the pear. Brush the pear slices with lemon juice, then lay them in a single layer on the prepared trays. Dust with caster sugar and dry in the oven for several hours, or until the pears are crisp. Cool and store in an airtight container until required (they will stay crisp for 1–2 days).

To make the poached pears, combine the sugar and 1 litre (35 fl oz/4 cups) water in a large heavy-based saucepan and bring to the boil. Add the whole unpeeled pears, lemon zest and cinnamon stick and cover with a sheet of baking paper and a plate to keep them completely submerged during poaching. Poach for 20–25 minutes, or until tender when pierced with a knife. Cool, then refrigerate in the poaching liquid until required.

Preheat the oven to 180°C (350°F/Gas 4). Grease eight round 10 cm (4 inch) cake tins or ceramic dishes, about 2 cm (¾ inch) deep.

Using a slotted spoon, remove the pears from the poaching liquid and drain on paper towels. Dice the pears and set aside.

Pour the rested clafoutis batter into the moulds to about three-quarters full. Scatter over the poached pear — it will sink into the batter. Bake for 15 minutes, or until the clafoutis springs back to the touch. Cool slightly in the tins before turning out.

To make the honey cream, whisk together the cream, icing sugar and honey.

Serve the pear and hazelnut clafoutis warm, topped with a good dollop of the honey cream, a scoop of vanilla bean ice cream and the pear crisps alongside.

Grilled bananas, banana bread & burnt butter ice cream

SERVES 6
1 loaf banana bread (Basics, page 240)
6 bananas (see Note)
a knob of unsalted butter
1 tablespoon soft brown sugar
burnt butter ice cream (Basics, page 244), to serve
icing (confectioners') sugar, for dusting

BUTTERSCOTCH SAUCE
150 g (5½ oz) caster (superfine) sugar
150 ml (5 fl oz) pouring (whipping) cream
100 g (3½ oz) unsalted butter, diced

To make the butterscotch sauce, put the sugar and 60 ml (2 fl oz/¼ cup) water in a small saucepan over medium heat and stir until the sugar dissolves. Bring to the boil and boil, without stirring, until the syrup becomes a dark golden caramel. Immediately remove from the heat and very carefully, as hot caramel spits, stir in the cream. Return the saucepan to medium heat. Whisk in the butter, one piece at a time, and stir until the caramel is smooth. Remove from the heat. Set aside and keep warm.

Slice the banana bread into 1.5 cm (⅝ inch) thick slices. Place on a baking tray lined with baking paper and gently warm in a moderate oven or under a hot grill (broiler).

Meanwhile, peel and cut the bananas in half, then slice each half lengthways to give four thin slices. Melt the butter and the brown sugar in a nonstick frying pan over medium heat. Add the banana slices and cook on both sides until tender and golden.

To serve, place a slice of banana bread in the centre of each serving plate. Spoon over a little of the butterscotch sauce. Arrange the bananas on the bread and top with a scoop of burnt butter ice cream. Drizzle over a little extra butterscotch sauce and dust with icing sugar.

Note: Only ever cook this dish with just-ripe cavendish bananas, as the smaller lady finger and sugar banana varieties will toughen once heated. They also tend to go quite floury and grainy, which can be unpleasant. I also suggest you squirrel away some banana bread to enjoy with your coffee the next day.

Steamed golden syrup & ginger puddings

SERVES 6

240 g (8½ oz) unsalted butter, diced
240 g (8½ oz) caster (superfine) sugar
4 eggs
80 ml (2½ fl oz/⅓ cup) full-cream (whole) milk
350 g (12 oz/2⅓ cups) self-raising flour
3 teaspoons ground ginger
a pinch of salt
175 g (6 oz/½ cup) golden syrup or light corn syrup
100 g (3½ oz/½ cup) crystallised ginger, chopped
pouring (whipping) cream, to serve

Grease six 125 ml (4 fl oz/½ cup) metal dariole moulds or ramekins and line the base of each with a small square of baking paper.

In the bowl of an electric mixer, cream together the butter and sugar until light and pale. Add the eggs, one at a time, beating well after each addition. Stir in the milk. Sift together the flour, ground ginger and salt, then fold into the creamed mixture.

Place a spoonful of golden syrup and diced ginger in the base of each mould. Spoon the pudding mixture on top to about three-quarters full. Cover each pudding loosely with a layer of baking paper, then a layer of foil. Sit the puddings in a steamer basket over a saucepan of simmering water and cook for 30–40 minutes — the cooked puddings should spring back like a sponge when done.

To serve, remove the puddings from the steamer, loosen with a knife from the moulds and turn out onto serving plates. Serve with a drizzle of cream.

Hazelnut meringue, Frangelico custard & hazelnut caramel sauce
(*pictured page 178*)

SERVES 6

250 ml (9 fl oz/1 cup) pouring (whipping) cream, softly whipped, to serve

HAZELNUT MERINGUES
4 egg whites
190 g (6¾ oz) caster (superfine) sugar
100 g (3½ oz) ground hazelnuts

HAZELNUT CARAMEL SAUCE
150 g (5½ oz/1 cup) chopped good-quality milk chocolate, such as couverture
30 g (1 oz) honey
200 g (7 oz) caster (superfine) sugar
3 tablespoons light corn syrup
½ teaspoon salt
250 ml (9 fl oz/1 cup) pouring (whipping) cream
225 g (8 oz/1⅔ cups) hazelnuts, roasted, skinned and chopped

FRANGELICO CUSTARD
6 egg yolks
120 g (4¼ oz) caster (superfine) sugar
50 g (1¾ oz/⅓ cup) plain (all-purpose) flour, sifted
500 ml (17 fl oz/2 cups) full-cream (whole) milk
1 vanilla bean, split lengthways, seeds scraped
30 ml (1 fl oz) Frangelico liqueur

Preheat the oven to 180°C (350°F/Gas 4). Grease and line two baking trays with baking paper.

To make the hazelnut meringues, whisk the egg whites in the bowl of an electric mixer until soft peaks form. Gradually add one-third of the sugar and whisk until all the sugar has been used and stiff peaks form.

In a separate bowl, combine the remaining sugar with the ground hazelnuts, mixing well. Fold into the beaten egg whites. Spread the meringue evenly over the prepared trays. Bake for 12–15 minutes, or until the meringue is golden and firm. Set aside to cool completely.

Use a round pastry cutter, about 4.5 cm (1¾ inches) in diameter, to stamp out twelve discs. Break the remaining meringue into small pieces and reserve for garnish. Store both separately in airtight containers until required.

To make the hazelnut caramel sauce, put the chocolate and honey in a small saucepan over low heat, stirring until the chocolate melts. Set aside.

Put the sugar, corn syrup and salt in a saucepan over medium heat, and stir until the sugar has dissolved. Bring to the boil and boil, without stirring, until the syrup becomes a dark golden colour. Immediately remove from the heat and very carefully, as hot caramel spits, stir in the cream. Pour the caramel over the melted chocolate, stirring well to combine, then fold through the hazelnuts. Cool, then store in an airtight container until required.

To make the Frangelico custard, beat the egg yolks and sugar in a bowl until thick and pale, then stir in the flour.

Put the milk, vanilla bean and seeds in a large saucepan over medium heat and slowly bring to the boil. Pour a little hot milk onto the egg mixture, whisking until smooth. Add the remaining hot milk and return to a clean saucepan over medium heat. Cook, stirring continuously with a wooden spoon, until the mixture has thickened and comes to the boil. Add the Frangelico, then whisk for a further minute to ensure it is smooth. Strain into a bowl and place plastic wrap directly over the custard surface to prevent a skin forming. Cool.

To serve, place a large spoonful of Frangelico custard in the bases of six 250 ml (9 fl oz/1 cup) capacity serving glasses. Top with a large spoonful of the hazelnut caramel sauce, then sprinkle over a small handful of the reserved meringue pieces. Finish with a spoonful of cream on top. Serve the hazelnut meringues alongside.

Hazelnut meringue, Frangelico custard & hazelnut caramel sauce
Opposite: Coconut pain perdu, raspberry sorbet & macadamia nut brittle

Coconut pain perdu, raspberry sorbet & macadamia nut brittle

Pain perdu is French toast and means 'lost bread', although it is actually a way of reclaiming lost bread by soaking it in egg and milk and frying it. This recipe uses brioche soaked in a coconut custard before being cooked, then drizzled with warm coconut sauce and served with a scoop of cleansing raspberry sorbet.

(*pictured page 179*)

SERVES 6
unsalted butter, for pan-frying
raspberry sorbet (Basics, page 244), to serve
store-bought macadamia nut brittle, to serve

BRIOCHE
2 teaspoons dried yeast
350 g (12 oz) strong flour, sifted (see Note)
4 eggs, beaten
3 tablespoons caster (superfine) sugar
a pinch of salt
100 g (3½ oz) unsalted butter, diced and softened
1 egg, beaten, for glazing

COCONUT SAUCE
250 ml (9 fl oz/1 cup) pouring (whipping) cream
65 g (2½ oz/¾ cup) desiccated coconut, toasted
finely grated zest of 1 orange
1 egg yolk
115 g (4 oz/½ cup) caster (superfine) sugar

COCONUT CUSTARD
½ vanilla bean, split lengthways
250 ml (9 fl oz/1 cup) coconut milk
125 ml (4 fl oz/½ cup) pouring (whipping) cream
2 tablespoons Malibu
3 eggs
170 g (6 oz/¾ cup) caster (superfine) sugar

To make the brioche, put the yeast, flour, eggs, sugar, salt and 2 tablespoons water and salt in a large bowl and mix well to combine. Knead, either by hand or in an electric mixer fitted with a dough hook attachment, for 8–10 minutes, or until the dough is smooth and elastic. Add the butter and continue to knead until all the butter is incorporated. Cover the bowl with a clean damp cloth and leave in a warm place for 1 hour, or until doubled in size.

Preheat the oven to 200°C (400°F/Gas 6). Grease a 28 x 10 x 8 cm (11¼ x 4 x 3¼ inch) loaf (bar) tin. Place the dough into the prepared tin. Brush with the beaten egg and bake for 30–35 minutes, or until cooked and golden.

To make the coconut sauce, put the cream, coconut and orange zest in a heavy-based saucepan and bring to the boil. Remove from the heat. In a mixing bowl, beat the egg yolk and sugar until thick and pale. Whisk in the hot cream mixture, then return to a clean saucepan over medium heat. Using a wooden spoon, stir constantly until the sauce thickens and coats the back of the spoon — do not let the mixture boil. Refrigerate until cold.

To make the coconut custard, scrape the seeds from the vanilla bean into a mixing bowl. Add the remaining ingredients and whisk together until well combined. Cover and refrigerate until required.

Cut the brioche into 2 cm (¾ inch) thick slices, trim and discard the crusts, then cut each slice into three batons — you'll need 18 pieces in total. The remaining brioche can be kept for up to 1 week in an airtight container.

Soak the brioche batons, a few at a time, in the custard for 2 minutes, without allowing the brioche to become too soft. Heat a large nonstick frying pan over medium heat, add a good knob of butter and fry the brioche on both sides until golden.

Gently reheat the coconut sauce.

To serve, arrange three slices of the coconut pain perdu on each plate and drizzle over the warm coconut sauce. Serve with a scoop of sorbet and the brittle on the side.

Note: If strong flour is unavailable, you can use plain (all-purpose) flour, but you may need to use about 30 g (1 oz) more as it has less gluten in it. Strong flour is also known as baker's flour.

Ruby grapefruit granita, lemonade sorbet, mint jelly & rosewater

While there are a few components to this recipe, it is still a fairly easy one to serve at a dinner party as everything can be made in advance. The only thing to be mindful of when plating the dessert is to act quickly to avoid the granita melting and to keep the foam aerated — make sure your bowls are well chilled in the freezer before serving.

SERVES 6

500 g (1 lb 2 oz) caster (superfine) sugar
2 ruby grapefruit, peeled and segmented, to serve
1 small handful of mint leaves, torn, to serve

RUBY GRAPEFRUIT GRANITA
80 g (2¾ oz/⅓ cup) caster (superfine) sugar
250 ml (9 fl oz/1 cup) boiling water
625 ml (21½ fl oz/2½ cups) freshly squeezed ruby grapefruit juice, strained

LEMONADE SORBET
260 ml (9¼ fl oz) freshly squeezed lemon juice
250 ml (9 fl oz/1 cup) soda water

MINT JELLY
2 large handfuls of mint leaves
2 x 2 g gelatine leaves

ROSEWATER FOAM
6 x 2 g gelatine leaves
2 teaspoons rosewater (Glossary)
1 drop red food colouring

Place the sugar and 500 ml (17 fl oz/2 cups) water in a saucepan over medium heat and stir until dissolved. Bring to the boil, then remove from the heat. Cool the sugar syrup to room temperature and refrigerate until needed.

To make the ruby grapefruit granita, combine the sugar and boiling water in a bowl, stirring until the sugar dissolves. Stir in the juice, then pour into a shallow metal tray and freeze for several hours, or until set.

To make the lemonade sorbet, pour 130 ml (4½ fl oz) chilled sugar syrup, the lemon juice and soda water into a bowl and stir to combine. Transfer to an ice-cream machine and churn according to the manufacturer's instructions, then freeze. Alternatively, transfer to a shallow metal tray and freeze, whisking every couple of hours until smooth and frozen.

To make the mint jelly, blanch the mint in a saucepan of salted boiling water for 90 seconds. Drain, then immediately refresh in iced water. Drain again, squeezing out any excess moisture. Put the mint and 60 ml (2 fl oz/¼ cup) chilled sugar syrup in a blender and blend until smooth. Soften the gelatine in cold water and squeeze to remove any excess water. Put 60 ml (2 fl oz/¼ cup) chilled sugar syrup in a small saucepan over medium heat, bring almost to the boil, then remove from the heat. Whisk in the gelatine, allow to cool slightly, then stir in the mint syrup. Pour into a small plastic container, then refrigerate for several hours, or until the jelly is set.

To make the rosewater foam, bring the remaining chilled sugar syrup almost to the boil, then remove from the heat. Soften the gelatine in cold water and squeeze to remove any excess water. Whisk the gelatine, rosewater and food colouring into the syrup, then strain through a fine sieve and set aside to cool. This can be prepared several hours ahead and refrigerated in an airtight container.

To serve, bring the rosewater mixture to just above room temperature. Aerate using a stick blender or hand-held milk frother to form a foam. Remove the grapefruit granita from the freezer and scratch the surface with a fork to form flakes. Spoon over the bases of chilled serving bowls. Arrange three grapefruit segments and three teaspoons of jelly around the granita. Scatter over the mint, then top with a scoop of sorbet. Aerate the rosewater foam again, if necessary, then spoon over the sorbet, allowing it to fall into the granita. Serve immediately.

Ginger bavarois & poached pear with sesame & ginger wafer

SERVES 6
6 sesame and ginger wafers (Basics, page 241), to serve

GINGER BAVAROIS
500 ml (17 fl oz/2 cups) pouring (whipping) cream
3 egg yolks
60 g (2¼ oz/¼ cup) caster (superfine) sugar
2 x 2 g gelatine leaves
125 g (4½ oz) glacé ginger

POACHED PEARS
750 g (1 lb 10 oz/3¼ cups) caster (superfine) sugar
3 beurre bosc pears
zest of 1 lemon, removed in strips
1 cinnamon stick

To make the ginger bavarois, put 250 ml (9 fl oz/1 cup) of the cream in a saucepan over medium heat and bring just to the boil. In a mixing bowl, lightly whisk together the egg yolks and sugar. Whisk the hot cream into the egg yolks, then return to a clean saucepan over medium heat. Using a wooden spoon, stir constantly until the custard thickens and coats the back of the spoon — do not let it boil. Remove from the heat.

Soften the gelatine leaves in cold water and squeeze to remove any excess water, then whisk the gelatine into the custard and stir to completely dissolve. Strain through a fine sieve into a bowl, add the ginger, then set aside and allow to cool to room temperature, stirring occasionally — the mixture will start to thicken. Once the mixture is completely cool, blend in a blender until the ginger is well incorporated into the custard. Softly whip the remaining cream, then fold through the custard.

Rinse six 125 ml (4 fl oz/½ cup) plastic dariole moulds with cold water. Divide the bavarois mixture among the moulds. Refrigerate until set, preferably overnight.

To make the poached pears, combine the sugar and 1 litre (35 fl oz/4 cups) water in a large heavy-based saucepan and bring to the boil. Add the whole unpeeled pears, lemon zest and cinnamon and cover with a sheet of baking paper and a plate to keep them completely submerged during poaching. Poach for 20–25 minutes, or until tender when pierced with a knife. Cool in the poaching liquid. Remove the pears from the poaching liquid, reserving the liquid. Drain the pears on paper towels. Cut each pear in half, scoop out the core, then cut each half into wedges. Refrigerate in an airtight container until required.

Strain the poaching liquid into a clean saucepan, discarding the aromatics, reserving the lemon zest for garnish, if desired. Bring to the boil, then reduce the heat and simmer until the liquid reduces to a syrup consistency. Refrigerate until required.

To serve, run a paring knife around the edge of each mould to loosen the bavarois, then invert and gently squeeze onto one side of each serving plate. Arrange the pear wedges and lemon zest (if using) alongside and drizzle with a little of the syrup. Serve with sesame and ginger wafers.

Flourless chocolate cake, poached rhubarb & raspberry sorbet

SERVES 8–10

icing (confectioners') sugar, for dusting
raspberry sorbet (Basics, page 244), to serve

FLOURLESS CHOCOLATE CAKE
250 g (9 oz/1⅔ cups) chopped good-quality dark (bittersweet) chocolate, such as couverture
2 tablespoons brandy or cognac
2 tablespoons strong espresso coffee
200 g (7 oz) unsalted butter, softened
200 g (7 oz) caster (superfine) sugar
200 g (7 oz/2 cups) ground almonds
6 eggs, separated

POACHED RHUBARB
460 g (1 lb/2 cups) caster (superfine) sugar
6 rhubarb stalks, cut into 4 cm (1½ inch) lengths

Preheat the oven to 160°C (315°F/Gas 2–3). Grease and line the base of a round 28 cm (11¼ inch) spring-form cake tin with baking paper.

Put the chocolate, brandy and coffee in a heatproof bowl over a saucepan of simmering water, stirring to melt the chocolate. Add the butter and sugar, mixing well. Remove from the heat, then fold in the ground almonds.

In a bowl, whisk the egg yolks and add to the chocolate mixture, stirring well.

In the bowl of an electric mixer, whisk the egg white to stiff peaks. Stir a spoonful into the chocolate mixture, mixing well, then fold in the remaining beaten egg white.

Spoon the cake mixture into the prepared tin and bake for 40–45 minutes. The cake should have a delicate crust but will be fudge-like in the centre. Cool completely in the tin before turning out.

To make the poached rhubarb, put the sugar and 500 ml (17 fl oz/2 cups) water in a saucepan over medium heat, stirring until the sugar dissolves. Bring to a simmer, then add the rhubarb. Poach gently for 2–3 minutes, or until the rhubarb has softened but still holds its shape. Remove from the heat. Use a slotted spoon to remove the rhubarb from the syrup and set aside to cool.

To serve, cut the cake into wedges, dust with icing sugar and place on serving plates.

Arrange the rhubarb and a scoop of raspberry sorbet alongside.

Pumpkin cheesecake, ginger custard & maple syrup ice cream

This is a rich but surprisingly refreshing way to end a meal. We use butternut, grey or Queensland blue pumpkin for this as they are naturally dry and allow the filling to set firm.

SERVES 8–10

maple syrup ice cream (Basics, page 243), to serve

CHEESECAKE BASE

100 g (3½ oz) unsalted butter, melted
115 g (4 oz) dark treacle
1 egg
½ teaspoon natural vanilla extract
375 g (13 oz/2½ cups) plain (all-purpose) flour
1½ teaspoons baking powder
a pinch each of ground nutmeg, ginger, cinnamon and cloves
100 g (3½ oz) unsalted butter, melted and cooled

PUMPKIN FILLING

900 g (2 lb) cream cheese, at room temperature
115 g (4 oz/½ cup) caster (superfine) sugar
a pinch each of ground ginger, nutmeg and cinnamon
1 teaspoon natural vanilla extract
5 eggs, at room temperature
2 tablespoons plain (all-purpose) flour
80 ml (2½ oz/⅓ cup) thick (double/heavy) cream
450 g (1 lb) steamed butternut pumpkin (winter squash), puréed, cold

GINGER CUSTARD

325 ml (11 fl oz) thick (double/heavy) cream
250 ml (9 fl oz/1 cup) full-cream (whole) milk
100 g (3½ oz) fresh ginger, chopped
½ teaspoon ground ginger
5 egg yolks
80 g (2¾ oz/⅓ cup) caster (superfine) sugar

To make the cheesecake base, whisk together the butter, treacle, egg and vanilla in a large bowl. Sift together the dry ingredients, then add to the butter mixture, mixing well until it comes together to form a soft dough. Wrap in plastic wrap and rest in the refrigerator for at least 30 minutes.

Preheat the oven to 160°C (315°F/Gas 2–3). Grease and line two baking trays with baking paper. Grease and line the base of a round 26 cm (10½ inch) cake tin.

Divide the rested dough into two even-sized pieces and place each between two sheets of plastic wrap or baking paper. Roll the dough out to 3 mm (⅛ inch) thick all over. Place on the prepared trays and bake for about 10–12 minutes, or until golden. Remove from the oven and set aside to cool. Once cool, put in a food processor and pulse to create fine crumbs.

In a large mixing bowl, combine 2 heaped cups of the crumbs with the cooled melted butter — it should look like wet sand — add more butter or crumbs, if necessary. Press the crumbs into the base of the prepared tin and bake for 8 minutes. Remove from the oven and cool completely.

Reduce the oven temperature to 150°C (300°F/Gas 2).

To make the pumpkin filling, whip the cream cheese in the bowl of an electric mixer. Add the sugar, spices and vanilla and beat on low speed until smooth, scraping down the sides of the bowl. Add the eggs, one at a time, beating well after each addition. Add the flour, mix well, then slowly add the cream. Fold in the pumpkin purée. Pour the filling into the tin over the cooked and cooled base. Sit the cake tin in a large roasting tray and pour in enough boiling water to come halfway up the side of the tin. Carefully place in the oven and bake for about 1 hour, or until the filling is set. The cheesecake should look firm with a slight wobble in the centre. Cool. The cheesecake should ideally be refrigerated overnight before serving.

To make the ginger custard, put the cream, milk, fresh and ground ginger in a saucepan and bring almost to the boil. Remove from the heat and set aside for 20 minutes for the flavours to infuse. Strain through a fine sieve.

In a bowl, lightly whisk together the egg yolks and sugar. Whisk in the infused cream mixture then return to a clean saucepan over medium heat. Using a wooden spoon, stir constantly until the custard thickens and coats the back of the spoon — do not let it boil. Strain through a fine sieve, then refrigerate until cold.

To serve, cut the cheesecake into wedges and serve with a little ginger custard and a scoop of maple syrup ice cream.

Coconut cake with mango mousse & milk gelato

SERVES 8–10

2 large or 3 small mangoes, peeled and sliced, to serve
caster (superfine) sugar, for glazing (optional)
milk gelato (Basics, page 245), to serve

COCONUT CAKE
300 g (10½ oz/2 cups) self-raising flour, sifted
110 g (3¾ oz) ground almonds
550 g (1 lb 4 oz) caster (superfine) sugar
220 g (7¾ oz) desiccated coconut
250 g (9 oz) unsalted butter, melted
6 eggs, separated
125 ml (4 fl oz/½ cup) buttermilk

MANGO MOUSSE
110 g (3¾ oz/½ cup) caster (superfine) sugar
1 tablespoon glucose syrup
1 kg (2 lb 4 oz) frozen mango cheeks, thawed and puréed
12 x 2 g gelatine leaves
4 egg whites
750 ml (26 fl oz/3 cups) pouring (whipping) cream, softly whipped

Preheat the oven to 160°C (315°F/Gas 2–3). Grease and line the base and sides of a 30 x 23 x 4 cm (12 x 9 x 1½ inch) baking tin with baking paper.

To make the coconut cake, combine the flour, ground almonds, sugar and coconut in a large mixing bowl. Make a well in the centre and add the butter, egg yolks and buttermilk, stirring well to combine.

In the bowl of an electric mixer, whisk the egg white to soft peaks. Fold through the cake mixture. Spread the cake mixture into the prepared tin and bake for 10–15 minutes, or until golden — the cake is cooked when a skewer inserted into the centre comes out clean. Set aside and cool in the tin.

Once cool, use an 8 cm (3¼ inch) metal pastry ring to cut the cake into discs. Grease and line eight 8 cm (3¼ inch) tart rings with a wide piece of baking paper so the paper sits at least 5–6 cm (2–2½ inches) above the base. Sit a cake disc inside each ring and place on a baking tray lined with baking paper.

To make the mango mousse, put the sugar, glucose syrup and 100 ml (3½ fl oz) water in a saucepan over medium heat, stirring until the sugar dissolves. Bring to the boil, then remove from the heat.

In a bowl, combine the mango purée and 170 ml (5½ fl oz/⅔ cup) of the warm sugar syrup until well combined. Soften the gelatine in cold water and squeeze out, then add to the purée, stirring to dissolve. Allow to cool.

In the bowl of an electric mixer, whisk the egg white to stiff peaks, then fold through the mango mixture. Lastly fold through the cream. Pour the mango mousse evenly into the tart rings over the coconut cake, tapping lightly on the tray to flatten the mousse. Refrigerate for 3 hours to set.

To serve, carefully remove the tart rings and baking paper from the coconut cake and mousse, and place one in the centre of each serving plate. Serve with slices of fresh mango, sprinkled with a little caster sugar and caramelised under a hot grill (broiler), if desired, and a scoop of milk gelato.

Green apple, raisin & polenta crumble pie

SERVES 6

100 g (3½ oz) unsalted butter, diced
6 green apples, peeled, cored and thickly sliced
185 g (6½ oz/1 cup) soft brown sugar
60 g (2¼ oz/½ cup) raisins
1 cinnamon stick
1 vanilla bean, split lengthways, seeds scraped
a pinch of freshly grated nutmeg
2 teaspoons chopped glacé ginger
finely grated zest and juice of 1 lemon
24 x 4 cm (9½ x 1½ inch) blind-baked sweet shortcrust pastry case (Basics, page 239)
whipped cream with vanilla seeds or crème fraîche, to serve

POLENTA CRUMBLE

100 g (3½ oz/⅔ cup) polenta
80 g (2¾ oz/¾ cup) ground almonds
90 g (3¼ oz) plain (all-purpose) flour
80 g (2¾ oz/⅓ cup) caster (superfine) sugar
finely grated zest of 1 lemon
160 g (5¾ oz) unsalted butter, softened

Melt the butter in a heavy-based saucepan over medium heat. Increase the heat to high, add the apple and cook for 2–3 minutes. Add the sugar and raisins and continue to cook for several minutes. Add the spices and ginger and continue to cook until the apple has softened, but still holds its shape. Stir through the lemon zest and juice. Remove from the heat. Use a slotted spoon to transfer the apple mixture to a shallow tray to cool, reserving the liquid.

Strain the reserved liquid into a heavy-based saucepan and discard the aromatics. Bring to the boil and boil until it reduces to a syrup consistency. Set aside.

To make the polenta crumble, combine the dry ingredients and lemon zest in a large bowl. Use your fingers to evenly rub in the butter. The mixture should have a coarse texture.

Preheat the oven to 180°C (350°F/Gas 4).

Spoon the cooled apple mixture into the blind-baked pastry case. Sprinkle an even layer of the crumble over the top, about 5 mm (¼ inch) thick. Do not pack down, as this will stop the crumble cooking properly. Bake for 15–20 minutes, or until the crumble is crisp and golden and the filling is hot.

To serve, gently remove the pie from the tin and drizzle with the reduced apple syrup. Serve with crème fraîche on the side.

Dark chocolate dumplings with cinnamon ice cream

These piping hot little balls of lightly deep-fried dough, with a wickedly molten centre of liquid chocolate, can be made well in advance, stored in the freezer and cooked frozen. Remember to cook just a few at a time.

SERVES 10—12

200 g (7 oz) unsalted butter, diced
1 teaspoon table salt
130 g (4½ oz) caster (superfine) sugar
275 g (9¾ oz) plain (all-purpose) flour, sifted
8 eggs
75 g (2¾ oz/½ cup) chopped dark (bittersweet) chocolate, such as couverture
vegetable oil, for deep-frying
½ teaspoon ground cinnamon
cinnamon ice cream (Basics, page 242), to serve

Put the butter, salt, 1 tablespoon of the sugar and 500 ml (17 fl oz/2 cups) water in a saucepan over low heat, stirring until the butter has melted. Remove from the heat. Add the flour, return to low heat and stir constantly until the mixture is smooth and comes away from the side of the pan. Transfer the mixture to the bowl of an electric mixer fitted with a paddle attachment and add the eggs, one at a time, beating well between each addition, until the mixture is cool and holds its shape.

Grease and line two baking trays with baking paper. Spoon the dumpling mixture into a piping (icing) bag fitted with a plain nozzle and pipe 30—35 evenly sized balls onto the lined trays. Push some chocolate into the centre of each ball, then pipe over a little extra dumpling mixture to cover the hole. Freeze. (Dumplings will keep stored in the freezer for up to 1 month.)

To cook the dumplings, fill a deep-fryer or large, deep heavy-based saucepan one-third full of vegetable oil and heat to 150°C (300°F). Carefully add the dumplings a few at a time straight from the freezer into the hot oil, allowing three dumplings per person.

Cook until the dumplings are golden and slightly puffed. Remove from the hot oil using a slotted spoon and drain on paper towels.

Combine the remaining sugar and cinnamon and toss the dumplings gently through the sugar mixture to coat. Serve immediately with scoops of cinnamon ice cream.

Note: As an alternative, fill half of the dumplings with white chocolate and the other half with dark chocolate, then freeze and cook them in separate batches so that you can serve a combination of the two. It may be a little more time consuming and require some careful labelling, however it's well worth the trouble.

Saffron & almond cake with milk gelato & saffron syrup

SERVES 10

170 ml (5½ fl oz/⅔ cup) full-cream (whole) milk
½ teaspoon saffron threads
150 g (5½ oz/1 cup) plain (all-purpose) flour
55 g (2 oz/½ cup) ground almonds
230 g (8½ oz/1 cup) caster (superfine) sugar
1 teaspoon baking powder
½ teaspoon bicarbonate of soda (baking soda)
finely grated zest and juice of 1 orange
½ teaspoon ground mixed (pumpkin pie) spice
1 egg
25 g (1 oz/¼ cup) flaked almonds
milk gelato (Basics, page 245), to serve

SAFFRON SYRUP

170 g (6 oz/¾ cup) caster (superfine) sugar
a pinch of saffron threads
1 vanilla bean, split lengthways, seeds scraped

Preheat the oven to 190°C (375°F/Gas 5). Grease and line the base of a round 20–22 cm (8–8½ inch) spring-form cake tin with baking paper.

Put 50 ml (1¾ fl oz) of the milk and the saffron in a small saucepan over medium heat, bring to a simmer, then remove from the heat and set aside to cool.

In a large bowl, use a fork to combine the flour, ground almonds, sugar, baking powder, bicarbonate of soda, orange zest and mixed spice, ensuring the ingredients are evenly distributed.

In a separate bowl, whisk together the remaining milk, the saffron-infused milk, egg and orange juice. Add to the dry ingredients and bring together with the fork, stirring until the mixture is just combined.

Pour into the prepared cake tin, scatter over the flaked almonds, then bake for 20–25 minutes, or until a skewer comes out clean when inserted into the centre of the cake. Cool briefly in the tin before turning out onto a wire rack to cool completely.

To make the saffron syrup, place the sugar, saffron, vanilla bean and seeds in a saucepan with 100 ml (3½ fl oz) water. Bring to the boil, stirring to dissolve the sugar, then reduce the heat and simmer for a further 5 minutes, or until the mixture has reduced to a syrup consistency. Remove from the heat, discard the vanilla bean and set aside to cool.

Drizzle half of the saffron syrup over the warm cake, then cool to room temperature.

To serve, cut the cake into wedges and place in the centre of serving plates. Drizzle over the remaining syrup and serve with a generous scoop of milk gelato.

Baked date tart, caramelised oranges & crème fraîche ice cream

I first came across this recipe watching a cooking demonstration at a food and wine festival at Noosa Heads by friend and fellow chef, Tony Kelly. I loved the simplicity of the recipe, coupled with the light yet indulgent flavours the dates, mascarpone and oranges produced. This is my version of that recipe.

SERVES 6

BAKED DATE TART
1 quantity sweet shortcrust pastry (Basics, page 239)
250 g (9 oz) fresh dates, pitted and chopped
90 ml (3 fl oz) brandy
finely grated zest of 1 orange
375 g (13 oz) mascarpone
3 eggs
½ vanilla bean, split lengthways, seeds scraped
50 g (1¾ oz/¼ cup) caster (superfine) sugar, plus extra for glazing
crème fraîche ice cream (Basics, page 243), to serve

CARAMELISED ORANGES
5 oranges, peeled and segmented
200 g (7 oz) caster (superfine) sugar

Prepare the pastry as directed, resting for 1 hour in the refrigerator. Roll out the rested pastry into a rectangle, about 3 mm (⅛ inch) thick all over, then gently ease it into a greased 35 x 12 x 3 cm (14 x 4½ x 1¼ inch) rectangular tart tin. Refrigerate for 30 minutes.

Preheat the oven to 180°C (350°F/Gas 4). Blind-bake the pastry as directed on page 239.

To make the caramelised oranges, put the orange segments in a bowl. Combine the sugar with 50 ml (1¾ fl oz) water in a heavy-based saucepan over medium heat, stirring until the sugar has dissolved. Bring to the boil and boil, without stirring, until the syrup becomes a dark golden colour. Immediately remove from the heat. Pour the caramel over the orange and set aside to cool.

Combine the dates, brandy, orange zest and 200 ml (7 fl oz) water in a saucepan over very low heat. Cook until the dates are very soft and have collapsed to form a paste. Set aside.

Reduce the oven temperature to 150°C (300°F/Gas 2).

Whisk together the mascarpone, eggs, vanilla seeds and sugar until well combined.

Spread the date paste about 5 mm (¼ inch) thick over the base of the cooled tart shell. Pour the mascarpone filling over the date paste to the top of the tart shell. Bake for 25–30 minutes, or until the filling is just set. Cool before serving.

To serve, sprinkle the tart with caster sugar, then use a kitchen blowtorch to caramelise the top to a rich golden colour. Cut into slices and top with the caramelised oranges and a scoop of crème fraîche ice cream.

Coconut tapioca, caramelised bananas, pineapple sorbet & sesame cookies

SERVES 8–10

200 g (7 oz/1 cup) tapioca pearls
750 ml (26 fl oz/3 cups) coconut milk
110 g (3¾ oz/½ cup) caster (superfine) sugar
1 vanilla bean, split lengthways, seeds scraped
grated zest of 1 lime
2 egg yolks
pineapple sorbet (Basics, page 244), to serve
finely grated lime zest, extra to garnish

SESAME COOKIES (OPTIONAL)
90 g (3¼ oz) unsalted butter, softened
140 g (5 oz/¾ cup) soft brown sugar
1 egg
½ teaspoon natural vanilla extract
80 g (2¾ oz/½ cup) sesame seeds, toasted
90 g (3¼ oz) plain (all-purpose) flour
¼ teaspoon baking powder

CARAMELISED BANANAS
5 bananas (see Note, page 175)
50 g (1¾ oz) unsalted butter
100 g (3½ oz) soft brown sugar
juice of ½ lemon

Put the tapioca in a bowl with enough water to cover. Leave to soak overnight in the refrigerator.

Rinse the tapioca thoroughly in clean water, drain, then place in a large saucepan with the coconut milk, sugar and vanilla bean and seeds. Bring to a simmer, stirring constantly, and cook slowly for 15–20 minutes, or until the tapioca is completely cooked. Remove from the heat and cool briefly. Add the lime zest and egg yolks, stirring well to combine. Remove the vanilla bean. Divide the coconut tapioca among individual serving glasses or one large glass bowl and refrigerate for 2 hours, or until set.

Preheat the oven to 180°C (350°F/Gas 4). Line two baking trays with baking paper.

To make the sesame cookies, cream the butter and sugar together in the bowl of an electric mixer until light and pale. Add the egg and vanilla, mixing well to combine. On low speed, add the sesame seeds, flour and baking powder. Roll teaspoons of the mixture into small balls and place on the prepared trays, leaving space between them, as the mixture will spread. Bake for 5 minutes, or until golden. Transfer to a wire rack to cool.

To caramelise the bananas, slice them diagonally into three or four even slices. Melt the butter in a heavy-based frying pan over medium-high heat. As the butter begins to foam, add the banana slices and sprinkle with the brown sugar. Cook briefly, turning, until the banana is just soft — do not overcook. Lastly, add the lemon juice to taste.

To serve, spoon the warm bananas and the caramel over the coconut tapioca. Grate the lime zest over the pineapple sorbet and serve alongside.

Pistachio & caramel ice cream, poached pears & butterscotch sauce

SERVES 8–10

POACHED PEARS
375 ml (13 fl oz/1½ cups) light-bodied dessert wine
3 cardamom pods, roasted, crushed and sieved
1 cinnamon stick
1 vanilla bean, split lengthways, seeds scraped
6 pears, unpeeled, halved and cored

BUTTERSCOTCH SAUCE
250 g (9 oz) caster (superfine) sugar
250 ml (9 fl oz/1 cup) pouring (whipping) cream

PISTACHIO & CARAMEL ICE CREAM
300 g (10½ oz/1⅓ cups) caster (superfine) sugar
500 ml (17 fl oz/2 cups) full-cream (whole) milk
500 ml (17 fl oz/2 cups) pouring (whipping) cream
10 egg yolks
300 g (10½ oz/2 cups) shelled pistachio nuts, blanched, skins removed

To make the poached pears, put the dessert wine, cardamom, cinnamon, vanilla bean and seeds in a large saucepan. Bring to the boil, then reduce the heat to a simmer. Immerse the pears in the syrup and cover with baking paper and a plate to keep them submerged. Poach for about 8–10 minutes, or until tender. Remove from the heat. Cool and cut into wedges, then store in the poaching liquid until required.

To make the pistachio and caramel ice cream, combine 200 g (7 oz) of the sugar and 125 ml (4 fl oz/½ cup) water in a large saucepan over medium heat and stir until the sugar dissolves. Bring to the boil and boil, without stirring, until the syrup turns a dark golden colour. Immediately remove from the heat and very carefully, as hot caramel spits, stir in the milk and cream. Place back over medium heat and bring almost to the boil.

In a bowl, lightly whisk together the egg yolks and remaining sugar. Whisk the hot milk mixture into the egg yolks, then return to a clean saucepan over medium heat. Using a wooden spoon, stir constantly until the custard thickens and coats the back of the spoon — do not let it boil. Strain through a fine sieve into a bowl.

Spread 225 g (8 oz/1½ cups) of the pistachio nuts over a baking tray and toast lightly in a moderate oven. While still warm, briefly pulse the nuts in a food processor to roughly chop, then add to the strained warm custard. Set aside for the custard to cool to room temperature and the flavours to infuse. Strain, discarding the pistachios, then refrigerate until cold.

Transfer the cold ice-cream mixture to an ice cream machine and churn according to the manufacturer's instructions, then freeze. Alternatively, transfer to a shallow metal tray and freeze, whisking every couple of hours until creamy and frozen.

To make the butterscotch sauce, combine the sugar and 60 ml (2 fl oz/¼ cup) water in a small saucepan over medium heat and stir until the sugar dissolves. Bring to the boil and boil, without stirring, until the syrup becomes a light golden colour. Immediately remove from the heat and very carefully, as hot caramel spits, stir in the cream. Return to the heat and stir until the caramel is smooth. Remove from the heat and set aside.

To serve, scoop some pistachio and caramel ice cream into a bowl with the poached pears. Place the butterscotch sauce on the side and sprinkle over the remaining pistachios. Serve immediately.

Cherry soufflé with chocolate sauce

A soufflé you can make in advance? Surely not! However, the use of Italian meringue in this recipe stabilises the mixture so that it can be prepared 2 to 3 hours ahead of time and refrigerated in the moulds until you're ready to serve.

SERVES 6

icing (confectioners') sugar, for dusting

CHERRY SOUFFLÉS

125 ml (4 fl oz/½ cup) cherry purée (see Note)
finely grated zest and juice of ½ lemon
1 tablespoon cornflour (cornstarch)
unsalted butter, softened, for brushing
185 g (6½ oz) caster (superfine) sugar, plus extra for dusting
15 g (½ oz) glucose syrup (Glossary)
3 egg whites
a pinch of salt

CHOCOLATE SAUCE

300 g (10½ oz/2 cups) chopped good-quality dark (bittersweet) chocolate, such as couverture
550 ml (19 fl oz) thick (double/heavy) cream
30 g (1 oz) glucose syrup (Glossary)

POACHED CHERRIES

250 g (9 oz) caster (superfine) sugar
2 tablespoons kirsch
finely grated zest and juice of ½ lemon
18 ripe cherries, pitted and cut in half

To make the chocolate sauce, put the chocolate in a mixing bowl. Put the cream and glucose in a saucepan and bring to the boil, then remove from the heat and pour over the chocolate, stirring to melt the chocolate. Strain through a fine sieve and refrigerate until required.

To make the poached cherries, put the sugar, kirsch, lemon zest and juice with 250 ml (9 fl oz/1 cup) water in a saucepan over medium heat, stirring until the sugar dissolves. Bring to the boil, then reduce the heat and add the cherries. Simmer for 3–4 minutes. Set aside to cool.

To make the soufflé, put the cherry purée, lemon zest and juice in a saucepan and bring to the boil. Reduce the heat and simmer for 2 minutes. Mix the cornflour together with 2 tablespoons water to form a paste, then drizzle into the cherry mixture, stirring constantly. Bring back to the boil, then remove from the heat and cool.

Preheat the oven to 200°C (400°F/Gas 6). Brush six 185 ml (6 fl oz/¾ cup) capacity ramekins with butter, then dust with caster sugar, shaking out any excess.

Combine the caster sugar, glucose syrup and a dash of water in a small saucepan over medium heat and stir until the sugar has dissolved. Bring to the boil, then reduce the heat and simmer, stirring constantly, for 5 minutes, or until the temperature reaches 120°C (235°F) on a sugar thermometer (known as 'soft ball' stage).

Meanwhile, whisk the egg white and salt in the bowl of an electric mixer until stiff peaks form. Gradually add the sugar syrup in a steady stream, whisking constantly until cold. Fold in the cooled cherry purée mixture.

Put about six poached cherry halves in the base of each ramekin. Spoon the soufflé mixture in over the cherries, filling each dish to the top. Level off the tops with a spatula. Gently run your thumb or a paring knife around the inside rim of each dish to loosen the mixture away from the top — this will allow the soufflés to rise cleanly. Bake for 8 minutes, or until the soufflés have risen 1–2 cm (½–¾ inch) out of the dishes and are coloured.

Meanwhile, gently reheat the chocolate sauce. Dust the soufflés with icing sugar and place on serving plates. Serve immediately with the warm chocolate sauce on the side.

Note: To make the cherry purée put 350 g (12 oz/2⅓ cups) whole pitted cherries into a food processor and process until smooth, then strain through a fine sieve.

Date-stuffed saffron pears with cinnamon yoghurt

SERVES 6
460 ml (16 fl oz) white wine
340 g (11¾ oz/1½ cups) caster (superfine) sugar
2 tablespoons freshly squeezed lemon juice
4 whole cloves
1 cinnamon stick
½ teaspoon saffron threads
6 large or 9 small ripe but firm pears, peeled and cored
6–9 fresh dates, pitted (see Note)
250 g (9 oz/1 cup) Greek-style yoghurt
a pinch of ground cinnamon

Combine the white wine, sugar, lemon juice and spices in a large saucepan over medium heat and stir until the sugar dissolves. Bring to the boil, then reduce the heat to a simmer. Immerse the pears in the syrup and cover with baking paper and a plate to keep them submerged. Poach for 12–15 minutes, or until almost tender. Remove from the heat. Set aside to cool slightly in the poaching liquid.

Preheat the oven to 180°C (350°F/Gas 4).

Remove the pears from the poaching liquid, reserving the liquid. Place a date in the core of each pear, wrap in foil, then place on a baking tray and bake for 7–8 minutes. Remove from the oven.

Meanwhile, strain the poaching liquid through a fine sieve into a clean saucepan, discarding the aromatics. Place the pan over medium heat and simmer until reduced by one-third.

Whisk together the yoghurt and ground cinnamon.

To serve, carefully remove the foil from the pears. Slice the pears in half, slicing carefully through the dates, and arrange in the base of serving bowls. Pour some of the reduced poaching syrup around the pears and top with a spoonful of the cinnamon yoghurt.

Note: Fresh dates are available all year round and are usually found in the fresh produce section of supermarkets or at your greengrocer's. They should be deep brown, plump and moist. Fresh dates are lower in sugar content than dried dates though just as sweet, making them a perfect match to the sweet spiced pears. Dried dates are simply no substitute for fresh in this recipe.

Ginger kisses with espresso cream

A well-made coffee accompanied by a little sweet morsel is my favourite way to end a great meal. These delicious little treats also make a great accompaniment to the milk chocolate brûlée on page 220, or as part of a dessert platter.
(pictured page 204)

MAKES ABOUT 24
40 g (1½ oz) unsalted butter, softened
125 g (4½ oz) caster (superfine) sugar
1 tablespoon golden syrup or light corn syrup
225 g (8 oz/1½ cups) plain (all-purpose) flour
1 teaspoon baking powder
1 teaspoon ground cinnamon
1 teaspoon ground ginger
2 eggs, beaten
icing (confectioners') sugar, sifted, for dusting

ESPRESSO CREAM
150 g (5½ oz) unsalted butter, softened
300 g (10½ oz) icing (confectioners') sugar, sifted
3 teaspoons hot espresso or strong plunger coffee

Preheat the oven to 200°C (400°F/Gas 6). Grease and line two baking trays with baking paper.

In the bowl of an electric mixer, cream together the butter, sugar and golden syrup until light and pale.

In a separate bowl, sift together the flour, baking powder, cinnamon and ginger. Gradually add the beaten eggs to the creamed butter mixture, alternating with the dry ingredients, mixing well to combine.

Roll teaspoons of the biscuit dough into balls and press down gently on the prepared baking trays (or use a piping bag with a small plain nozzle). Bake for 10–12 minutes, or until golden. Cool completely on the trays.

To make the espresso cream, cream the butter and sugar together in a bowl until light and pale. Add the hot espresso and mix well to combine. Spread a small amount of the espresso cream on the base of a ginger biscuit and sandwich together with another biscuit. Repeat with the remaining biscuits and espresso cream. Dust with icing sugar to serve. Ginger kisses will keep for 1–2 days stored in an airtight container.

Ginger kisses with espresso cream
Opposite: Trio of chocolate — white chocolate sorbet, milk chocolate mousse & dark chocolate delice

Trio of chocolate — white chocolate sorbet, milk chocolate mousse & dark chocolate delice

(pictured page 205)

SERVES 10

WHITE CHOCOLATE SORBET

400 g (14 oz/1¾ cups) caster (superfine) sugar

250 g (9 oz/1⅔ cups) chopped good-quality white chocolate, such as couverture

MILK CHOCOLATE MOUSSE

375 g (13 oz/2½ cups) chopped good-quality milk chocolate, such as couverture

100 g (3½ oz) caster (superfine) sugar

4 egg whites

750 ml (26 fl oz/3 cups) pouring (whipping) cream, softly whipped

To make the white chocolate sorbet, combine the sugar and 600 ml (21 fl oz) water in a large saucepan over medium heat and stir until the sugar dissolves. Bring to the boil, then remove from the heat. In a separate heavy-based saucepan, melt the white chocolate with 600 ml (21 fl oz) water. Bring to the boil, then remove from the heat. Stir in the sugar syrup and set aside to cool. Transfer to an ice-cream machine and churn according to the manufacturer's instructions, then freeze. Alternatively, transfer to a shallow metal tray and freeze, whisking every couple of hours until smooth and frozen.

To make the milk chocolate mousse, put the chocolate in a heatproof bowl over a saucepan of simmering water and allow to melt, stirring occasionally, until smooth. Set aside to cool slightly. Combine the sugar and 60 ml (2 fl oz/¼ cup) water in a small saucepan over medium heat and stir until the sugar dissolves. Bring to the boil, then reduce the heat and simmer, stirring constantly, for 5 minutes, or until the temperature reaches 120°C (235°F) on a sugar thermometer (known as 'soft ball' stage). Meanwhile, whisk the egg white in the bowl of an electric mixer until soft peaks form. When the sugar syrup reaches 120°C (235°F), gradually add it to the beaten egg white in a steady stream, whisking constantly until cold. Use a whisk to carefully fold in the melted chocolate, then fold in the whipped cream. Transfer the mousse to a shallow tray, cover with plastic wrap and refrigerate until required.

To make the dark chocolate delice, put the chocolate in a heatproof bowl over a saucepan of simmering water and allow to melt, stirring occasionally, until smooth. Set aside to cool slightly. Put the egg, egg yolks, sugar and 1 tablespoon water in a heatproof bowl over a saucepan of simmering water, whisking constantly until the mixture becomes thick and foamy and doubles in volume. Remove from the heat. Fold in the melted chocolate, then fold in the whipped cream. Line a 28 x 10 x 8 cm (11¼ x 4 x 3¼ inch) loaf (bar) tin with plastic wrap, allowing a 4 cm (1½ inch) overhang around the sides. Pour the mixture into the tin, then tap the tin lightly to remove any air bubbles. Cover the top with the overhanging plastic wrap and refrigerate for several hours or overnight until set.

To make the chocolate tuiles, cream the butter and sugar together in a bowl until light and pale. Add the flour, cocoa and egg white, beating until smooth. Refrigerate the tuile mixture for 1 hour before using.

DARK CHOCOLATE DELICE

220 g (7¾ oz/1½ cups) chopped good-quality dark (bittersweet) chocolate, such as couverture
1 egg
2 egg yolks
80 g (2¾ oz/⅓ cup) caster (superfine) sugar
250 ml (9 fl oz/1 cup) pouring (whipping) cream, softly whipped

CHOCOLATE TUILES

100 g (3½ oz) unsalted butter, softened
220 g (7¾ oz/1 cup) caster (superfine) sugar
200 g (7 oz/1⅓ cups) plain (all-purpose) flour, sifted
30 g (1 oz/¼ cup) unsweetened cocoa powder, sifted, plus extra for dusting
4 egg whites

Preheat the oven to 180°C (350°F/Gas 4). Draw three 10 cm (4 inch) circles on baking paper and invert the paper onto a baking tray. Using a spatula, smear a thin layer of tuile batter onto each circle and bake for 3–5 minutes, or until brown at the edges and golden in the centre. Cool completely on the trays. Repeat until all the batter has been used. Select the ten best-shaped tuiles and store them in an airtight container until required. Crush the remaining tuiles using a mortar and pestle to use as garnish. Store in an airtight container.

To serve, turn the dark chocolate delice out of the tin onto a work surface. Cut the delice with a hot knife into about 1.5 cm (⅝ inch) thick slices and then cut each slice into two triangles to serve. Place a slice of the delice to one side of each serving plate with a large scoop of the milk chocolate mousse and a spoonful of the chocolate tuile crumbs. Rest a scoop of the white chocolate sorbet on the tuile crumbs, then top with a whole tuile dusted with cocoa powder.

White chocolate bavarois & chocolate chilli soup

It is said the first bavarois, a soft mousse dessert, was made by French chefs working in the court of the Wittelsbach Princes of Bavaria. Soft, smooth and silky, they prove to be the perfect foil for the lightly spiced chocolate chilli soup, a pre-Columbian speciality of the Aztecs that still works in today's kitchen.

SERVES 8–10

shaved good-quality white chocolate, such as couverture, to serve

WHITE CHOCOLATE BAVAROIS
300 g (10½ oz/2 cups) chopped good-quality white chocolate, such as couverture
250 ml (9 fl oz/1 cup) full-cream (whole) milk
4 x 2 g gelatine leaves
2 eggs
2 tablespoons caster (superfine) sugar
500 ml (17 fl oz/2 cups) pouring (whipping) cream, whipped to soft peaks

CHOCOLATE CHILLI SOUP
140 g (5 oz/⅔ cup) caster (superfine) sugar
2 red chillies, seeded and chopped
120 g (4¼ oz) good-quality dark (bittersweet) chocolate, such as couverture, chopped
80 g (2¾ oz/⅔ cup) unsweetened cocoa powder, sifted

To make the white chocolate bavarois, put the chocolate and 200 ml (7 fl oz) of the milk in a heatproof bowl over a saucepan of simmering water and allow to melt, stirring occasionally, until smooth. Remove from the heat and cool to room temperature.

Heat the remaining milk in a small saucepan. Soften the gelatine leaves in cold water and squeeze to remove any excess water. Whisk the gelatine into the milk, stirring to completely dissolve.

In a separate mixing bowl, whisk together the eggs and sugar until thick and pale. Fold the cooled chocolate into the egg mixture. Stir in the gelatine mixture, mixing well to combine, then lastly fold in the whipped cream. Rinse eight to ten 125 ml (4 fl oz/½ cup) capacity plastic dariole moulds with cold water. Pour the bavarois mixture into the moulds, filling to the top. Refrigerate for 2–3 hours, or until set.

To make the chocolate chilli soup, put the sugar, chilli and 400 ml (14 fl oz) water in a saucepan over low heat and bring to a simmer, stirring until the sugar dissolves. Add the chocolate and cocoa and continue to simmer for 10 minutes, stirring occasionally. Remove from the heat and set aside to cool to room temperature.

Strain the soup through a fine sieve. If you prefer, you can prepare the soup in advance and refrigerate it in an airtight container until required. It can be reheated in a heatproof bowl over a saucepan of simmering water.

To serve, run the tip of a paring knife around the edge of the dariole moulds, then dip the base of the mould in very hot water and gently shake the bavarois into the middle of serving bowls. Carefully pour the chocolate chilli soup around the bavarois and serve topped with the shaved white chocolate.

Basil crème brûlée & strawberry compote with vanilla madeleines

(*pictured page 212*)

SERVES 8

vanilla bean ice cream (Basics, page 241), to serve
icing (confectioners') sugar, for dusting

BASIL CRÈME BRÛLÉE

1.2 litres (44 fl oz) pouring (whipping) cream
300 ml (10½ fl oz) full-cream (whole) milk
2 large handfuls of basil leaves
12 egg yolks
250 g (9 oz) caster (superfine) sugar, plus extra for glazing

STRAWBERRY COMPOTE

1 kg (2 lb 4 oz) fresh strawberries, hulled
2 tablespoons icing (confectioners') sugar

VANILLA MADELEINES

4 eggs
2 egg yolks
140 g (5 oz/⅔ cup) caster (superfine) sugar
1 teaspoon natural vanilla extract
125 g (4½ oz) plain (all-purpose) flour
1¼ teaspoons baking powder
150 g (5½ oz) unsalted butter, melted

To make the basil crème brûlée, put the cream, milk and basil in a saucepan over medium heat and bring to the boil. Remove from the heat. Set aside for 30 minutes to allow the flavours to infuse.

In a large mixing bowl, whisk the egg yolks and sugar until thick and pale. Strain the cream mixture through a fine sieve, discarding the basil. Whisk the cream into the eggs, then return the mixture to a clean saucepan over medium heat. Using a wooden spoon, stir constantly, until the custard thickens and coats the back of the spoon — do not let it boil. Remove from the heat. Strain the brûlée mixture through a fine sieve into a jug. Cool to room temperature, then refrigerate overnight to allow any air bubbles to rise and then skim them from the surface.

Preheat the oven to 170°C (325°F/Gas 3). Lightly grease two madeleine tins.

To make the vanilla madeleines, whisk the eggs, egg yolks, sugar and vanilla together in the bowl of an electric mixer until thick and pale. Sift the flour and baking powder together, then on slow speed, gradually add to the egg mixture until incorporated. Gradually stir in the melted butter.

Spoon the madeleine mixture into the tins and bake for 8–10 minutes, or until the madeleines spring back to the touch. Cool in the tins, then transfer to an airtight container until required. The madeleines will keep for 2–3 days.

To make the strawberry compote, cut the strawberries lengthways into 4–6 pieces, depending on the size. Put 1 heaped cup of the sliced strawberries into a food processor with the icing sugar and blend until smooth. Transfer to a saucepan over medium heat and bring to a gentle boil until it reduces by one-quarter. Reduce the heat to low, add the remaining strawberries and continue to cook for several minutes, until the strawberries have just softened. Remove from the heat and set aside to cool. Strain through a fine sieve, discarding the cooking liquid.

Reduce the oven temperature to 120°C (235°F/Gas ½).

Spoon the cooled strawberry compote evenly into eight 185 ml (6 fl oz/¾ cup) capacity ramekins. Use the back of a large metal spoon to slowly pour the brûlée mixture into the moulds over the strawberry compote. Sit the ramekins in a large roasting tray and pour in enough boiling water to reach halfway up the sides of the ramekins. Bake for 30 minutes, or until the brûlée is just set. Cool, then refrigerate until ready to serve.

To serve, sprinkle the brûlée liberally with caster sugar, cleaning the edges to avoid burning. Using a kitchen blowtorch, caramelise the tops to a rich golden colour. Dust the madeleines with icing sugar, then arrange two alongside the brûlée with a scoop of vanilla ice cream.

Note: A grill (broiler) can be used to caramelise the brûlée tops though the brûlées tend to soften before they glaze. Kitchen blowtorches can be purchased from all good kitchen shops. Use with care.

Basil crème brûlée & strawberry compote with vanilla madeleines

Cherry & Drambuie semifreddo

Cherry & Drambuie semifreddo
(pictured page 213)

SERVES 6

100 g (3½ oz) fresh cherries, pitted
300 g (10½ oz) caster (superfine) sugar
9 egg yolks
finely grated zest of 1 orange
80 ml (2½ fl oz/⅓ cup) Drambuie
1 teaspoon natural vanilla extract
670 ml (23 fl oz/2⅔ cup) pouring (whipping) cream
poached cherries, to serve

Line a 30 x 12 x 10 cm (12 x 4½ x 4 inch) loaf (bar) tin with plastic wrap, allowing a 4 cm (1½ inch) overhang around the sides.

Put the cherries, 100 g (3½ oz) of the sugar and 100 ml (3½ fl oz) water in a small saucepan over low heat. Gently cook the cherries until soft and reduced to a pulp. Set aside to cool.

Put the remaining sugar and 125 ml (4 fl oz/½ cup) water in a saucepan over medium heat and stir until the sugar dissolves. Bring to the boil, then reduce the heat and simmer, stirring constantly, for 5 minutes, or until the temperature reaches 120°C (235°F) on a sugar thermometer (known as 'soft ball' stage).

Meanwhile, in the bowl of an electric mixer, whisk the egg yolks until thick and pale. With the machine running, gradually drizzle in the sugar syrup, whisking constantly, until the mixture has cooled. Stir in the orange zest, Drambuie and vanilla.

In a separate bowl, whisk the cream to soft peaks. Using a large balloon whisk, carefully fold the whipped cream through the egg mixture. Lastly, fold through the cherry mixture to form a ripple effect.

Pour the mixture into the prepared tin, cover with the overhanging plastic wrap and freeze overnight.

To serve, turn the semifreddo out of the tin onto a work surface. Using a hot knife, cut into slices about 1.5 cm (⅝ inch) thick. Arrange the semifreddo in the centre of each plate and serve with poached cherries.

Chocolate panna cotta, poached pears & gingerbread

SERVES 6

icing (confectioners') sugar, for dusting
chocolate shavings, to garnish

CHOCOLATE PANNA COTTA
160 ml (5¼ fl oz) full-cream (whole) milk
500 ml (17 fl oz/2 cups) pouring (whipping) cream
120 g (4¼ oz) caster (superfine) sugar
150 g (5½ oz/1 cup) chopped good-quality dark (bittersweet) chocolate, such as couverture
5 x 2 g gelatine leaves
400 ml (14 fl oz) pouring (whipping) cream, whipped to soft peaks

POACHED PEARS
750 ml (26 fl oz/3 cups) white wine
300 g (10½ oz) caster (superfine) sugar
1 vanilla bean, split lengthways
6 cm (2½ inch) piece of ginger, crushed
6 ripe but firm pears, preferably Williams' pears, peeled

GINGERBREAD
75 g (2¾ oz) unsalted butter, softened
125 g (4½ oz) caster (superfine) sugar
25 g (1 oz) golden syrup or light corn syrup
1 teaspoon ground ginger
2 teaspoons ground cinnamon
¼ teaspoon ground cloves
½ teaspoon ground cardamom
1 teaspoon bicarbonate of soda (baking soda)
25 ml (1 fl oz) full-cream (whole) milk
250 g (9 oz/1⅔ cups) plain (all-purpose) flour, sifted, plus extra for dusting

To make the chocolate panna cotta, put the milk, cream and sugar in a saucepan over medium heat. Bring to just below boiling, reduce the heat to low, then add the chocolate and stir until melted. Remove from the heat. Soften the gelatine leaves in cold water and squeeze to remove any excess water. Whisk the gelatine into the chocolate mixture and stir to completely dissolve. Strain the mixture into a bowl and allow to cool. Before the mixture reaches setting point, fold through the whipped cream. Pour the panna cotta mixture into six 125 ml (4 fl oz/½ cup) capacity ramekins. Refrigerate for several hours, or until set.

To make the gingerbread, put the butter, sugar, golden syrup, spices and bicarbonate of soda in the bowl of an electric mixer and beat with the paddle attachment until well combined. Gradually pour in the milk and 25 ml (1 fl oz) water, mixing well to combine, then slowly add the flour. Shape the dough into a circle, wrap in plastic wrap, and refrigerate for at least 1 hour.

Preheat the oven to 180°C (350°F/Gas 4). Grease and line a baking tray with baking paper. On a lightly floured surface, roll out the rested gingerbread dough so that it is 3 mm (⅛ inch) thick all over. Using a large dinner plate as a stencil, cut the gingerbread into a large circle, then cut into twelve wedges. Carefully transfer to the prepared tray and bake for 10–12 minutes, or until golden. Turn out onto a wire rack to cool completely.

To make the poached pears, select a saucepan that will fit the pears snugly. Place the wine, sugar, vanilla bean, ginger and 300 ml (10½ fl oz) water in the pan over medium heat and bring to the boil. Add the pears, then cover with baking paper and a plate to keep them completely submerged. Reduce the heat to low and gently poach for 20–30 minutes, or until tender. Cool the pears in the syrup. Once cooled the pears can be stored in an airtight container with the syrup in the refrigerator for up to 2–3 days.

To serve, drain the pears from the syrup and cut in half. Place a panna cotta to the side of each serving plate. Arrange two pear halves alongside, one on top of each other. Dust the gingerbread with icing sugar and rest against the panna cotta. Scatter the top of the panna cotta with the chocolate shavings.

Lemon & white chocolate mousse with lemon curd

Not only do these individual mousses look spectacular, they're a great alternative to a full dessert if all you want is something a little sweet to finish. Serve them simply on their own or as part of a dessert tasting plate.

MAKES 20–25 SHOT GLASSES

LEMON & WHITE CHOCOLATE MOUSSE
185 g (6½ oz/1¼ cups) chopped good-quality white chocolate, such as couverture
2 egg whites
50 g (1¾ oz/¼ cup) caster (superfine) sugar, plus 1 tablespoon extra
375 ml (13 fl oz/1½ cups) pouring (whipping) cream, softly whipped
grated zest of 2 lemons
½ tablespoon limoncello (Glossary)
1 lemon

LEMON CURD
2 egg yolks
2 eggs
60 ml (2 fl oz/¼ cup) freshly squeezed lemon juice
125 g (4½ oz) caster (superfine) sugar
125 g (4½ oz) unsalted butter, melted

To make the lemon and white chocolate mousse, put the chocolate in a heatproof bowl over a saucepan of simmering water and allow to melt, stirring occasionally, until smooth. Cool to room temperature.

In the bowl of an electric mixer, whisk the egg white until soft peaks form, then gradually add the sugar and continue to whisk until all the sugar is incorporated and the mixture is thick and glossy.

Fold the cooled chocolate into the beaten egg white, then fold in the cream, lemon zest and limoncello. Pipe the mousse into shot glasses to three-quarters full. Place on a baking tray and refrigerate until required.

To make the lemon curd, whisk together the egg yolks, eggs, lemon juice and sugar in a heatproof bowl. Add the melted butter, then place over a saucepan of simmering water, stirring constantly until the mixture thickens and coats the back of a wooden spoon — do not let it boil. Strain into an airtight container and refrigerate until required.

Peel the zest from the lemon in wide strips, then use a sharp knife to remove the white pith from the zest, discarding the pith. (Reserve the lemon for another use.) Blanch the lemon zest in a small saucepan of boiling water for 2 minutes. Refresh in iced water. Blanch the zest for a further 2 minutes, refresh in iced water once again, then cut into thin strips. Toss the lemon zest in the extra caster sugar.

To serve, use a teaspoon dipped in hot water to place a small spoonful of lemon curd on top of each mousse. Top with a little candied lemon zest.

Rhubarb fool

Rhubarb fool is classic English summer food. The original spelling was 'foole' and has nothing to do with stupidity — just traditional summer fruit, such as raspberries or gooseberries, and lots of lovely fresh cream.

SERVES 6

70 g (2½ oz) unsalted butter, melted
100 g (3½ oz) soft brown sugar
6 rhubarb stalks, chopped
a good pinch of ground cinnamon
750 ml (26 fl oz/3 cups) pouring (whipping) cream
1 vanilla bean, split lengthways, seeds scraped
biscotti (Basics, page 240), to serve

Combine the butter and sugar in a saucepan over low heat, stirring until the sugar dissolves. Add the rhubarb and cinnamon. Cook slowly until the rhubarb is tender and begins to break down. Remove from the heat and set aside to cool.

In the bowl of an electric mixer, whisk the cream and vanilla seeds to soft peaks. Fold through the cooled rhubarb, reserving a little of the syrup for garnish.

Spoon the rhubarb fool into six 250 ml (9 fl oz/1 cup) capacity serving glasses. Drizzle over the reserved rhubarb syrup and serve with biscotti.

Note: Cream with vanilla and sugar added is often called chantilly cream. In this case we haven't added any extra sugar as the rhubarb should be sweet enough. However, if you have a sweet tooth, or just prefer your rhubarb a little sweeter, add a little extra sugar when cooking the rhubarb rather than to the cream. This way, you can just add enough of the sweet rhubarb syrup, to taste.

Milk chocolate brûlée

SERVES 6–8

1.2 litres (44 fl oz) pouring (whipping) cream
170 g (6 oz) good-quality milk chocolate,
   such as couverture, chopped
9 egg yolks
100 g (3½ oz) caster (superfine) sugar,
   plus extra for glazing

Preheat the oven to 120°C (235°F/Gas ½).

Put the cream and chocolate in a saucepan over medium heat, stirring to melt the chocolate. Bring to the boil, then remove from the heat.

In a large mixing bowl, whisk the egg yolks and sugar until thick and pale. Whisk the hot chocolate cream mixture into the eggs, then strain through a fine sieve into a jug.

Pour the mixture into six 185 ml (6 fl oz/¾ cup) capacity ramekins. Sit the ramekins in a large roasting tray and pour in enough boiling water to reach halfway up the side of the ramekins. Bake for 30 minutes, or until the brûlées are just set. Cool.

To serve, sprinkle the brûlée liberally with the extra sugar, cleaning the edges to avoid burning. Use a kitchen blowtorch to caramelise the tops to a rich golden colour, then serve.

Note: A grill (broiler) can be used to caramelise the brûlée tops though the brûlées tend to soften before they glaze. Kitchen blowtorches can be purchased from all good kitchen shops. Use with care.

Orange & coconut syrup cake

SERVES 6

450 g (1 lb) Greek-style yoghurt
130 g (4¾ oz) shredded coconut
finely grated zest and juice of 2 oranges
200 g (7 oz/1⅓ cups) self-raising flour
½ teaspoon bicarbonate of soda (baking soda)
200 g (7 oz) unsalted butter, softened
320 g (11¼ oz) caster (superfine) sugar
5 eggs
icing (confectioners') sugar, for dusting
shaved fresh coconut, to serve
whipped cream or vanilla bean ice cream
   (Basics, page 241), to serve

ORANGE SYRUP

200 g (7 oz) caster (superfine) sugar
juice of 2 oranges

Preheat the oven to 150°C (300°F/Gas 2). Grease the base of a round 26 cm (10½ inch) spring-form cake tin and line the base and side with baking paper.

In a bowl, mix together the yoghurt, shredded coconut, orange zest and juice until well combined.

Sift together the flour and bicarbonate of soda in a separate bowl.

In the bowl of an electric mixer, cream the butter and sugar together until light and pale. Add the eggs, one at a time, beating well after each addition. Fold through the yoghurt mixture, incorporating well, then fold in the dry ingredients.

Pour the cake mixture into the prepared tin and bake for 45–50 minutes, or until a skewer inserted into the centre of the cake comes out clean. Remove from the oven.

Meanwhile, make the orange syrup by combining the sugar and just enough water to cover in a small saucepan over medium heat and stir until the sugar dissolves. Add the orange juice, then remove from the heat.

Drizzle the syrup in a slow, steady stream over the top of the warm cake until the syrup is absorbed, using a pastry brush to distribute the syrup evenly. Cool the cake to room temperature before removing from the tin.

Dust the cake with icing sugar and cut into wedges. Top each wedge with a little shaved coconut and serve with a spoonful of whipped cream or a scoop of ice cream.

Chocolate, rum & almond pithiviers

This recipe calls for ready-rolled butter puff pastry. There's some really good quality boutique, ready-to-use frozen pastry on the market these days. For this recipe I recommend you try a brand called Carême.

SERVES 6

60 g (2¼ oz) good-quality dark (bittersweet) chocolate, such as couverture
120 g (4¼ oz) caster (superfine) sugar
2 tablespoons unsweetened cocoa powder
150 g (5½ oz/1½ cups) ground almonds
100 g (3½ oz) unsalted butter, diced
2 eggs
2 teaspoons dark rum
6 sheets ready-rolled store-bought butter puff pastry
1 egg, extra, beaten

In a food processor, combine the chocolate, sugar, cocoa and ground almonds until the chocolate is finely chopped. Add the butter and process until the mixture just comes together — do not overwork. Add the eggs and rum, mixing well to combine. Transfer to a bowl, cover with plastic wrap and refrigerate for a couple of hours or until the mixture is firm.

Preheat the oven to 200°C (400°F/Gas 6). Grease and line two baking trays with baking paper.

Use a pastry cutter or plate to stamp out sixteen 10 cm (4 inch) rounds of pastry. Place eight of the pastry rounds in a single layer on the prepared baking trays — do not overlap.

Divide the chocolate filling between eight pastry rounds on the trays, leaving a 2 cm (¾ inch) border. Brush the border with beaten egg, then place the remaining pastry rounds over the filling. Crimp together the edges using your thumb and forefinger. Using the back of a small knife, make circular patterns on the top of each pithivier, taking care not to cut through the pastry. Brush the tops with the beaten egg and refrigerate for 15 minutes.

Bake for 10 minutes, then reduce the oven temperature to 180°C (350°F/Gas 4) and bake for 15 minutes, or until the pastry is golden and has risen.

Pithiviers can be eaten warm or at room temperature and are best on the day they are baked.

Mixed nut tartlets with rum & raisin purée & coconut ice cream

I can't tell you the number of times I've tasted a great dish that's been ruined by stale nuts. This beautifully rich tart is best when it's made using fresh nuts. Buy them from a dedicated nut supplier or health food store to ensure a high turnover of stock to get them at their freshest.

SERVES 6
500 g (1 lb 2 oz) soft brown sugar
50 g (1¾ oz) glucose syrup (Glossary)
500 ml (17 fl oz/2 cups) pouring (whipping) cream
50 g (1¾ oz) honey
9 eggs
280 g (10 oz/2 cups) mixed nuts (such as pecans, brazil nuts, cashews, almonds, macadamias and hazelnuts), toasted and roughly chopped
6 x 8 cm (3¼ inch) blind-baked sweet shortcrust tartlet cases (Basics, page 239)
coconut ice cream (Basics, page 242), to serve

RUM & RAISIN PURÉE
250 g (9 oz/2 cups) raisins
100 ml (3½ fl oz) dark rum
60 g (2¼ oz/¼ cup) caster (superfine) sugar
finely grated zest and juice of 1 orange

To make the rum and raisin purée, soak the raisins in the rum for 1 hour. Put the sugar and 80 ml (2½ fl oz/⅓ cup) water in a small saucepan over medium heat, stirring until the sugar dissolves. Bring to the boil and simmer for 2 minutes. Remove from the heat and set aside. Put the raisins and rum in a small saucepan and gently warm over low heat. Remove from the heat and add the orange zest and juice. Set aside to cool. Blend the raisins in a food processor to form a smooth paste, adding enough of the cooking liquid to taste. Refrigerate until required.

Preheat the oven to 180°C (350°F/Gas 4).

To make the tartlet filling, put the brown sugar, glucose syrup, cream, honey and eggs in a large bowl and whisk together until well combined.

Spread the nuts over the base of the blind-baked tartlet cases. Pour the filling over the nuts to completely fill each pastry case. Bake for 10–15 minutes, or until the filling is just set and golden. Leave to cool in the tins before gently turning out.

To serve, place a tartlet in the centre of each serving plate with a spoonful of rum and raisin purée and two scoops of coconut ice cream to one side.

Chocolate meringues with cassis cream & fresh raspberries

MAKES ABOUT 25
3 egg whites
½ teaspoon natural vanilla extract
165 g (5¾ oz/¾ cup) caster (superfine) sugar
25 g (1 oz) unsweetened cocoa powder, sifted, plus extra for dusting
fresh raspberries (optional), to serve

CASSIS CREAM
300 ml (10½ fl oz) thick (double/heavy) cream
2 tablespoons icing (confectioners') sugar, sifted
60 ml (2 fl oz/¼ cup) crème de cassis

Preheat the oven to 140°C (275°F/Gas 1). Grease and line two baking trays with baking paper.

In the bowl of an electric mixer, whisk the egg white and vanilla on high speed. Gradually add the sugar and continue to whisk to stiff peaks. Fold in the cocoa powder. Spoon the mixture into a piping (icing) bag with a plain nozzle. Pipe the meringue into about fifty even-sized circles, each with a diameter of about 4 cm (1½ inch). If you don't have a piping bag, spoon the mixture onto lined trays then use a fork to shape the meringues. Bake for 45–60 minutes, then turn the oven off and allow the meringues to dry for a further 2 hours in the oven. The meringues will keep for 2–3 days when stored in an airtight container without the cassis cream filling.

To make the cassis cream, lightly whisk the cream in the bowl of an electric mixer, add the icing sugar and crème de cassis and continue to whisk to soft peaks.

Sandwich the meringues together with the cassis cream. Arrange on a serving platter and lightly dust with a small amount of cocoa powder. Scatter with fresh raspberries, if using.

Note: You can vary the size of the meringues depending on what you are making them for. This size is ideal as a petit four or dessert canapé, but you could double the size of each meringue to make larger biscuits to have with morning coffee, or even larger again to serve them as a dessert.

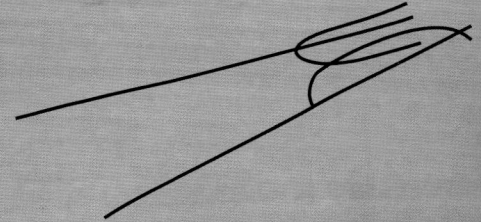

Basics

Vegetable stock

MAKES ABOUT 2 LITRES (70 FL OZ)
olive oil
1 onion, chopped
1 leek, white part only, chopped
sea salt
3 celery stalks, chopped
2 tomatoes
1 small fennel bulb (optional), chopped
3 garlic cloves
1 bay leaf
3 black peppercorns

Heat a little olive oil in a large heavy-based saucepan or stockpot over low heat. Sauté the onion, leek and a good pinch of sea salt for several minutes, with little or no colour, until the onion is soft. Add the remaining vegetables, the bay leaf, peppercorns and 2.5 litres (87 fl oz) water, bring to the boil, then reduce the heat and simmer for 1 hour.

Remove the pan from the heat, cool, then strain, discarding the vegetables and aromatics. Vegetable stock will keep for 2–3 days refrigerated, or several months in the freezer.

White chicken stock

MAKES ABOUT 2 LITRES (70 FL OZ)
2 kg (4 lb 8 oz) chicken bones and carcasses
1 carrot, diced
1 onion, diced
1 leek, white part only, sliced
3 garlic cloves, unpeeled, lightly crushed
4 thyme sprigs
2 fresh bay leaves
3–4 white peppercorns
3–4 parsley sprigs

Rinse the chicken bones in cold water and place in a large saucepan or stockpot with all the remaining ingredients. Cover well with cold water and bring to the boil, skimming off any impurities that rise to the surface. Reduce the heat to low and simmer for 90 minutes, skimming regularly.

Strain the stock, allow to cool, then refrigerate or freeze until ready to use. The stock will keep for 2–3 days refrigerated, or several months in the freezer.

Fish stock

MAKES ABOUT 2 LITRES (70 FL OZ)
50 g (1¾ oz) unsalted butter
2 onions, sliced
1 bay leaf
3–4 white peppercorns
3–4 parsley sprigs
juice of ½ lemon
1 kg (2 lb 4 oz) fresh fish bones, rinsed

....

Melt the butter in a large heavy-based saucepan or stockpot over low heat. Add the onion, bay leaf, peppercorns, parsley and lemon juice. Sauté for several minutes, without colour, until the onion is soft. Add the fish bones and 2.5 litres (87 fl oz) water, bring to the boil, then reduce the heat and cook for 20 minutes, skimming the surface for any impurities that rise to the surface.

Remove from the heat, cool, then strain, discarding the fish bones and aromatics. Fish stock will keep for 1–2 days refrigerated, or several months in the freezer.

Beef stock

MAKES ABOUT 4 LITRES (140 FL OZ)
2.5 kg (5 lb 8 oz) beef neck bones
2.5 kg (5 lb 8 oz) oxtail pieces
2 tablespoons olive oil
2 onions, diced
2 carrots, diced
2 celery stalks, diced
2 leeks, white part only, sliced
½ garlic bulb, cut in half horizontally, unpeeled
90 g (3¼ oz) field or Swiss brown mushrooms, sliced
125 g (4½ oz/½ cup) tomato paste (concentrated purée)
500 ml (17 fl oz/2 cups) red wine
1 pig's trotter
1 teaspoon white peppercorns
3 bay leaves
6 thyme sprigs
6 parsley sprigs

....

Preheat the oven to 220°C (425°F/Gas 7).

Put the bones and oxtail pieces in a roasting tray and roast for 30–40 minutes, or until well browned. Drain off the rendered fat.

Heat the olive oil in a large saucepan or stockpot over high heat. Add the onion, carrot, celery, leek, garlic and mushrooms and sauté for about 10 minutes, or until well coloured. Add the tomato paste and cook, stirring, for 2 minutes. Add the wine and simmer for 15 minutes, or until the liquid is reduced by half.

Add the roasted bones, pig's trotter, peppercorns and herbs and cover well with cold water. Bring to the boil, skimming off any impurities that rise to the surface, then reduce the heat and gently simmer for 4–6 hours. The saucepan may need topping up with water to keep the bones submerged. Continue to skim occasionally to remove any impurities that rise to the surface.

Strain the stock, allow to cool, then refrigerate or freeze until ready to use. The stock will keep for 1 week refrigerated or several months in the freezer.

Jus

MAKES ABOUT 1.25 LITRES (44 FL OZ)
4 litres (140 fl oz) beef stock (Basics, page 229)
1–2 tablespoons arrowroot or cornflour (cornstarch), optional

Put the stock in a large saucepan or stockpot and bring to the boil. Boil for 20–30 minutes, or until the stock is reduced by two-thirds, occasionally skimming off any impurities that rise to the surface. The sauce should be thick and glossy.

If, after obtaining the required flavour, the jus is still not of coating consistency, blend the arrowroot with 60 ml (2 fl oz/¼ cup) cold water, then, whisking constantly, gradually drizzle just enough of the mixture into the boiling stock until the sauce coats the back of a spoon.

Strain the jus while still hot, allow to cool, then store for about 1 week in the refrigerator, or several months in the freezer.

Clarified butter

MAKES 250 ML (9 FL OZ/1 CUP)
250 g (9 oz) unsalted butter

Put the butter in a small saucepan over low heat and allow it to melt and separate. Alternatively, melt the butter in a microwave on medium heat for 3–4 minutes, or until completely melted and the butter has settled on top.

Carefully pour off the melted butter into a container, leaving the milk solids behind. Discard the milk solids, seal and refrigerate the clarified butter to use as required. Clarified butter will keep for 2 weeks stored in an airtight container in the refrigerator.

Beurre blanc

Beurre blanc, translated from the French to mean 'white butter', is made from a reduction of white vinegar and French shallots to which cold butter can be added, piece by piece, to produce a rich, glossy, butter sauce. Adding a little cream helps to stabilise the sauce and prevent it from splitting. Creamy, yet light and tangy, beurre blanc is the perfect accompaniment to fish and seafood and can also work well with some poultry and vegetable dishes.

MAKES 375 ML (13 FL OZ/1½ CUPS)
125 ml (4 fl oz/½ cup) good-quality white wine vinegar
125 ml (4 fl oz/½ cup) white wine
2 French shallots (eschalots), thinly sliced
1 garlic clove
3 white peppercorns
1 bay leaf
1 thyme sprig
60 ml (2 fl oz/¼ cup) pouring (whipping) cream
150 g (5½ oz) chilled unsalted butter, diced
juice of ½ lemon
sea salt and freshly ground white pepper

Combine the vinegar, wine, eschalot, garlic, peppercorns, bay leaf and thyme in a small saucepan over medium heat. Bring to the boil and simmer until reduced by two-thirds. Strain into a clean saucepan, return to the heat and whisk in the cream. Return to the boil and simmer until reduced by one-third.

Briskly whisk in the butter, piece by piece — the sauce should appear thick and glossy. Season with the lemon juice, sea salt and a pinch of white pepper to taste. Keep warm until required.

Once beurre blanc is made it can't be reheated as it will split, so it's a good idea to always make it just slightly ahead of time and keep it warm in a preheated thermos.

Variations: To make saffron and vanilla beurre blanc, add a pinch of saffron threads to the vinegar mixture.

To make vanilla beurre blanc, add 1 vanilla bean, split lengthways, after the cream has been added. Once the mixture has reduced by one-third, remove the vanilla bean, whisk in the butter, then continue to prepare as directed.

To make lemon beurre blanc, use a vegetable peeler to remove 2 strips of zest from 1 lemon and extract the juice. Add the zest to the vinegar mixture. Continue to prepare as above, adding all the lemon juice.

Mayonnaise

MAKES 500 G (1 LB 2 OZ/2 CUPS)
3 egg yolks
2 teaspoons Dijon mustard
2 tablespoons white wine vinegar
1 tablespoon freshly squeezed lemon juice
250 ml (9 fl oz/1 cup) extra virgin olive oil
250 ml (9 fl oz/1 cup) olive oil
sea salt
a pinch of cayenne pepper

....

Put the egg yolks, mustard, vinegar and lemon juice in a food processor and blend until the mixture doubles in volume. Combine the oils and, with the machine running, slowly drizzle in the oils until the mayonnaise becomes well blended and thick. Transfer the mayonnaise to a bowl. Season with sea salt and cayenne pepper. You may need to adjust the acidity with extra lemon juice.

Alternatively, you can use a whisk to beat the egg yolks, mustard, vinegar and lemon juice until well combined and slightly risen in volume. Slowly drizzle in the olive oil while constantly beating. Oil must be added slowly and a lot of care taken so the mayonnaise does not split (separate). If it does, whisk 1 fresh egg yolk and a little boiling water together until light and fluffy, then gradually add the split mayonnaise, a little at a time, until the mixture comes back together.

....

Variation: To make lime mayonnaise grate the zest of 1 lime and extract the juice. Use the method above, but replace the lemon juice with lime juice. If needed you can adjust the acidity with a little hot water or the remaining lime juice. Fold in the lime zest after seasoning.

Salsa verde

MAKES 165 G (5¾ OZ/1 CUP)
2 large handfuls of basil leaves
2 large handfuls of flat-leaf (Italian) parsley leaves
2 garlic cloves
1½ tablespoons salted capers, rinsed and squeezed dry
3 anchovy fillets, drained, rinsed and dried
1 tablespoon red wine vinegar
2½ tablespoons extra virgin olive oil
2 teaspoons Dijon mustard
sea salt and freshly ground black pepper

....

Finely chop the herbs, garlic, capers and anchovies and place in a bowl. Alternatively, all of the ingredients can be pounded using a mortar and pestle or blended together in a food processor. Whisking well, or with the machine running, drizzle in the vinegar, then add the extra virgin olive oil. Whisk in the mustard, then season with sea salt and black pepper, to taste.

Salsa verde is best used freshly made and at room temperature, although it will keep for 1–2 days stored in an airtight container in the refrigerator.

Red wine vinaigrette

MAKES 200 ML (7 FL OZ)
1 garlic clove, crushed
1 tablespoon freshly squeezed lemon juice
50 ml (1¾ fl oz) good-quality red wine vinegar
150 ml (5 fl oz) extra virgin olive oil
sea salt and freshly ground black pepper

Put the garlic, lemon juice and vinegar in a bowl. Whisk in the extra virgin olive oil, then season to taste with sea salt and black pepper. The vinaigrette can be made ahead of time and stored in the refrigerator for 2–3 weeks.

Balsamic dressing

MAKES 250 ML (9 FL OZ/1 CUP)
60 ml (2 fl oz/¼ cup) good-quality balsamic vinegar
1 garlic clove, crushed
a pinch of caster (superfine) sugar
sea salt and freshly ground black pepper
185 ml (6 fl oz/¾ cup) extra virgin olive oil

Put the vinegar, garlic and sugar in a bowl with some sea salt and black pepper. Gradually whisk in the extra virgin olive oil until well blended. The dressing can be made ahead of time and stored in an airtight container in the refrigerator for 2–3 weeks.

Verjuice dressing

MAKES ABOUT 400 ML (14 FL OZ)
600 ml (21 fl oz) verjuice (Glossary)
200 ml (7 fl oz) extra virgin olive oil
1 teaspoon Dijon mustard
sea salt and freshly ground black pepper

Put the verjuice in a small saucepan, bring to the boil, then reduce the heat and simmer until it reduces by two-thirds. Remove from the heat and set aside to cool.

In a bowl, whisk together the verjuice reduction, extra virgin olive oil and mustard. Season to taste with sea salt and black pepper. The dressing can be made ahead of time and stored in the refrigerator for 2–3 weeks.

Roasted red capsicums

red capsicums (peppers)
olive oil
sea salt and freshly ground black pepper

Preheat the oven to 250°C (500°F/Gas 9). Wash and dry several capsicums and rub well with olive oil. Season with sea salt and freshly ground black pepper. Place on a baking tray and roast until the skins are well blistered, turning once or twice. You can also roast capsicums on a barbecue or under a hot grill (broiler).

Place the capsicums in a bowl, cover with plastic wrap and allow to cool. When the skins have steamed away from the flesh, peel them off and discard along with the membranes and seeds. Use the roasted flesh as directed in each recipe. Roasted capsicums will keep in an airtight container, stored in the refrigerator, for several days.

Salsa Romesco

MAKES 600 G (1 LB 5 OZ/2 CUPS)
8 roma (plum) tomatoes, cut in half lengthways
1 tablespoon soft brown sugar
100 ml (3½ fl oz) olive oil
4 slices white bread, crusts removed, diced
4 dried red chillies
2 garlic cloves
2 roasted red capsicums, peeled, seeded and chopped (Basics, page 234)
2 long red chillies, seeded and chopped
80 ml (2½ fl oz/⅓ cup) sherry vinegar
1–2 teaspoons smoked Spanish paprika
sea salt and freshly ground black pepper
120 g (4¼ oz/¾ cup) blanched almonds, roasted and roughly chopped
120 g (4¼ oz) hazelnuts, roasted, skinned and roughly chopped

....

Preheat the oven grill (broiler) to medium. Lay the tomato halves, cut-side up, on a baking tray lined with baking paper. Sprinkle with the sugar, then place under the hot grill for several minutes to caramelise, being careful they don't burn. Remove from the heat and set aside.

Heat 60 ml (2 fl oz/¼ cup) of the oil in a heavy-based frying pan over medium heat. Add the bread, tossing to coat in oil, and cook until crisp and golden. Set aside.

Soak the dried chillies in hot water to soften, then cut in half lengthways and remove the seeds; finely chop the flesh. In a food processor, blend the dried chilli, garlic, roasted capsicum and tomato until well combined. Add the bread and blend until smooth. Add the chilli, vinegar and paprika to taste. With the motor running, drizzle in the remaining oil and process until the sauce is emulsified. Season with sea salt and black pepper, then fold through the nuts. This is best used the day it is made but it will keep for 2–3 days stored in an airtight container in the refrigerator.

....

Note: Salsa Romesco makes a great accompaniment to grilled fish and poultry dishes.

Red pepper jam

MAKES 500 G (1 LB 2 OZ/2 CUPS)
6 roasted red capsicums (peppers), peeled and seeds removed (Basics, page 234)
olive oil
2 French shallots (eschalots), roughly chopped
1 garlic clove, finely chopped
1 tablespoon soft brown sugar, to taste
1 tablespoon best-quality red wine vinegar, to taste
sea salt and freshly ground black pepper

....

Roughly dice the capsicums into 2 cm (¾ inch) squares. Heat a little olive oil in a large heavy-based saucepan over medium heat. Gently sauté the eschalot and garlic until tender. Add the capsicum and cook for 50 minutes, stirring often to ensure the mixture doesn't stick or burn — reduce the heat, if necessary. Add the sugar and vinegar and season to taste with sea salt and black pepper. Cook for a further 10 minutes. Remove from the heat.

Blend the jam in a food processor or using a stick blender to break the mixture down to a jam-like consistency, being careful not to purée the jam — it should still have a little texture. The jam can be made in advance and stored in an airtight container in the refrigerator for up to 1 week.

....

Note: Red pepper jam makes a great accompaniment to grilled meats and seafood, egg and vegetable dishes, or as a topping for toasted sourdough or grilled polenta.

Harissa

MAKES ABOUT 250 G (9 OZ/1½ CUPS)
2 teaspoons roasted caraway seeds
2 teaspoons roasted cumin seeds
6 large red chillies, cut in half lengthways, seeded
3 garlic cloves
1 roasted red capsicum (pepper), sliced (Basics, page 234)
2 teaspoons tomato paste (concentrated purée)
1 teaspoon smoked Spanish paprika
best-quality red wine vinegar
80 ml (2½ fl oz/⅓ cup) olive oil
sea salt and freshly ground black pepper

....

Pound the caraway and cumin seeds using a mortar and pestle. In a food processor, combine the chilli, garlic, capsicum, tomato paste and paprika. Scrape down the sides of the bowl.

With the machine running, add a splash of vinegar and the olive oil until well combined. Lastly, add the ground caraway and cumin seeds, process briefly and season with sea salt and black pepper.

Harissa will keep for several days stored in an airtight container in the refrigerator.

Red curry paste

MAKES 1 KG (2 LB 4 OZ/4 CUPS)
60 g (2¼ oz) shrimp paste
2 teaspoons ground paprika
2 dried red chillies
1½ teaspoons ground white pepper
1 tablespoon cumin seeds
1 teaspoon coriander seeds
½ cinnamon stick
3 star anise
6 garlic cloves, chopped
100 g (3½ oz) French shallots (eschalots), chopped
3 lemongrass stems, white part only, chopped
20 g (¾ oz) galangal, chopped
200 ml (7 fl oz) vegetable oil
400 ml (14 fl oz) coconut cream
100 g (3½ oz) palm sugar (jaggery), grated
2 makrut (kaffir lime) leaves

....

Preheat the oven to 180°C (350°F/Gas 4).

Wrap the shrimp paste in foil and roast for about 20 minutes. Set aside to cool. Spread the spices over a nonstick baking tray and lightly roast in the oven until fragrant. Cool to room temperature, then grind using a mortar and pestle or in a spice grinder.

Put the garlic, eschalot, lemongrass, galangal and shrimp paste in a food processor and blend to form a smooth paste. Add the ground spices, mixing well to combine.

Heat the vegetable oil and coconut cream in a saucepan over medium heat until the coconut cream splits. Add the spice paste and cook for 20 minutes, stirring frequently. Add the palm sugar, stirring until the sugar caramelises, then add the makrut leaves and cook for a further 5 minutes. Remove from the heat and set aside to cool completely. Use as the recipe directs.

....

Note: This recipe makes a large quantity. You could reduce the quantities to make a smaller amount, however this could affect the texture and taste. Any left-over curry paste can be stored in an airtight container for up to 1 month in the refrigerator, or several months frozen.

Celeriac rémoulade

MAKES 750 G (1 LB 10 OZ/3 CUPS)
juice of 2 lemons
500–600 g (1 lb 2 oz–1 lb 5 oz) celeriac
8 anchovies, finely chopped
1 tablespoon salted capers, rinsed and squeezed dry
60 g (2¼ oz/½ cup) gherkins (cornichons), chopped
1 handful of flat-leaf (Italian) parsley leaves, finely chopped
juice of ½ lemon
250 g (9 oz/1 cup) mayonnaise (Basics, page 232)
sea salt and freshly ground black pepper

Add the lemon juice to a bowl of cold water to make acidulated water. Peel the celeriac, thinly slice lengthways and immediately place into the acidulated water as it will discolour quickly once cut. Drain, then pat dry with paper towels.

In a mixing bowl, combine the celeriac, anchovies, capers, gherkins, parsley and lemon juice with enough mayonnaise to moisten. Season to taste with sea salt and black pepper. The celeriac can be stored for 1–2 days in an airtight container in the refrigerator.

Salted lemons

MAKES 6 SALTED LEMONS
6 lemons
160 g (5¾ oz) grey salt, such as Sel Gris, or damp grey salt (see Note, page 83)
1 tablespoon fennel seeds
1 tablespoon honey
¾ tablespoon brown mustard seeds
1 teaspoon white peppercorns
1 clove
2 bay leaves
3–4 thyme sprigs

Slice the lemons into quarters, without cutting all the way through, leaving the base of the lemon intact to hold it together. Freeze overnight.

Remove the lemons from the freezer and thaw completely. Put the remaining ingredients and 1.25 litres (44 fl oz) water in a large saucepan over medium heat and bring to a gentle simmer, stirring to dissolve the salt and infuse the water with the aromatics.

Put the lemons into a large sterilized jar (choose one that will fit the lemons snugly) and pour the simmering salt brine over the lemons to completely cover, adding a little extra water if necessary. Cover with a sheet of baking paper and a small plate or shallow ramekin (it must be small enough to fit inside the jar opening) to keep them completely submerged. Fit the lid tightly, then invert the jar — this will help to create a vacuum seal once cooled. Cool to room temperature. Once completely cool, refrigerate for a minimum of 3 weeks before using. Salted lemons will keep for 5–6 months in the refrigerator.

Potato gnocchi

SERVES 8

1.5 kg (3 lb 5 oz) pink-skinned waxy potatoes, such as desiree, skin on
3 egg yolks, lightly beaten
sea salt and freshly ground black pepper
150–225 g (5½–8 oz/1–1½ cups) plain (all-purpose) flour, sifted

Preheat the oven to 190°C (375°F/Gas 5).

Bake the potatoes whole for 25–35 minutes, or until you can skewer them easily with a thin knife. Remove from the oven and allow to cool slightly. Cut the potatoes in half, scoop out the flesh using a metal spoon, discarding the skins. Pass the flesh through a mouli or sieve into a bowl — you should have 900 g (2 lb) of cooked potato.

Working quickly, fold in the egg yolks and season with sea salt and black pepper. Add 150 g (5½ oz/1 cup) of the flour and stir into the potato using a 'cutting' action. Once the flour has been incorporated, bring the dough together using your hands — do not overwork. Add more flour, if required, bearing in mind the dough should be soft and light.

To shape the gnocchi, place the dough in a piping (icing) bag with a 1.5 cm (⅝ inch) nozzle. Pipe the dough onto a lightly floured surface (it will need a good squeeze to get it through the nozzle). Using a spatula or blunt, floured, knife, cut the gnocchi into 2.5 cm (1 inch) pieces.

Blanch the gnocchi briefly (30–60 seconds) in a large saucepan of boiling water until they float to the top. Drain, then refresh in iced water, allowing the gnocchi to cool completely. Drain again, then place the gnocchi on baking trays lined with baking paper. Freeze until required.

Note: Using freshly made gnocchi is best, although it's not always practical, even in a commercial kitchen. A recent dish at e'cco saw us making a fresh batch twice, sometimes three times a day, which became very time consuming. One of our chefs decided to freeze it to see if it would alter the texture and quality of the dough. To our surprise it worked, and cooked perfectly straight from the freezer.

Fresh gnocchi will keep for a couple of days, although it soon starts to discolour; we found the freezing method also preserved its pure white colour.

Candied walnuts

MAKES 230 G (8½ OZ/2 CUPS)
200 g (7 oz) caster (superfine) sugar
200 g (7 oz/2 cups) walnuts
vegetable oil, for deep-frying
sea salt

Combine the sugar and 200 ml (7 fl oz) water in a heavy-based saucepan over medium–high heat and stir until the sugar has dissolved. Add the walnuts, bring to the boil, then reduce the heat to medium. Simmer very gently, adjusting the heat as necessary, for 45–55 minutes, or until the liquid reduces and the nuts are glazed. Stir occasionally so the nuts cook evenly. Remove from the heat.

Fill a deep-fryer or large heavy-based saucepan one-third full of oil and heat to 165°C (320°F). In small batches, use a slotted spoon to scoop the walnuts from the saucepan into the hot oil, allowing any excess syrup to drain off. Fry for 2 minutes, moving them around, until they become a rich golden colour. Remove from the hot oil using a slotted spoon and place on baking paper. Repeat with the remaining nuts. Season the candied walnuts with sea salt while hot, then cool completely before storing in an airtight container. Candied walnuts will keep for 1–2 weeks stored in an airtight container.

Blind-baked sweet shortcrust pastry

MAKES ONE 24 X 4 CM (9½ X 1½ INCH) TART CASE
OR SIX 8 CM (3¼ INCH) TARTLET CASES
150 g (5½ oz) unsalted butter, at room temperature
100 g (3½ oz) icing (confectioners') sugar
1 egg yolk
250 g (9 oz/1⅔ cups) plain (all-purpose) flour
1 egg, beaten

Lightly grease a round 24 x 4 cm (9½ x 1½ inch) tart tin or six 8 cm (3¼ inch) tartlet tins.

Cream the butter and icing sugar together in a food processor. Add the egg yolk, mix well, then add the flour — do not overwork. If necessary, add just enough chilled water to bring the pastry together on the blade. Knead lightly, then wrap in plastic wrap and refrigerate for 1 hour.

Roll out the rested pastry to 3 mm (⅛ inch) thick all over and gently ease into the prepared tart tin or cut to line the smaller tartlet tins. Place in the refrigerator or freezer for a further 30 minutes.

Once chilled, you can blind-bake the pastry or continue to store in the freezer until required. (There is no need to thaw frozen pastry cases before using.)

To blind-bake, preheat the oven to 180°C (350°F/Gas 4). Line the pastry case or tartlet cases with baking paper or foil, fill with pastry weights, such as uncooked rice or split peas, then bake for 10–12 minutes. Remove the pastry weights and lining, brush with the beaten egg and bake for a further 5–8 minutes, or until golden. Use as directed in recipes.

Banana bread

MAKES 1 LOAF

220 g (7¾ oz/1½ cups) plain (all-purpose) flour
1 teaspoon baking powder
½ teaspoon salt
300 g (10½ oz/1⅓ cups) caster (superfine) sugar
2 eggs
80 ml (2½ fl oz/⅓ cup) buttermilk
125 ml (4 fl oz/½ cup) vegetable oil
3 bananas, mashed
30 ml (1 fl oz) dark rum
50 g (1¾ oz/½ cup) pecans or walnuts, chopped

Preheat the oven to 165°C (320°F/Gas 2–3). Grease and line a 28 x 10 x 8 cm (11¼ x 4 x 3¼ inch) loaf (bar) tin with baking paper.

In a large mixing bowl, sift together the flour, baking powder and salt. Stir in the sugar.

In a separate bowl, whisk together the eggs, buttermilk and oil, then stir in the mashed banana. Make a well in the centre of the dry ingredients and add the banana mixture, mixing well to combine. Fold through the rum and nuts. Pour the mixture into the prepared tin and bake for 1 hour, or until a skewer inserted into the centre of the banana bread comes out clean. Leave in the tin for 10 minutes before turning out onto a wire rack to cool completely.

Banana bread will keep for 2–3 days when stored in an airtight container.

Biscotti

MAKES ABOUT 30–40

300 g (10½ oz/2 cups) plain (all-purpose) flour, sifted, plus extra for dusting
270 g (9½ oz) caster (superfine) sugar
¾ teaspoon baking powder
2 eggs
2 egg yolks
¾ teaspoon natural vanilla extract
grated zest of ½ orange
grated zest of ½ lemon
135 g (4¾ oz) almonds

Preheat the oven to 160°C (315°F/Gas 2–3). Grease and line a baking tray with baking paper.

Combine the flour, sugar and baking powder in a large mixing bowl and make a well in the centre. In a separate bowl, whisk together the eggs, egg yolks, vanilla extract, orange and lemon zest. Add to the dry ingredients, gently mix to combine, then add the almonds.

On a floured surface, form the mixture into a rectangular shape measuring about 30 x 10 cm (12 x 4 inches). Place on the prepared tray. Bake for 35 minutes, or until golden, then remove from the oven and allow to cool completely.

Reduce the oven temperature to 80°C (175°F/Gas ¼). Line several baking trays with baking paper.

Cut the biscotti into very thin slices, about 2–3 mm (1/16–1/8 inch) thick, and lay flat on the prepared trays. Return to the oven and slowly dry the biscotti for 1–2 hours, or until very crisp, checking occasionally. Allow to cool. Store for several days in an airtight container.

Note: You can use any combination of nuts (such as hazelnuts and pistachios) for this recipe. Simply substitute the same weight of nuts for the almonds.

Sesame & ginger wafers

MAKES ABOUT 20
80 g (2¾ oz/⅓ cup) caster (superfine) sugar
grated zest of 1 orange
2 tablespoons freshly squeezed orange juice
40 g (1½ oz/¼ cup) plain (all-purpose) flour
¼ teaspoon ground ginger
40 g (1½ oz/¼ cup) sesame seeds
40 g (1½ oz) unsalted butter, melted
1 tablespoon finely chopped glacé ginger

Preheat the oven to 170°C (325°F/Gas 3).
   In a bowl, combine the sugar, orange zest and orange juice and stir until the sugar has dissolved.
   In a separate bowl, sift together the flour and ground ginger, then add the sesame seeds. Make a well in the centre and stir in the melted butter and the orange mixture, mixing well to combine. Lastly add the glacé ginger. Refrigerate the wafer mixture for 1 hour before using.
   Draw three 8 cm (3¼ inch) triangles on a sheet of baking paper and invert the paper onto a baking tray. Repeat with another sheet of baking paper and baking tray. Using a spatula, smear a thin layer of wafer mixture onto each triangle and bake for 7–10 minutes, or until golden. Slide the sheets of baking paper onto a wire rack and allow the wafers to cool completely before removing. Repeat the process with the remaining wafer mixture.
   Sesame wafers will keep for several days, stored in an airtight container.

Vanilla bean ice cream

MAKES 1.25 LITRES (44 FL OZ)
2 vanilla beans, split lengthways
500 ml (17 fl oz/2 cups) full-cream (whole) milk
500 ml (17 fl oz/2 cups) pouring (whipping) cream
12 egg yolks
300 g (10½ oz/1⅓ cups) caster (superfine) sugar

Scrape the seeds from the vanilla beans into a large saucepan. Add the vanilla beans, milk and cream and bring almost to the boil.
   Meanwhile, in a bowl, lightly whisk together the egg yolks and sugar. Whisk the hot milk mixture into the egg yolks, then return to a clean saucepan over medium heat.
   Using a wooden spoon, stir constantly until the custard thickens and coats the back of the spoon — do not let it boil. Strain through a fine sieve. Allow to cool to room temperature, then refrigerate until cold.
   Transfer to an ice cream machine and churn according to the manufacturer's instructions, then freeze. Alternatively, transfer to a shallow metal tray and freeze, whisking every couple of hours until creamy and frozen.

Cinnamon ice cream

MAKES 1.25 LITRES (44 FL OZ)
2 vanilla bean, split lengthways
2 cinnamon sticks
500 ml (17 fl oz/2 cups) full-cream (whole) milk
500 ml (17 fl oz/2 cups) pouring (whipping) cream
12 egg yolks
300 g (10½ oz/1⅓ cups) caster (superfine) sugar

Scrape the seeds from the vanilla beans into a large saucepan. Add the vanilla beans, cinnamon sticks, milk and cream and bring almost to the boil.

Meanwhile, in a bowl, lightly whisk together the egg yolks and sugar. Whisk the hot milk mixture into the egg yolks, then return to a clean saucepan over medium heat.

Using a wooden spoon, stir constantly until the custard thickens and coats the back of the spoon — do not let it boil. Strain through a fine sieve. Allow to cool to room temperature, then refrigerate until cold.

Transfer to an ice-cream machine and churn according to the manufacturer's instructions, then freeze. Alternatively, transfer to a shallow metal tray and freeze, whisking every couple of hours until creamy and frozen.

Coconut ice cream

MAKES 1.25 LITRES (44 FL OZ)
150 g (5½ oz/2½ cups) shredded coconut
500 ml (17 fl oz/2 cups) full-cream (whole) milk
500 ml (17 fl oz/2 cups) pouring (whipping) cream
12 egg yolks
300 g (10½ oz/1⅓ cups) caster (superfine) sugar

Put the shredded coconut, milk and cream in a large saucepan and bring almost to the boil.

Meanwhile, in a bowl, lightly whisk together the egg yolks and sugar. Whisk the hot milk mixture into the egg yolks, then return to a clean saucepan over medium heat.

Using a wooden spoon, stir constantly until the custard thickens and coats the back of the spoon — do not let it boil. Allow to cool to room temperature, then refrigerate until cold.

Transfer to an ice-cream machine and churn according to the manufacturer's instructions, then freeze. Alternatively, transfer to a shallow metal tray and freeze, whisking every couple of hours until creamy and frozen.

Crème fraîche ice cream

MAKES 1.25 LITRES (44 FL OZ)
1 litre (35 fl oz/4 cups) full-cream (whole) milk
300 g (10½ oz/1⅓ cups) caster (superfine) sugar
70 g (2½ oz) glucose syrup
5 egg yolks
335 g (11¾ oz) crème fraîche
200 ml (7 fl oz) pouring (whipping) cream

....

Combine the milk, sugar and glucose syrup in a large saucepan over medium heat and stir until the sugar dissolves. Bring almost to the boil, then remove from the heat.

Meanwhile, in a bowl, lightly whisk the egg yolks. Whisk the hot milk mixture into the egg yolks, then return the mixture to a clean saucepan over medium heat. Using a wooden spoon, stir constantly until the custard thickens and coats the back of the spoon — do not let it boil. Strain through a fine sieve, allow to cool to room temperature, then refrigerate until cold.

Whisk the crème fraîche and cream into the cooled custard. Transfer to an ice-cream machine and churn according to the manufacturer's instructions, then freeze. Alternatively, transfer to a shallow metal tray and freeze, whisking every couple of hours until creamy and frozen.

Maple syrup ice cream

MAKES 1.25 LITRES (44 FL OZ)
1 litre (35 fl oz/4 cups) pouring (whipping) cream
12 egg yolks
200 g (7 oz) soft brown sugar
150 ml (5 fl oz) maple syrup

....

Put the cream in a large heavy-based saucepan and bring almost to the boil.

Meanwhile, in a bowl, lightly whisk together the egg yolks and sugar. Whisk the hot cream into the egg yolks, stir in the maple syrup, then return to a clean saucepan over medium heat. Using a wooden spoon, stir constantly until the custard thickens and coats the back of the spoon — do not let it boil. Strain through a fine sieve, allow to cool to room temperature, then refrigerate until cold.

Transfer to an ice-cream machine and churn according to the manufacturer's instructions, then freeze. Alternatively, transfer to a shallow metal tray and freeze, whisking every couple of hours until creamy and frozen.

Burnt butter ice cream

MAKES 1.25 LITRES (44 FL OZ)
400 g (14 oz) unsalted butter
500 ml (17 fl oz/2 cups) full-cream (whole) milk
200 ml (7 fl oz) pouring (whipping) cream
12 egg yolks
300 g (10½ oz/1⅓ cups) caster (superfine) sugar

Melt the butter in a large saucepan over medium heat, then slowly bring to the boil. Simmer and cook until the butter turns a rich golden colour. Remove from the heat. Stir in the milk and cream.

Meanwhile, lightly whisk together the egg yolks and sugar in a bowl. Whisk the warm butter mixture into the egg yolks, then return the mixture to a clean saucepan over medium heat. Using a wooden spoon, stir constantly until the custard thickens and coats the back of the spoon — do not let it boil. Strain through a fine sieve, allow to cool to room temperature, then refrigerate until cold.

Transfer to an ice-cream machine and churn according to the manufacturer's instructions, then freeze. Alternatively, transfer to a shallow metal tray and freeze, whisking every couple of hours until creamy and frozen.

Raspberry sorbet

MAKES ABOUT 1 LITRE (35 FL OZ/4 CUPS)
460 g (1 lb/2 cups) caster (superfine) sugar
500 ml (17 fl oz/2 cups) raspberry purée (see Note)

Combine the sugar and 500 ml (17 fl oz/2 cups) water in a saucepan over medium heat, stirring until the sugar dissolves. Bring to the boil, then remove from the heat and add the raspberry purée. Refrigerate until cold.

Transfer the mixture to an ice-cream machine and churn according to the manufacturer's instructions, then freeze. Alternatively, transfer to a shallow metal tray and freeze, whisking every couple of hours until smooth and frozen.

Note: To make raspberry purée, blend 850 g (1 lb 14 oz) fresh or frozen raspberries in a food processor until smooth, then strain through a fine sieve, forcing the mixture through the sieve with the back of a wooden spoon. You can store the purée in an airtight container in the refrigerator for up to 2 days.

Pineapple sorbet

MAKES 1.5 LITRES (52 FL OZ)
500 g (1 lb 2 oz) caster (superfine) sugar
800 ml (28 fl oz) strained fresh pineapple juice (see Note)

Combine the sugar and 500 ml (17 fl oz/2 cups) water in a saucepan over medium heat and stir until the sugar has dissolved. Bring to the boil, then remove from the heat and add the pineapple juice. Refrigerate until cold.

Transfer the mixture to an ice-cream machine and churn according to the manufacturer's instructions, then freeze. Alternatively, transfer to a shallow metal tray and freeze, whisking every couple of hours until smooth and frozen.

Note: To prepare the pineapple juice, dice the flesh from two fresh pineapples. Juice the pineapple flesh using a vegetable juicer, or purée in a food processor, then pass through a fine sieve before measuring the required quantity. You can also use bottled pineapple juice, preferably with no added sugar.

Milk gelato

MAKES ABOUT 1 LITRE (35 FL OZ/4 CUPS)
175 g (6 oz/¾ cup) caster (superfine) sugar
100 g (3½ oz) glucose syrup
700 ml (24 fl oz) full-cream (whole) milk

Put the sugar, glucose syrup and 250 ml (9 fl oz/1 cup) of the milk in a large saucepan over medium heat and stir until the sugar dissolves — do not let the mixture boil. Remove from the heat. Stir in the remaining milk, then refrigerate until cold.

Transfer to an ice-cream machine and churn according to the manufacturer's instructions, then freeze. Alternatively, transfer to a shallow metal tray and freeze, whisking every couple of hours until creamy and frozen.

Glossary & Index

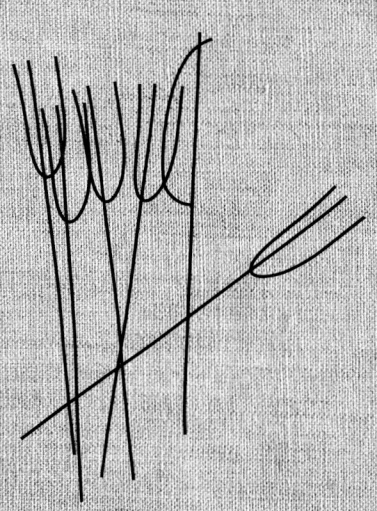

bacon lardons
Small strips of thick-cut bacon, usually available ready-chopped from delicatessens. Alternatively, cut thick slices of bacon lengthways into strips, then cut into 5 mm (¼ inch) long pieces.

balsamic vinegar
A northern Italian speciality vinegar originally from Modena. Vinegar is aged over many years, using a solera system where it darkens and becomes sweet and syrupy. Good balsamic is expensive — beware of imitation vinegar where caramel is added to a lesser vinegar to enrich it.

blanching and peeling tomatoes
To remove the skins from tomatoes, make a small incision in the base of each tomato, plunge into salted boiling water, then transfer to a bowl of iced water. Peel the skins and discard. Use the peeled tomatoes as directed.

buttermilk
Lightly acidic liquid that is left after churning butter. It is often used to lighten cake batters.

couverture
Good-quality chocolate with a high proportion of cocoa butter. It should melt easily on the tongue and not leave a fatty residue on the roof of the mouth. Avoid compound cooking chocolate.

crème fraîche
A distinctly sharp, semi-sour cream that can be used as a substitute for sour cream.

devein
To remove the intestinal tract from prawns (shrimp), firstly remove the shell. Using a knife, cut down the back of the prawn, then discard the intestinal tract.

escalope
Pieces of boneless meat that have been thinned out using a mallet or rolling pin for faster cooking.

gelatine
Half a teaspoon of gelatine powder is equal to one 2 g gelatine leaf. Dissolve the powder in 1 tablespoon cold water. This will form a jelly that can be added to hot liquid, as you would with gelatine leaves. Leaf gelatine is available from good delicatessens and food emporiums, and is considered superior to gelatine powder.

glucose syrup
The most common form of sugar is dextroglucose, a naturally occurring form, generally referred to as dextrose. It has about half the sweetening power of regular sugar and is used to make commercial sweets and frostings, as well as baked goods and other processed foods.

harissa
A North African and Middle Eastern condiment based on dried red chillies, garlic and other spices, such as ground red capsicum, caraway, cumin and coriander. Available from good delicatessens or you can make your own.

jus
Sauce or gravy, reduced from stock.

kefalograviera
A Greek sheep's milk cheese, similar to haloumi that is available from most good supermarkets or delicatessens. Otherwise substitute with haloumi.

Ligurian olives
Small, mild-tasting brownish black olives from north-western Italy. A good eating olive that is also used for making olive oil.

limoncello
A lemon liqueur produced in southern Italy. It is made from lemon rind (traditionally from the Sorrento lemon, though most lemons will produce satisfactory limoncello), alcohol, water and sugar. It is bright yellow in colour, sweet and lemony, but not sour as it doesn't contain any lemon juice.

mouli
A mill that is used to purée fruit, soup or vegetables.

palm sugar (jaggery)
Asian-style sugar produced from palm sap, available as dark brown or light golden in colour.

pin-boning
To remove bones from a fish or salmon fillet with tweezers or pliers. You can ask your fishmonger to do this.

porcini mushroom
A meaty type of mushroom, originating in Italy and translating as 'little pig'. It is the same variety as the French cep and is available mostly dried, but also frozen and fresh.

risotto rice
Arborio, carnaroli and vialone nano are all good Italian risotto rice varieties. They cook to a creamy consistency and the grains remain separate with a firm centre.

rosewater
This is the left-over liquid when rose petals and water are distilled together to make rose oil. It has a very strong flavour so you only need to use a small amount. It's available from delicatessens and most health food stores.

salted black beans
Small black soy beans dried and fermented in salt. Their distinctive yeasty smell and salty flavour pairs well with other strong flavours. Soak for 1 hour, then rinse well before use or they will impart too much saltiness.

Sichuan peppercorns
Native to the Sichuan province of China, these bear some resemblance to black peppercorns, but aren't actually from the pepper family. They are a dried berry from a tree of the prickly ash family. Also called anise pepper, they have a mild, peppery, citrus bouquet and flavour.

silica crystals
A highly absorbent form of silica dioxide used to prevent damage or deterioration from moisture and humidity.

star anise
Aniseed-flavoured, eight-pointed pod of an evergreen Asian tree. Buy whole star anise then roast and grind as required.

strong flour
Flour of any type made from a hard wheat, usually containing between 11 and 12 per cent protein, which is mostly gluten. Used mainly in bread-making and for puff and choux pastry.

sweetbreads
The pancreas and thymus glands from cows, calves and lambs. Usually prepared by washing, blanching, refreshing and trimming, then braising with stock.

verjuice
The juice extracted from large unripened grapes, which imparts a subtle tartness and acidity to vinaigrettes and sauces. Verjuice must be refrigerated once opened.

A

Asian-style barbecued pork & lychee salad 70
asparagus, pan-fried, with Ligurian olives, garlic & chilli 154
Atlantic salmon in brik pastry with betel leaves, eggplant,
    lime & coconut 94

B

balsamic dressing 233
banana bread 240
barbecue bug tails with a salad of green mango, chilli,
    coriander & lime 41
barbecue seafood skewers with papaya, lemongrass,
    lime & chilli salad 91
barramundi, pan-fried potatoes, leeks & vanilla
    beurre blanc 85
barramundi with a salad of globe artichokes, broad beans
    & lemon beurre blanc 90
basil crème brûlée & strawberry compote with vanilla
    madeleines 210
beef
    beef stock 229
    braised beef cheeks, Paris mash, baby carrots, asparagus
        & fresh horseradish 132
    carpaccio of beef, horseradish cream & chorizo oil 74
    eye fillet of beef, pommes allumettes, crisp pancetta
        & horseradish cream 98
    eye fillet of beef, truffled kipfler potatoes, buttered
        spinach, sauce soubise & crisp sweetbreads 124
    soy-braised beef cheek, Asian herb salad & fried shallots 61
beetroot
    beetroot risotto, goat's cheese, pickled golden beetroot
        & candied walnuts 20
    roast baby beetroot with blue cheese, walnuts & chervil 158
    shaved baby beetroot, goat's cheese & hazelnut salad 143
beurre blanc 231
biscotti 240
blue cheese soufflé with a pear, hazelnut & truffle
    honey salad 32
blue-eye trevalla, roast, saffron potatoes, baby leeks & peas 84
brussels sprouts, sautéed, pancetta & garlic 168
bug wontons, kecap manis, coriander & Thai basil 55
burnt butter ice cream 244
butter, clarified 230

C

candied walnuts 239
capsicums, roasted 234
carpaccio of beef, horseradish cream & chorizo oil 74
carrots, baby, with cumin, orange & thyme 161
celeriac rémoulade 237
cheese
    blue cheese soufflé with a pear, hazelnut & truffle
        honey salad 32
    mozzarella pan-fried with prosciutto & rosemary 35
    parmesan wafer stack, lobster, watercress
        & limemayonnaise 36
    roast baby beetroot with blue cheese, walnuts
        & chervil 158
cherry & Drambuie semifreddo 214
cherry soufflé with chocolate sauce 200
chicken
    chicken breast wrapped in Parma ham with salsa Romesco 99
    palliard of chicken with a mixed leaf salad 130
    roast chicken, baby carrots, eschalots, salted lemon
        & pine nuts 104
    soy-poached chicken, hokkien noodles, ginger
        & springonion 116
    warm chicken salad with avocado, apple, celery & pecans 64
    white chicken stock 228
chocolate
    chocolate, rum & almond pithiviers 222
    chocolate meringues with cassis cream & fresh
        raspberries 225
    chocolate panna cotta, poached pears & gingerbread 215
    dark chocolate dumplings with cinnamon
        ice cream 190
    flourless chocolate cake, poached rhubarb
        & raspberry sorbet 185
    lemon & white chocolate mousse with lemon curd 216
    milk chocolate brûlée 220
    trio of chocolate 206
    white chocolate bavarois & chocolate chilli soup 209
cinnamon ice cream 242
clarified butter 230
coconut cake with mango mousse & milk gelato 187
coconut ice cream 242
coconut pain perdu, raspberry sorbet
    & macadamia nut brittle 180
coconut tapioca, caramelised bananas, pineapple sorbet
    & sesame cookies 198
crème fraîche ice cream 243
crisp cabbage salad with feta, mint & chilli 138

D

date-stuffed saffron pears with cinnamon yoghurt 202
desserts
    baked date tart, caramelised oranges
        & crème fraîche ice cream 195
    basil crème brûlée & strawberry compote
        with vanilla madeleines 210
    cherry & Drambuie semifreddo 214
    cherry soufflé with chocolate sauce 200
    chocolate, rum & almond pithiviers 222
    chocolate meringues with cassis cream & fresh
        raspberries 225
    chocolate panna cotta, poached pears & gingerbread 215

coconut cake with mango mousse & milk gelato 187
coconut pain perdu, raspberry sorbet
   & macadamia nut brittle 180
coconut tapioca, caramelised bananas, pineapple sorbet
   & sesame cookies 198
dark chocolate dumplings with cinnamon
   ice cream 190
date-stuffed saffron pears with cinnamon yoghurt 202
flourless chocolate cake, poached rhubarb & raspberry
   sorbet 185
ginger bavarois & poached pear with sesame
   & ginger wafer 182
ginger kisses with espresso cream 203
green apple, raisin & polenta crumble pie 188
grilled bananas, banana bread & burnt butter
   ice cream 175
hazelnut meringue, Frangelico custard
   & hazelnut caramel sauce 177
lemon & white chocolate mousse with lemon curd 216
milk chocolate brûlée 220
mixed nut tartlets with rum & raisin purée
   & coconut ice cream 224
orange & coconut syrup cake 221
pear & hazelnut clafoutis with pear crisps
   & honey cream 174
pistachio & caramel ice cream, poached pears
   & butterscotch sauce 197
pumpkin cheesecake, ginger custard & maple syrup
   ice cream 186
rhubarb fool 219
ruby grapefruit granita, lemonade sorbet, mint jelly
   & rosewater 181
saffron & almond cake with milk gelato & saffron
   syrup 193
steamed golden syrup & ginger puddings 176
trio of chocolate - white chocolate sorbet, milk
   chocolate mousse & dark chocolate delice 206
white chocolate bavarois & chocolate chilli soup 209
dressings 232–4
duck
   duck breast, brussels sprouts, baby onions, bacon
      lardons & sauce diable 134
   duck breast, pumpkin purée, balsamic braised
      red cabbage & candied walnuts 100
   duck liver crostini with fried duck egg 72
   Peking duck salad, seared scallops, ginger & peanuts 65
   slow-cooked duck, roast kipflers, caramelised onions
      & bacon 116

E
eggplant, marinated, with labneh & balsamic 145
eggplant & feta agnolotti, cherry tomatoes, spinach
   & olives 30

F
fennel
   braised fennel, pine nuts, raisins, wild rocket,
      Persian feta & vincotto 171
   roasted fennel, kipfler potatoes & pancetta 150
figs
   baked fig & goat's curd with a salad of rocket,
      hazelnuts & vincotto 23
   roast quail, fresh figs, frisée, salted ricotta & mint
      with a honey & vanilla dressing 58
   salad of grilled figs, radicchio & gorgonzola 153
fish
   Atlantic salmon in brik pastry with betel leaves,
      eggplant, lime & coconut 94
   barramundi, pan-fried potatoes, leeks
      & vanilla beurre blanc 85
   barramundi with a salad of globe artichokes, broad beans
      & lemon beurre blanc 90
   fish stock 229
   grilled swordfish with warm kipfler potato salad & salsa
      verde 87
   pan-fried whiting, curry-spiced cauliflower, wild rocket,
      raisins & flaked almonds 96
   rare-seared tuna, zucchini, pecorino, salted lemon,
      olives & salsa verde 78
   roast blue-eye trevalla, saffron potatoes, baby leeks
      & peas 84
   roast snapper, jerusalem artichokes, pine mushrooms
      & sorrel 88
   seared ocean trout, colcannon, sauce matelote &
      horseradish crème fraîche 81
   steamed whiting fillets with iceberg lettuce & anchovy
      mayonnaise 80
   whole rainbow trout baked in sea salt with salsa verde 83
   see also seafood

G
ginger bavarois & poached pear with sesame
   & ginger wafer 182
ginger kisses with espresso cream 203
green apple, raisin & polenta crumble pie 188

H
ham, Ibérico, burrata, rocket, vincotto, tomato
   fondue & toasted ciabatta 66
harissa 236
hazelnut meringue, Frangelico custard & hazelnut
   caramel sauce 177

I
Ibérico ham, burrata, rocket, vincotto, tomato fondue
   & toasted ciabatta 66
ice creams 241–4

J

jus 230

L

lamb
    braised lamb shanks, red wine risotto & roast garlic 131
    lamb cutlets, scorched tomatoes, sumac croutons,
        Persian feta, sugarsnap peas & olives 119
    lamb tagine with couscous & harissa 115
    rack of lamb with herb–mustard crust & a salad
        of Ligurian olives, parsley & onion 102
leek tart, roasted pears, blue cheese & hazelnuts 25
lemon & white chocolate mousse with lemon curd 216
lemons, salted 237

M

maple syrup ice cream 243
mayonnaise 232
menus 10–13
milk gelato 245
Moroccan spiced quail, carrot purée, feta & olives 62
mozzarella pan-fried with prosciutto & rosemary 35

O

ocean trout, seared, colcannon, sauce matelote
    & horseradish crème fraîche 81
orange & coconut syrup cake 221

P

palliard of chicken with a mixed leaf salad 130
pancetta-wrapped scallops, parsnip purée
    & curry vinaigrette 56
Paris mash 156
parmesan wafer stack, lobster, watercress
    & lime mayonnaise 36
parsnips, roast, rocket, lemon, honey & thyme 167
party advice 14–17
pastry, blind-baked sweet shortcrust 239
pear & hazelnut clafoutis with pear crisps
    & honey cream 174
Peking duck salad, seared scallops, ginger & peanuts 65
pineapple sorbet 245
pistachio & caramel ice cream, poached pears
    & butterscotch sauce 197
polenta 157
pommes écrasées 166
pork
    Asian-style barbecued pork & lychee salad 70
    pork loin with prunes, sage, sautéed apples & hazelnuts 112
    pork neck with chilli & lime 126
    roast pork belly, caramelised pear purée, potato
        fondant, silverbeet & pomegranate jus 106
    Sichuan pork belly, black bean broth & Asian greens 103

potatoes
    pommes écrasées 166
    potato gnocchi 238
    potato gnocchi, pine mushrooms, cavalo nero,
        porcini butter, peas & pecorino 31
    roast kipflers with artichokes, olives & lemon 159
    salad of sautéed potatoes, mixed leaves, pancetta porcini
        & poached egg 29
    shaved kipfler potatoes, green beans, eschalots,
        parmesan & truffle cream 163
    warm potato salad with lemon & grain mustard 152
prawns
    prawn & chickpea fritters, tomato & coriander salsa 54
    Thai red curry of prawns with Asian salad & peanuts 44
pumpkin
    pumpkin, feta, sage & walnut dumplings 24
    pumpkin cheesecake, ginger custard & maple syrup
        ice cream 186
    roast pumpkin, wild rocket, pine nuts, honey
        & cumin dressing 164
    spiced pumpkin, spinach & harissa salad 149

Q

quail
    Moroccan spiced quail, carrot purée, feta & olives 62
    roast quail, carrot & cumin salad with a coriander
        & mint dressing 71
    roast quail, fresh figs, frisée, salted ricotta & mint
        with a honey & vanilla dressing 58
    roast quail, frisée, Manchego, salted almonds
        & quince dressing 75
    roast quail with a salad of witlof, dates, hazelnuts
        & saffron dressing 69

R

rabbit, slow-cooked risotto, peas & mascarpone 135
rainbow trout, whole, baked in sea salt with salsa verde 83
raspberry sorbet 244
ravioli, open, with artichokes, pan-roasted tomatoes,
    basil, goat's curd & olives 26
red curry paste 236
red pepper jam 235
red wine vinaigrette 233
rhubarb fool 219
ruby grapefruit granita, lemonade sorbet, mint jelly
    & rosewater 181

S

saffron & almond cake with milk gelato & saffron syrup 193
saganaki & lemon 148
salads
    Asian-style barbecued pork & lychee salad 70
    crisp cabbage salad with feta, mint & chilli 138

Peking duck salad, seared scallops, ginger & peanuts 65
roast quail, frisée, Manchego, salted almonds
    & quince dressing 75
salad of apple, fennel, frisée, pancetta & ricotta 141
salad of grilled figs, radicchio & gorgonzola 153
salad of sautéed potatoes, mixed leaves, pancetta
    & poached egg 29
salad of shaved jerusalem artichokes, rocket, orange
    & feta 140
scallops, seared, jerusalem artichokes, parsley
    & radish salad with mandarin sauce 38
shaved baby beetroot, goat's cheese & hazelnut salad 143
shaved nashi pear & crab salad with peanuts,
    watercress & pomelo 48
spiced pumpkin, spinach & harissa salad 149
tomato salad with salted ricotta & basil 144
warm chicken salad with avocado, apple, celery & pecans 64
warm potato salad with lemon & grain mustard 152
salsa verde 232
salted lemons 237
seafood
    barbecue bug tails with a salad of green mango, chilli,
        coriander & lime 41
    barbecue seafood skewers with papaya, lemongrass,
        lime & chilli salad 91
    bug wontons, kecap manis, coriander & Thai basil 55
    pancetta-wrapped scallops, parsnip purée
        & curry vinaigrette 56
    parmesan wafer stack, lobster, watercress
        & lime mayonnaise 36
    Peking duck salad, seared scallops, ginger & peanuts 65
    prawn & chickpea fritters, tomato & coriander salsa 54
    seared prawns, sautéed potatoes, fennel, watercress,
        avocado, saffron & vanilla beurre blanc 50
    seared prawns with a salad of melon, ginger, lime & mint 47
    seared scallops, jerusalem artichokes, parsley & radish
        salad with mandarin sauce 38
    seared scallops, saffron potatoes, tomato, fresh peas,
        pine nuts & basil ravigotte 53
    shaved nashi pear & crab salad with peanuts, watercress
        & pomelo 48
    steamed scallops, leeks, rice wine vinegar & soy 45
    sugar-cured ocean trout, celeriac rémoulade, salted
        lemon & basil oil 51
    Thai red curry of prawns with Asian salad & peanuts 44
    wet polenta, sand crab, chilli, garlic & basil 42
    see also fish
sesame & ginger wafers 241
Sichuan pork belly, black bean broth & Asian greens 103
sides
    baby carrots with cumin, orange & thyme 161
    braised fennel, pine nuts, raisins, wild rocket,
        Persian feta & vincotto 171
    crisp cabbage salad with feta, mint & chilli 138
    pan-fried asparagus with Ligurian olives, garlic & chilli 154
    Paris mash 156
    pommes écrasées 166
    roast baby beetroot with blue cheese, walnuts & chervil 158
    roast kipflers with artichokes, olives & lemon 159
    roast parsnip, rocket, lemon, honey & thyme 167
    roast pumpkin, wild rocket, pine nuts, honey
        & cumin dressing 164
    roasted fennel, kipfler potatoes & pancetta 150
    saganaki & lemon 148
    sautéed brussels sprouts, pancetta & garlic 168
    shaved kipfler potatoes, green beans, eschalots,
        parmesan & truffle cream 163
    steamed greens with salted lemon, white anchovies
        & toasted almonds 162
    warm potato salad with lemon & grain mustard 152
    see also salads
snapper, roast, jerusalem artichokes, pine mushrooms
    & sorrel 88
soy-braised beef cheek, Asian herb salad & fried shallots 61
soy-poached chicken, hokkien noodles, ginger
    & spring onion 116
spatchcock, open pie, eschalots, peas, mushrooms,
    tarragon & brandy cream 120
stocks 228–9
sugar-cured ocean trout, celeriac rémoulade, salted
    lemon & basil oil 51
swordfish, grilled, with warm kipfler potato salad
    & salsa verde 87

T
Thai red curry of prawns with Asian salad & peanuts 44
tomato salad with salted ricotta & basil 144
tuna, rare-seared, zucchini, pecorino, salted lemon,
    olives & salsa verde 78

V
vanilla bean ice cream 241
veal escalope with Marsala, beans & pancetta 117
vegetable stock 228
venison, rare-roasted, balsamic beetroot, ruby chard
    & smoked eggplant 129
verjuice dressing 234

W
walnuts, candied 239
wet polenta, sand crab, chilli, garlic & basil 42
whiting, pan-fried, curry-spiced cauliflower, wild rocket,
    raisins & flaked almonds 96
whiting fillets, steamed, with iceberg lettuce & anchovy
    mayonnaise 80

Eating In

Dedication

To all my staff, past and present, who have made e'cco what it is today. Restaurants are always the sum of many, not one.

To my wife Shirley, who has always been there for me and has never once questioned the time, energy and commitment that it takes to run a restaurant.

To Tracey Rayner, my manager, for her enormous efforts on this book, our fourth together. She has spent countless hours on this project, as well as looking after the day-to-day running of e'cco. She really is as good as they get.

To Sam Brading, my sous chef, who did so much of the organising and cooking during the testing and photography phase of this book — I couldn't have done it without you.

To Krista Graham, a gifted pastry chef who assisted with desserts during the production stage — every kitchen needs a Krista.

To Richard Cornish, for his invaluable contribution; putting my thoughts onto paper, I assure you, isn't an easy task. Cooking may be an art, but being able to write well is equally so.

To Jared Fowler, our photographer, and our stylist, Emma Ross, two of the very best in their field.

To Mathias Andersson, my friend and head chef, who has, and continues to bring so much to e'cco.

To Tanya, Melinda and Alan, who along with Tracey, have been with me forever. To have one of them you'd consider yourself lucky, to have them all I guess I'm blessed.

To Kay Scarlett, Juliet Rogers, Jacqueline Blanchard, Belinda So and the rest of the Murdoch Books team who care so much.

And to the rest of the e'cco team, both kitchen and front-of-house, for the passion and dedication they bring with them every day.

Published in 2010 by Murdoch Books Pty Limited

Murdoch Books Australia
Pier 8/9
23 Hickson Road
Millers Point NSW 2000
Phone: +61 (0) 2 8220 2000
Fax: +61 (0) 2 8220 2558
www.murdochbooks.com.au

Murdoch Books UK Limited
Erico House, 6th Floor
93–99 Upper Richmond Road
Putney, London SW15 2TG
Phone: +44 (0) 20 8785 5995
Fax: +44 (0) 20 8785 5985
www.murdochbooks.co.uk

Publisher: Kay Scarlett
Concept and Design: Chi Lam
Project Editor: Belinda So
Photographer: Jared Fowler
Stylist: Emma Ross
Editor: Jacqueline Blanchard
Production: Kita George

IMPORTANT: Those who might be at risk from the effects of salmonella poisoning (the elderly, pregnant women, young children and those suffering from immune deficiency diseases) should consult their doctor with any concerns about eating raw eggs.

OVEN GUIDE: You may find cooking times vary depending on the oven you are using. For fan-forced ovens, as a general rule, set the oven temperature to 20°C (35°F) lower than indicated in the recipes.

Text copyright © Murdoch Books 2010
The moral right of the author has been asserted.
Design copyright © Murdoch Books 2010
Photography copyright © Murdoch Books 2010

All rights reserved. No part of this publication may be reproduced, stored in a retrieval system or transmitted in any form or by any means, electronic, mechanical, photocopying, recording or otherwise, without the prior written permission of the publisher.

National Library of Australia
Cataloguing-in-Publication Data
Author: Johnson, Philip.
Title: Eating In: food to share from
                the e'cco kitchen.
ISBN: 978-1-74196-749-4 (hbk.)
Notes: Includes index.
Subjects: E'cco (Restaurant: Brisbane, Qld.)
                Cookery--Australia.
Dewey Number: 641.5

A catalogue record for this book is available from the British Library.

Colour reproduction by Splitting Image, Clayton, Victoria
Printed by 1010 Printing International Ltd. PRINTED IN CHINA.

The publisher would like to thank Georg Jensen, Wheel&Barrow, Waterford Wedgwood, Villeroy & Boch, Country Road, Simon Johnson, Black Pearl Epicure and Batstones Stone Masonry for lending equipment for use.